Class Counts: Student Edition

This book provides students with a lively and penetrating exploration of the concept of class and its relevance for understanding a
wide range of issues in contemporary society. What unites the topics
is not a preoccupation with a common object of explanation, but
rather a common explanatory factor: class. Three broad themes are
explored: class structure, class and gender, and class consciousness.
Specific empirical studies include such diverse topics as class
variations in the gender division of labor in housework; friendship
networks across class boundaries; transformations of the American
class structure since 1960; and cross-national variations in class
structure and class consciousness. The author evaluates these studies
in terms of how they confirm certain expectations within the Marxist
tradition of class analysis and how they pose challenging surprises.
This Student Edition of *Class Counts* thus combines Erik Olin
Wright's sophisticated account of central and enduring questions in
social theory with detailed empirical analyses of social issues.

Erik Olin Wright is Vilas Research Professor and C. Wright Mills
Professor of Sociology at the University of Wisconsin, Madison. He is
the author of eight books, most recently *Reconstructing Marxism* (with
Elliott Sober and Andrew Levin, 1992), *Interrogating Inequality* (1995),
and *Class Counts* (1997).

Studies in Marxism and Social Theory

Edited by G. A. COHEN, JON ELSTER AND JOHN ROEMER

The series is jointly published by the Cambridge University Press and the Editions de la Maison des Sciences de l'Homme, as part of the joint publishing agreement established in 1977 between the Fondation de la Maison des Sciences de l'Homme and the Syndics of the Cambridge University Press.

The books in the series are intended to exemplify a new paradigm in the study of Marxist social theory. They will not be dogmatic or purely exegetical in approach. Rather, they will examine and develop the theory pioneered by Marx, in the light of the intervening history, and with the tools of non-Marxist social science and philosophy. It is hoped that Marxist thought will thereby be freed from the increasingly discredited methods and presuppositions which are still widely regarded as essential to it, and that what is true and important in Marxism will be more firmly established.

Also in the series

Class Counts

Student Edition

Erik Olin Wright

CAMBRIDGE
UNIVERSITY PRESS

Maison des Sciences de l'Homme

PUBLISHED BY THE PRESS SYNDICATE OF THE UNIVERSITY OF CAMBRIDGE
The Pitt Building, Trumpington Street, Cambridge, United Kingdom

CAMBRIDGE UNIVERSITY PRESS
The Edinburgh Building, Cambridge CB2 2RU, UK   www.cup.cam.ac.uk
40 West 20th Street, New York, NY 10011-4211, USA   www.cup.org
10 Stamford Road, Oakleigh, Melbourne 3166, Australia
Ruiz de Alarcón 13, 28014 Madrid, Spain and Editions de la Maison des Sciences de
l'Homme, 54 Boulevard Raspail, 75270 Paris Cedex 06

First published 1997

Printed in the United Kingdom at the University Press, Cambridge

Set in Palatino 10/13   [CE]

A catalogue record for this book is available from the British Library

Library of Congress cataloguing in publication data
Wright, Erik Olin.
Class Counts: Student Edition / Erik Olin Wright.
    p. cm.
ISBN 0 521 66309 1 (hardback) – ISBN 0 521 66394 6 (paperback)
1. Social classes.   2. Social mobility.   3. Class consciousness.   I. Title.
HT609.W699   2000
305.5–dc21   99–42113   CIP

ISBN 0 521 66309 1 hardback
ISBN 0 521 66394 6 paperback
ISBN 2 7351 0863 5 hardback (France only)
ISBN 2 7351 0866 X paperback (France only)

Contents

Part IV Conclusion   249

Preface to student edition

The original edition of *Class Counts*, published in 1997, was intended as a research study oriented to technically sophisticated social scientists. The central ideas of the book, however, were potentially of interest to a much wider audience. The central objective of this abridged edition of *Class Counts* is thus to make the book more accessible and useful for students without advanced statistical training and without a specialist's interests in the details of the research literature and methodologies on each of the topics. To accomplish this, I have tried to follow four guiding principles in deciding what to cut, what to leave in and what to rewrite. First, I wanted none of the cuts to undermine the clarity and interest of the theoretical ideas and substantive arguments in the original book. As a result I have eliminated relatively little from the more theoretical sections of the book. Second, I wanted to eliminate virtually all technical statistical and methodological material. I have replaced this with simpler, graphical representations of results wherever possible. Where the technical details are important for specific arguments and analysis, I have included footnotes directing the reader to the pages in the original edition of *Class Counts* where the technical material can be found. Third, I have tried to eliminate most of the digressions and peripheral plots in the story. In many of the original empirical chapters I included extended discussions of empirical issues that were outside the main thrust of analysis. These I have mostly removed. I have also eliminated most of the footnotes which explored secondary themes and implications. Finally, I have eliminated most citations to the research literature on specific topics except in places where a discussion of a specific piece of work is needed to develop an idea or argument. One of the hallmarks of scholarly sociological research is the inclusion of long lists of citations for specific points being made. Often these serve mainly a ritualistic purpose, showing to the world that one has read the right stuff but not contributing anything to the substantive exposition of ideas. For readers of this abridged edition who wish to explore the broader literature linked to any specific topic in this book, they can consult the citations in the corresponding chapter of the original edition.

Even with all of these cuts I was unable to reduce the 576 pages of the original book to a reasonable length for this edition. It was therefore necessary to completely eliminate two of the chapters from the original edition: chapter 15 on the relationship between state employment and class consciousness, and chapter 16, on the relationship between class mobility and class consciousness. While I do think there are valuable ideas in these two chapters, in many ways the empirical investigations which accompanied them are less conclusive than in most of the rest of the book.

Elsie: "WHAT'S THAT, DADDY?"
Father: "A COW."
Elsie: "WHY?"

Punch

Preface to original edition

Like Elsie wondering why a cow is a "cow", I have spent an inordinate amount of time worrying about what makes a class a "class". Here is the basic problem. The Marxist concept of class is rooted in a polarized notion of antagonistic class relations: slave masters exploit slaves, lords exploit serfs, capitalists exploit workers. In the analysis of developed capitalist societies, however, many people do not seem to neatly fit this polarized image. In everyday language, many people are "middle class", and, even though Marxists generally do not like that term, nevertheless, most Marxist analysts are uncomfortable with calling managers, doctors and professors, "proletarians." Thus, the problem is this: how can the social categories which are commonly called "middle" class be situated within a conceptual framework built around a polarized concept of class? What does it mean to be in the "middle" of a "relation"? The diverse strands of research brought together in this book are all, directly or indirectly, ramifications of struggling with this core conceptual problem.

My empirical research on these issues began with my dissertation on class and income, completed in 1976. In that project, I used data gathered by the Michigan Panel Study of Income Dynamics, the Quality of Employment Survey and several other sources. None of these had been gathered with Marxist concepts in mind. When the data analysis failed to generate anticipated results I could therefore always say, "of course, the data were gathered in 'bourgeois categories' and this may explain why the hypotheses were not confirmed." It was therefore a natural next step to generate new data, data that would be directly tailored to quantitatively "testing" hypotheses on class and its consequences within the Marxist tradition, data that would leave me no excuses. This was the central idea behind my first grant proposal for this project to the National Science Foundation in 1977.

The original NSF proposal was framed as an attempt to generate a set of data in which the Marxist and Weberian traditions of class analysis could directly engage each other. I argued in the proposal that there was a tremendous gap between *theoretical debates* in class analysis – which largely revolved around a dialogue between Marx and Weber – and *quantitative research* – which largely ignored Marxism altogether. To close this gap required two things: first, generating systematic data derived from a Marxist conceptual framework, and, second, gathering the data comparatively. Since Marxist class analysis is, above all, rooted in the concept of class structure (rather than simply individual class attributes), we needed a sample of countries which varied structurally in certain ways in order to seriously explore Marxist themes.

As often occurs in research proposals, because of the need to frame issues in ways which the reviewers of the proposals will find compelling, this way of posing the agenda of the research did not really reflect my core reasons for wanting to do the project. Adjudication between general frameworks of social theory can rarely be accomplished in the form of head-to-head quantitative combat, since different theoretical frameworks generally are asking different questions. Furthermore, the gaps between concepts, questions and measures are nearly always too great for a direct adjudication between rival frameworks to yield robust and convincing results. The Marx/Weber debate, therefore, was always a somewhat artificial way of justifying the project, and it certainly has not (in my judgment) proven to be the most interesting line of empirical analysis. My theoretical motivations had much more to do with pushing Marxist class analysis forward on its own terrain – exploring problems such as cross-national variation in the permeability of class boundaries, the effects of class location and class biography on class consciousness, the variations across countries in patterns of ideological class formation, and so on.

Nevertheless, from the start a disproportionate amount of energy in the project in the United States as well as in many of the other countries has been devoted to the problem of *adjudicating conceptual issues* rather than *empirically investigating theoretical problems*. I have worried endlessly about the optimal way of conceptualizing the "middle class" which would be both coherent (i.e. be consistent with more abstract principles of Marxist theory) and empirically powerful. This preoccupation has sometimes displaced substantive theoretical concerns and it has been easy to lose sight of the real puzzles that need solving. Rather than delve deeply into the problem of trying to explain why workers in different countries display different degrees of radicalism, I have often worried more about how properly to define the category "working class" to be used in such an investigation. It was as if I felt that if only I could get the *concepts* right, then the theoretical issues would fall into place (or at least become more tractable). It now seems to me that often it is better to forge ahead and muddle through with somewhat less certain concepts than to devote such an inordinate amount of time attempting to reconstruct the concepts themselves. To paraphrase a comment once made about Talcott Parsons, it is a bad idea to keep repacking one's bags for a trip that one never takes. It is better to get out the door even if you may have left something important behind.

The initial plan when I began the comparative class analysis project was to do a survey of class structure and class consciousness in the US and Italy jointly with a close friend from graduate school, Luca Perrone. In fact, one of the initial motivations for the project was our mutual desire to embark on a research project that would make it easy for us to see each other regularly. By the time the final NSF grant was awarded, Sweden had been added to the project as the result of a series of lectures I gave in Uppsala in 1978. Soon, scholars in other countries learned of the project, and, through a meandering process, asked if they could replicate the survey. By 1982, surveys were completed or underway in the United Kingdom, Canada and Norway, and shortly thereafter additional surveys were carried out in Australia, Denmark, Japan, New Zealand and West Germany. Tragically, Luca Perrone died in a skin-diving accident in 1981 and so an Italian project was never completed. In the early 1990s, an additional round of projects were organized in Russia, South Korea, Spain, Taiwan and, most recently, Portugal. A second US survey was fielded in 1991 and a new Swedish survey in 1995.

Without really intending this to happen, the US project became the coordinating node of a rapidly expanding network of class analysis projects around the world. Originally, this was meant to be a focused, short-term project. In 1977 I had absolutely no intention of embarking on a megaproject that would eventually involve more than fifteen countries and millions of dollars. I thought that the project would take a few years, four or five at the most, and then I would return to other issues. It is now almost two decades later and the end is just now in sight.

Has it really been worth it to spend this amount of time and resources on a single research enterprise? If twenty years ago, when I was finishing my dissertation and contemplating whether or not to launch the class analysis project, I had been told that I would still be working on it in

1995, I would have immediately dropped the project in horror. Certainly there have been times during the years of this project when I was fed up with it, tired of worrying endlessly about the minutiae of measurement and only asking questions that could be answered with coefficients. Nevertheless, in the end, I do think that it has been worthwhile sticking with this project for so long. This is not mainly because of the hard "facts" generated by the research. If you simply made a list of all of the robust empirical discoveries of the research, it would be easy to conclude that the results were not worth the effort. While I hope to show in this book that many of these findings are interesting, I am not sure that by themselves they justify nearly two decades of work.

The real payoff from this project has come, I think, from the effects of thinking about the same ideas, concepts and puzzles for so long. I have returned countless times to the problem of the difference between Marxist and Weberian ideas about class, the meaning of exploitation and domination as analytical and normative issues in class analysis, the conceptual status of the "middle" class in a relational class framework, and so on. It is not that the simple "facts" generated by the regression equations directly inform these issues, but repeatedly grappling with the data has forced me to repeatedly grapple with these ideas. The long and meandering class analysis project has kept me focused on a single cluster of ideas for much longer than I would have otherwise done, and this has led – I hope – to a level of insight which I otherwise would not have achieved.

There are several limitations in the analyses of this book which should be mentioned. First, even though this is a book about class written from a Marxist perspective, there are no empirical analyses of two important segments of the class structure: substantial owners of capital, and the more marginalized, impoverished segments of population, often loosely labeled the "underclass". When I refer to the "capitalist class" in the empirical analyses I am, by and large, referring to relatively small employers, not to wealthy owners of investment portfolios. There is certainly no analysis of anything approaching the "ruling class". Similarly, the analysis of the working class largely excludes the unemployed and people who are outside of the labor force (discouraged workers, people on welfare, etc.). The irony, of course, is that within the Marxist tradition the critique of capitalism is directed above all against the wealthiest segments of the capitalist class, and the moral condemnation of capitalism is grounded to a significant extent on the ways it perpetuates poverty. The limitations of sample surveys simply make it impossible to seriously explore either of these extremes within the class structure with the methods we will use in this study.

Second, aside from relatively brief sections in chapter 2 and chapter 11, there is almost no discussion of the problem of race and class in the book. Given how salient the problem of race is for class analysis in the United States, this is a significant and unfortunate absence. However, the relatively small sample size meant that there were too few African-Americans in the sample to do sophisticated analyses of the interactions of race and class. What is more, even if we had had a significantly larger sample, the restriction of the American sample to the labor force and housewives would have precluded investigation of the crucial race/class issue of the "underclass". Given these limitations, I felt I would not be able to push the empirical analysis of race and class forward using the data from the Comparative Class Analysis Project.

Third, there is a methodological problem that affects the book as a whole. Most of the data analyses reported in this book were originally prepared for journal articles. The earliest of these appeared in 1987, the last in 1995. As often happens when a series of quite different analyses is generated from the same data over an extended period of time, small shifts in variable construction and operational choices are made. In preparing the book manuscript, therefore, I had to make a decision: should I redo most of the previously completed analyses in order to render all of the chapters strictly consistent, or should I simply report the findings in their original form and make note of the shifts in operationalizations? There is no question that, in the absence of constraints, the first of these options would be the best. But I figured that it would probably delay the completion of the book by a minimum of six months and probably more, and, given that there would be no substantive improvement in the ideas and insights of the research, this just did not seem worthwhile. So, in Ralph Waldo Emerson's spirit that "foolish consistency is the hobgoblin of small minds", I have retained nearly all of the original analyses (except in a few cases where I discovered actual errors of one sort or another).

This project would not have been possible without the financial support from the National Science Foundation, which funded the initial gathering and public archiving of the data and much of the data analysis. The Wisconsin Alumni Research Foundation also provided generous research support for data analysis throughout the research. In the late

1980s, grants from the Spencer Foundation and the MacArthur foundation made it possible to conduct the second US survey in conjunction
with the Russian class analysis project.

There are countless people to whom I am deeply indebted for the
research embodied in this book. Without the love and comradeship of
Luca Perrone, the project would never have been launched in the first
place. His quirky spirit is present throughout the book.

Michael Burawoy has been my most steadfast and supportive critic
over the years, encouraging me both to be a hard-nosed quantomaniac
and to keep the big ideas and political purposes always in mind. In
reading the draft of parts of this book he urged me to keep the overblown
concept-mongering to a minimum; too much grandiose theorizing, he
warned, would distract readers from the empirical message of the
research. I am afraid that I have only partially followed his advice: I have
not excised metatheoretical and conceptual discussions from the book,
but they are generally cordoned off in specific chapters.

My collaborators in the various national projects in the Comparative
Class Analysis Project contributed enormously to the development of
this research. Göran Ahrne, the principle director of the Swedish project
in the 1980s, was especially involved in formulating questions and
designing the intellectual agenda of the project from the start and always
provided sensible skepticism to my Marxist theoretical impulses.
Howard Newby, Gordon Marshall, David Rose, John Myles, Wallace
Clement, Markku Kivenen, Raimo Blom, Thomas Colbjornson, Håkon
Leilesfrud, Jens Hoff, John Western and Chris Wilkes were all involved
in the various international meetings where the project was framed and
analyses were discussed.

A series of extremely talented graduate student research assistants
were directly involved in many of these specific data analyses. In
particular, I would like to thank Cynthia Costello, Joey Sprague, David
Haken, Bill Martin, George Steinmetz, Donmoon Cho, Kwang-Young
Shin, Karen Shire, Cressida Lui and Sungkyun Lee. Two post-doctoral
fellows from the Australian project who spent two years in Madison –
Mark Western and Janeen Baxter – infused the data analysis with great
energy and imagination just at a time when my own enthusiasm was
beginning to wane.

A number of colleagues have provided invaluable feedback on specific
pieces of the analysis. Robert Hauser, Rob Mare, Michael Hout and
Charles Halaby were always generously helpful at rescuing me when I
ventured out of my depth in statistical techniques. Joel Rogers has been

extremely helpful in skeptically asking "so, what's the main point?" and providing an insightful sounding board for testing out the various punchlines in the book.

Finally, I would like to thank my wife, Marcia, for refusing to let the work on this book and other projects completely take over my life. She has managed with great skill the delicate balancing acts, being supportive of my academic work and yet not letting it get out of hand to encroach on everything else.

Acknowledgments

Some of the chapters in this book partially draw on previously published papers from the Comparative Class Analysis Project. In most cases, these earlier papers were substantially revised for this book: Chapter 3: "Proletarianization in Contemporary Capitalism" (with Joachim Singelmann), *American Journal of Sociology*, supplement to Vol. 83, 1982, and "The Transformation of the American Class Structure, 1960–1980" (with Bill Martin), *American Journal of Sociology*, July 1987. Chapter 4: "The Fall and Rise of the Petty Bourgeoisie" (with George Steinmetz), *The American Journal of Sociology*, March 1989. Chapter 5: "The Permeability of Class Boundaries to Intergenerational Mobility: a Comparative Study of the United States, Canada, Norway and Sweden" (with Mark Western), *American Sociological review*, June 1994, and "The Relative Permeability of Class Boundaries to Cross-Class Friendships: a comparative Analysis of the United States, Canada, Sweden and Norway" (with Donmoon Cho) *American Sociological Review*, February, 1992. Chapter 7: "Women in the Class Structure," *Politics & Society*, March, 1989. Chapter 8: "The Noneffects of Class on the Sexual Division of Labor in the Home: a Comparative Analysis of Sweden and the United States" (with Karen Shire, Shu-Ling Huang, Maureen Dolan and Janeen Baxter), *Gender & Society*, June 1992. Chapter 9. "The Gender Gap in Authority: a Comparative Analysis of the United States, Canada, The United Kingdom, Sweden, Norway and Japan" (with Janeen Baxter), *The American Sociological Review*, June, 1995. Chapter 11. "Class Structure and Class Formation" (with Carolyn Howe and Donmoon Cho), in Melvin Kohn (ed), *Comparative Sociology*, (Beverly Hills: Sage ASA Presidental Volume), 1989.

1. Class analysis

The empirical research in this book covers a wide range of substantive topics: from friendship patterns and class mobility to housework and class consciousness. What unites the topics is not a preoccupation with a common object of explanation, but rather a common explanatory factor: class. This is what class analysis attempts to do – explore the relationship between class and all sorts of social phenomena. This does not mean, of course, that class will be of explanatory importance for everything. Indeed, as we will discover, in some of the analyses of this book class turns out not to be a particularly powerful factor. Class analysis is based on the conviction that class is a pervasive social cause and thus it is worth exploring its ramifications for many social phenomena, but not that it is universally the most important. This implies deepening our understanding of the limits of what class can explain as well as of the processes through which class helps to determine what it does explain.

The most elaborated and systematic theoretical framework for class analysis is found in the Marxist tradition. Whatever one might think of its scientific adequacy, classical Marxism is an ambitious and elegant theoretical project in which class analysis provides a central part of the explanation of what can be termed the epochal trajectory of human history. The aphorism "class struggle is the motor of history" captures this idea. The argument of classical historical materialism was never that everything that happens in history is explainable by class analysis, although many critics of Marxism have accused Marxists of proposing such a monocausal theory. The claim is more restricted, yet still ambitious: that the overall trajectory of historical development can be explained by a properly constructed class analysis.

Many, perhaps most, contemporary Marxist scholars have pulled back from these grandiose claims of orthodox historical materialism. While

1

the idea that history has a comprehensible structure and that the dynamics of capitalism are frought with contradictions that point towards a socialist future may form part of the intellectual backdrop to Marxist scholarship, most actual research brackets these arguments and, instead, focuses on the ways in which class affects various aspects of social life. Class analysis thus becomes the core of a wide-ranging agenda of research on the causes and consequences of class relations.

Marxist-inspired class analysis, of course, is not the only way of studying class. There is also Weberian-inspired class analysis, stratification-inspired class analysis, eclectic common-sense class analysis. Before embarking on the specific empirical agenda of this book, therefore, we need to clarify the basic contours of the class concept which will be used in the analyses. In particular, we need to clarify the concept of class structure, since this plays such a pivotal role in class analysis. This is the basic objective of this chapter.

The concept of "class structure" is only one element in class analysis. Other conceptual elements include *class formation* (the formation of classes into collectively organized actors), *class struggle* (the practices of actors for the realization of class interests), and *class consciousness* (the understanding of actors of their class interests). The task of class analysis is not simply to understand class structure and its effects, but to understand the interconnections among all these elements and their consequences for other aspects of social life.

In chapter 10 we will explore a general model of the interconnections among these elements. The discussion in this chapter will be restricted to the problem of class structure. This is not because I believe that class structure is always the most important explanatory principle within class analysis. It could certainly be the case, for example, that the variation in class formations across time and place in capitalist societies may be a more important determinant of variations in state policies than variations in the class structures associated with those class formations. Rather, I initially focus on class structure because it remains *conceptually* pivotal to clarifying the overall logic of class analysis. To speak of *class* formation or *class* struggle as opposed to simply *group* formation or struggle implies that we have a definition of "class" and know what it means to describe a collective actor as an instance of class formation, or a conflict as a class conflict instead of some other sort of conflict. The assumption here is that the concept of class structure imparts the essential content of the adjective "class" when it is appended to "formation," "consciousness," and "struggle." Class formation is the formation of collective actors organized around class interests within class structures; class struggle is the struggle between such collectively organized actors over class interests; class consciousness is the understanding by people within a class of their class interests. In each case one must already have a definition of class structure before the other concepts can be fully specified. Elaborating a coherent concept of class structure, therefore, is an important conceptual precondition for developing a satisfactory theory of the relationship between class structure, class formation and class struggle.

1.1 The parable of the shmoo

A story from the *Li'l Abner* comic strips from the late 1940s will help to set the stage for the discussion of the concept of class structure. Here is the situation of the episode: Li'l Abner, a resident of the hill-billy community of Dogpatch, discovers a strange and wonderful creature, the "shmoo," and brings a herd of them back to Dogpatch. The shmoos' sole desire in life is to please humans by transforming themselves into the material things human beings need. They do not provide humans with luxuries, but only with the basic necessities of life. If you are hungry, they can become ham and eggs, but not caviar. What is more, they multiply rapidly so you never run out of them. They are thus of little value to the wealthy, but of great value to the poor. In effect, the shmoo restores humanity to the Garden of Eden. When God banished Adam and Eve from Paradise for their sins, one of their harshest punishments was that from then on they, and their descendants, were forced to "earn their bread by the sweat of their brow." The shmoo relieves people of this necessity and thus taps a deep fantasy in Western culture.

In the episode from *Li'l Abner* reproduced below, a manager working for a rich capitalist, P.U., does a study to identify the poorest place in America in order to hire the cheapest labor for a new factory. The place turns out to be Dogpatch. P.U. and the manager come to Dogpatch to recruit employees for the new factory. The story unfolds in the following sequence of comic strips from 1948 (Al Capp 1992: 134–136).

The presence of shmoos is thus a serious threat to both class relations and gender relations. Workers are more difficult to recruit for toilsome labor and no longer have to accept "guff" and indignities from their bosses. Women are no longer economically dependent on men and thus do not have to put up with sexist treatment.

In the episodes that follow, P.U. and his henchman organize a campaign to destroy the shmoo. They are largely successful, and its sinister influence is stopped. American capitalism can continue, un-threatened by the specter of the Garden of Eden.

The saga of the shmoo helps to clarify the sense in which the interests of workers and capitalists are deeply antagonistic, one of the core ideas of Marxist class analysis. Let us look at this antagonism a bit more closely by examining the preferences of capitalists and workers towards the fate of the shmoo. Consider four possible distributions of shmoos: everyone gets a shmoo; only capitalists get shmoos; only workers get shmoos; and the shmoos are destroyed so no one gets them. Table 1.1 indicates the preference orderings for the fate of shmoos on the assump-tion that both workers and capitalists are rational and only interested in their own material welfare.[1] They are thus neither altruistic nor spiteful; the actors are motivated only by the pure, rational egoism found typically in neoclassical economics. For capitalists, their first preference is that they alone get the shmoos, since they would obviously be slightly better off with shmoos then without them. Their second preference is

---

[1] This preference ordering assumes that the shmoo provides only for basic necessities. For a discussion of the issues in conditions where the generosity of shmoos can vary, see Wright (1997: 5–7).

Table 1.1. *Rank ordering of preferences for the fate of the shmoo by class*

Rank order	Capitalist class	Working class
1	Only capitalists get shmoos	Everyone gets shmoos
2	Destroy the shmoos	Only workers get shmoos
3	Everyone gets shmoos	Only capitalists get shmoos
4	Only workers get shmoos	Destroy the shmoo

that no one gets them. They would rather have the shmoo be destroyed than everyone get one. For workers, in contrast, their first preference is that everyone gets the shmoos. Given that the shmoo only provides for basic necessities, not luxuries, many workers will still want to work for wages in order to have discretionary income. Such workers will be slightly better off if capitalists have shmoos as well as workers, since this will mean that capitalists will have slightly more funds available for investment (because they will not have to buy basic necessities for themselves). Workers' second preference is that workers alone get the shmoos; their third preference is that only capitalists get the shmoos; and their least preferred alternative is that the shmoos be destroyed.

The preference ordering of workers corresponds to what could be considered universal human interests. This is one way of understanding the classical Marxist idea that the working class is the "universal class," the class whose specific material interests are equivalent to the interests of humanity as such. This preference ordering also corresponds to the what might be called Rawlsian preferences – the preferences that maximize the welfare of the worst off people in a society. With respect to the shmoo, at least, the material self-interests of workers corresponds to the dictates of Rawlsian principles of Justice. This is a remarkable correspondance, for it is derived not from any special assumptions about the virtues, high-mindedness or altruism of workers, but simply from the objective parameters of the class situation.

What the story of the shmoo illustrates is that the deprivations of the propertyless in a capitalist system are not simply an unfortunate by-product of the capitalist pursuit of profit; they are a necessary condition for that pursuit. This is what it means to claim that capitalist profits depend upon "exploitation." This does not imply that profits are solely "derived" from exploitation or that the degree of exploitation is the only determinant of the level of profits. But it does mean that exploitation is one of the necessary conditions for profits in a capitalist economy.

Exploiting classes thus have an interest in preventing the exploited from acquiring the means of subsistence even if, as in the case of the shmoo story, that acquisition does not take the form of a redistribution of wealth or income from capitalists to workers. To put it crudely, capitalism generates a set of incentives such that the capitalist class has an interest in destroying the Garden of Eden.

While in real capitalism capitalists do not face the problem of a threat from shmoos, there are episodes in the history of capitalism in which capitalists face obstacles not unlike the shmoo. Subsistence peasants have a kind of quasi-shmoo in their ownership of fertile land. While they have to labor for their living, they do not have to work for capitalists. In some times and places capitalists have adopted deliberate strategies to reduce the capacity of subsistence peasants to live off the land specifically in order to recruit them as a labor force. A good example is the use of monetized hut taxes in South Africa in the nineteenth century to force subsistence peasants to enter the labor market and work in the mines in order to have cash to pay their taxes. More generally, capitalist interests are opposed to social arrangements that have even a partial shmoo-like character. Capitalist class interests are thus opposed to such things as universal guaranteed basic income or durably very low rates of unemployment, even if the taxes to support such programs were paid entirely out of wages and thus did not directly come out of their own pockets. This reflects the sense in which capitalist exploitation generates fundamentally antagonistic interests between workers and capitalists.

1.2 The concept of exploitation

The story of the shmoo revolves around the linkage between class divisions, class interests and exploitation. There are two main classes in the story – capitalists who own the means of production and workers who do not. By virtue of the productive assets which they own (capital and labor power) they each face a set of constraints on how they can best pursue their material interests. The presence of shmoos fundamentally transforms these constraints and is a threat to the material interests of capitalists. Why? Because it undermines their capacity to exploit the labor power of workers. "Exploitation" is thus a key concept for understanding the nature of the antagonistic interests generated by the class relations.

Exploitation is a loaded theoretical term, since it suggests a moral condemnation of particular relations and practices, not simply an analytical description. To describe a social relationship as exploitative is to condemn it as both harmful and unjust to the exploited. Yet, while this moral dimension of exploitation is important, the core of the concept revolves around a particular type of antagonistic interdependency of material interests of actors within economic relations, rather than the injustice of those relations as such. As I will use the term, class exploitation is defined by three principle criteria:

(i)   *The inverse interdependent welfare principle*: the material welfare of exploiters causally depends on the material deprivations of the exploited. The welfare of the exploiter is at the expense of the exploited.

(ii) *The exclusion principle*: the causal relation that generates principle (i) involves the asymmetrical exclusion of the exploited from access to and control over certain important productive resources. Typically this exclusion is backed by force in the form of property rights, but in special cases it may not be.

(iii) *The appropriation principle*: the causal mechanism which translates (ii) exclusion into (i) differential welfare involves the appropriation of the fruits of labor of the exploited by those who control the relevant productive resources.[2] This appropriation is also often referred to as the appropriation of the "surplus product."

This is a fairly complex set of conditions. Condition (i) establishes the antagonism of material interests. Condition (ii) establishes that the antagonism is rooted in the way people are situated within the social organization of production. The expression "asymmetrical" in this criterion is meant to exclude "fair competition" among equals from the domain of possible exploitations. Condition (iii) establishes the specific mechanism by which the interdependent, antagonistic material interests are generated. The welfare of the exploiter depends upon the *effort* of the exploited, not merely the deprivations of the exploited.

If only the first two of these conditions are met we have what can be called "nonexploitative economic oppression," but not "exploitation." In nonexploitative economic oppression there is no transfer of the fruits of

---

[2] The expression "appropriation of the fruits of labor" refers to the appropriation of that which labor produces. It does not imply that the value of those products are exclusively determined by labor effort, as claimed in the labor theory of value. For a discussion of this way of understanding the appropriation of the fruits of labor, see Cohen (1988: 209–238). For a discussion of the concept of "surplus" as it bears on the problem of exploitation as defined here, see Wright (1997: 14–17).

labor from the oppressed to the oppressor; the welfare of the oppressor depends simply on the exclusion of the oppressed from access to certain resources, but not on their laboring effort. In both instances, the inequalities in question are rooted in ownership and control over productive resources.

The crucial difference between exploitation and nonexploitative oppression is that, in an exploitative relation, the exploiter *needs* the exploited since the exploiter depends upon the effort of the exploited. In the case of nonexploitative oppression, the oppressors would be happy if the oppressed simply disappeared. Life would have been much easier for the European settlers to North America if the continent had been uninhabited by people. Genocide is thus always a potential strategy for nonexploitative oppressors. It is not an option in a situation of economic exploitation because exploiters require the labor of the exploited for their material well-being. It is no accident that in the United States there is an abhorrent folk saying, "the only good Indian is a dead Indian," but not the saying "the only good worker is a dead worker" or "the only good slave is a dead slave." It makes sense to say "the only good worker is an obedient and conscientious worker," but not "the only good worker is a dead worker." The contrast between South Africa and North America in their treatment of indigenous peoples reflects this difference poignantly: in North America, where the indigenous people were oppressed (by virtue of being coercively displaced from the land) but not exploited, genocide was part of the basic policy of social control in the face of resistance; in South Africa, where the European settler population heavily depended upon African labor for its own prosperity, this was not an option.

Exploitation, therefore, does not merely define a set of *statuses* of social actors, but a pattern of ongoing *interactions* structured by a set of social relations, relations which mutually bind the exploiter and the exploited together. This dependency of the exploiter on the exploited gives the exploited a certain form of power, since human beings always retain at least some minimal control over their own expenditure of effort. Social control of labor which relies exclusively on repression is costly and, except under special circumstances, often fails to generate optimal levels of diligence and effort on the part of the exploited. As a result, there is generally systematic pressure on exploiters to moderate their domination and in one way or another to try to elicit some degree of consent from the exploited, at least in the sense of gaining some level of minimal cooperation from them. Paradoxically perhaps, exploitation is thus a constraining force on the practices of the exploiter. This constraint constitutes a basis of power for the exploited.

People who are oppressed but not exploited also may have some power, but it is generally more precarious. At a minimum, oppressed people have the power that comes from the human capacity for physical resistance. However, since their oppressors are not economically constrained to seek some kind of cooperation from them, this resistance is likely very quickly to escalate into quite bloody and violent confrontations. It is for this reason that the resistance of Native Americans to displacement from the land led to massacres of Native Americans by white settlers. The pressure on nonexploitative oppressors to seek accommodation is very weak; the outcomes of conflict therefore tend to become simply a matter of the balance of brute force between enemies moderated at best by moral qualms of the oppressor. When the oppressed are also exploited, even if the exploiter feels no moral compunction, there will be economic constraints on the exploiter's treatment of the exploited.

The conceptualization of exploitation proposed here has extension beyond the specific domain of class relations and economic exploitation. One can speak, for example, of the contrast between sexual exploitation and sexual oppression. In the former the sexual "effort," typically of women, is appropriated by men; in the latter the sexuality of some group is simply repressed. Thus, in heterosexist societies women are often sexually exploited, while homosexuals would typically be sexually oppressed.

Describing the material interests of actors generated by exploitation as antagonistic does not prejudge the moral question of the justice or injustice of the inequalities generated by these antagonisms. One can believe, for example, that it is morally justified to prevent poor people in Third World countries from freely coming into the United States and still recognize that there is an objective antagonism of material interests between US citizens and the excluded would-be Third World migrants. Similarly, to recognize the capital–labor conflict as involving antagonistic material interests rooted in the appropriation of labor effort does not necessarily imply that capitalist profits are unjust; it simply means that they are generated in a context of inherent conflict.

Nevertheless, it would be disingenuous to claim that the use of the term "exploitation" to designate this form of antagonistic interdependency of material interests is a strictly scientific, technical choice. Describing the appropriation of labor effort as "exploitation" rather than simply a "transfer" adds a sharp moral judgment to the analytical claim. Without at least a thin notion of the moral status of the appropriation, it would be impossible, for example, to distinguish such things as legitimate taxation from exploitation. Taxation involves coercive appropriation, and in many instances there is arguably a conflict of material interests between the taxing authorities and the taxpayer as a private individual. Even under deeply democratic and egalitarian conditions, many people would not voluntarily pay taxes since they would prefer to enhance their personal material interests by free-riding on other people's tax payments. Right-wing libertarians in fact do regard taxation as a form of exploitation because it is a violation of the sanctity of private property rights and thus an unjust, coercive appropriation. The motto "Taxation is theft" is equivalent to "taxation is exploitation." The claim that the capitalist appropriation of labor effort from workers is "exploitation," therefore, implies something more than simply an antagonism of material interests between workers and capitalists; it implies that this appropriation is unjust.

While I feel that a good moral case can be made for the kind of radical egalitarianism that provides a grounding for treating capitalist appropriation as unjust, it would take us too far afield here to explore the philosophical justifications for this claim. In any case, for purposes of sociological class analysis, the crucial issue is the recognition of the antagonism of material interests that are linked to class relations by virtue of the appropriation of labor effort, and on this basis I will refer to this as "exploitation."

1.3 Class and exploitation

Within the Marxist tradition of class analysis, class divisions are defined primarily in terms of the linkage between property relations and exploitation. Slave masters and slaves constitute classes because a particular property relation (property rights in people) generates exploitation (the appropriation of the fruits of labor of the slave by the slave master). Homeowners and the homeless would not constitute "classes" even though they are distinguished by property rights in housing since this division does not constitute a basis for the exploitation of the homeless by homeowners.

In capitalist society, the central form of exploitation is based on property rights in the means of production. These property rights generate three basic classes: *capitalists* (exploiters), who own the means of production and hire workers; *workers* (exploited), who do not own the means of production and sell their "labor power" (i.e. their capacity to work) to capitalists; and *petty bourgeois* (neither exploiter nor exploited), who own and use the means of production without hiring others. The Marxist account of how the capital–labor relation generates exploitation is a familiar one: propertyless workers, in order to acquire their means of livelihood, must sell their labor power to people who own the means of production. In this exchange relation, they agree to work for a specified length of time in exchange for a wage which they use to buy their means of subsistence. Because of the power relation between capitalists and workers, capitalists are able to force workers to produce more than is needed to provide them with this subsistence. As a result, workers produce a surplus which is owned by the capitalist and takes the form of profits. Profits, the amount of the social product that is left over after the costs of producing and reproducing all of the inputs (both labor power inputs and physical inputs) have been deducted, constitute an appropriation of the fruits of labor of workers.

Describing this relation as exploitative is a claim about the basis for the inherent conflict between workers and capitalists in the employment relation. It points to the crucial fact that the conflict between capitalists and workers is not simply over the *level of wages*, but over the *amount of work effort* performed for those wages. Capitalists always want workers to expend more effort than workers willingly want to do. As Bowles and Gintis (1990) have argued, "the whistle while you work" level of effort of workers is always suboptimal for capitalists, and thus capitalists have to adopt various strategies of surveillance and control to increase labor effort. While the intensity of overt conflict generated by these relations will vary over time and place, and class compromises may occur in which high levels of cooperation between labor and management take place, nevertheless, this underlying antagonism of material interests remains so long as the relationship remains exploitative.

For some theoretical and empirical purposes, this simple image of the class structure may be sufficient. For example, if the main purpose of an analysis is to explore the basic differences between the class structures of feudalism and capitalism, then an analysis of capitalist society which revolved entirely around the relationship between capitalists and workers might be adequate. However, for many of the things we want to study with class analysis, we need a more nuanced set of categories. In particular, we need concepts which allow for two kinds of analyses: first, the analysis of the variation across time and place in the class structures of concrete capitalist societies, and, second, the analysis of the ways individual lives are affected by their location within the class structure. The first of these is needed if we are to explore macro-variations in a fine-grained way; the second is needed if we are use class effectively in micro-analyses.[3]

Both of these tasks involve elaborating a concept of class structure in capitalist societies that moves beyond the core polarization between capitalists and workers. More specifically, this involves introducing new forms of complexity into the class concept by addressing four general problems in class structural analysis: first, the "middle class" within the class structure; second, people not in the paid labor force in the class structure; third, capitalist assets owned by employees; and fourth, the temporal dimension of class locations.

1.4 Adding complexities to the concept of class structure

1 The problem of the "middle class" among employees

If we limit the analysis of class structure in capitalism to the ownership of and exclusion from the means of production, we end up with a class structure in which there are only three locations – the capitalist class, the working class and the petty bourgeoisie – and in which around 85–90% of the labor force in most developed capitalist countries falls into a single class. While this may in some sense reflect a profound truth about capitalism – that the large majority of the population are separated from the means of production and must sell their labor power on the labor market in order to survive – it does not provide us with an adequate conceptual framework for explaining many of the things we want class to help explain. In particular, if we want class structure to help explain class consciousness, class formation and class conflict, then we need some way of understanding the class-relevant divisions within the employee population.

In ordinary language terms, this is the problem of the "middle class" – people who do not own their own means of production, who sell their labor power on a labor market, and yet do not seem part of the "working class." The question, then, is on what basis can we differentiate class locations among people who share a common location of nonownership

---

[3] For an extended discussion of the limitations of the overly abstract polarized concept of class structure, see Wright (1989: 271–278).

within capitalist property relations? In the analyses in this book, I will divide the class of employees along two dimensions: first, their relationship to authority within production, and second, their possession of skills or expertise.

Authority

There are two rationales for treating authority as a dimension of class relations among employees. The first concerns the role of *domination* within capitalist property relations. In order to insure the performance of adequate effort on the part of workers, capitalist production always involves an apparatus of domination involving surveillance, positive and negative sanctions and varying forms of hierarchy. Capitalists do not simply *own* the means of production and *hire* workers; they also *dominate* workers within production.

In these terms, managers and supervisors can be viewed as exercising delegated capitalist class powers in so far as they engage in the practices of domination within production. In this sense they can be considered *simultaneously* in the capitalist class and the working class: they are like capitalists in that they dominate workers; they are like workers in that they are controlled by capitalists and exploited within production. They thus occupy what I have called *contradictory locations within class relations* (see Wright 1978, 1985). The term "contradictory" is used in this expression rather than simply "dual" since the class interests embedded in managerial jobs combine the inherently antagonistic interests of capital and labor. The higher one moves in the authority hierarchy, the greater will be the weight of capitalist interests within this class location. Thus upper managers, and especially CEO's in large corporations will be very closely tied to the capitalist class, while the class character of lower level supervisor jobs will be much closer to the working class.

The second rationale for treating the authority dimension as a criterion for differentiating class locations among employees centers on the relationship between their earnings and the appropriation of surplus. The strategic position of managers within the organization of production enables them to make significant claims on a portion of the social surplus – the part of the socially produced product left over after all inputs have been paid for – in the form of relatively high earnings. In effect this means that the wages and salaries of managerial labor power are above the costs of producing and reproducing their labor power (including whatever skills they might have).

In an earlier work (Wright 1985) I argued that by virtue of this appropriation of surplus by managers they should generally be seen as exploiters. The problem with this formulation is that managers also contribute to the surplus through their own laboring activity, and thus their surplus income may simply reflect a capacity to appropriate part of the surplus which they contribute to production. Instead of being "exploiters," therefore, many managers may simply be less exploited than other employees. Because of this ambiguity, therefore, it is better simply to see managers as occupying a *privileged* position with respect to the process of exploitation which enables them to appropriate part of the social surplus in the form of higher incomes.

The specific mechanism through which this appropriation takes place can be referred to as a "loyalty rent." It is important for the profitability of capitalist firms that managers wield their power in an effective and responsible way. The difficulty is that a high level of surveillance and threats is generally not an effective strategy of eliciting this kind of behavior, both because managerial performance is generally rather hard to monitor and because repressive controls tend to intimidate initiative rather than stimulate creative behavior. What is needed, then, is a way of generating some level of real commitment on the part of managers to the goals of the organization. This is accomplished by relatively high earnings linked to careers and promotion ladders within authority hierarchies. These higher earnings involve a redistribution of part of the social surplus to managers in order to build their loyalty to the organization. Of course, negative sanctions are still present in the background: managers are sometimes fired, they are disciplined for poor work by failing to get promotions or raises, etc. But these coercive forms of control gain their efficacy from their link to the strong inducements of earnings that, especially for higher level managers, are significantly above the costs of producing the skills of managers.[4] Managers thus not only occupy *contradictory locations within class relations* by virtue of

[4] This rent component of the earnings of managers has been recognized in "efficiency wage" theory which acknowledges that the market-clearing wage may be suboptimal from the point of view of the goals of the employer. Because of the difficulty in enforcing labor contracts, employers have to pay employees more than the wages predicted by theories of competitive equilibria in order to gain compliance. While this mechanism may generate some small "employment rents" for all employees, it is especially salient for those employees who occupy strategic jobs requiring responsible, diligent performance of duties. For the mainstream economics discussion of efficiency wages, see Akerloff and Yellen (1986). For arguments that extend efficiency wage theory to Marxist arguments about the "extraction" of labor effort from workers, see Bowles and Gintis (1990).

domination, they occupy what might be termed a *privileged appropriation location within exploitation relations*. Both of these differentiate them from the working class.

Skills and expertise

The second axis of class differentiation among employees centers on the possession of skills or expertise. Like managers, employees who possess high levels of skills/expertise are potentially in a privileged appropriation location within exploitation relations. There are two primary mechanisms through which this can happen. First, skills and expertise are frequently scarce in labor markets, not simply because they are in short supply, but also because there are systematic obstacles in the way of increasing the supply of those skills to meet the requirements of employing organizations. One important form of these obstacles is credentials, but rare talents could also constitute the basis for sustained restrictions on the supply of a particular form of labor power.[5] The result of such restrictions on supply is that owners of the scarce skills are able to receive a wage above the costs of producing and reproducing their labor power. This "skill rent" is a way by which employees can appropriate part of the social surplus.

Second, the control over knowledge and skills frequently renders the labor effort of skilled workers difficult to monitor and control. The effective control over knowledge by such employees means that employers must rely to some extent on loyalty-enhancing mechanisms in order to achieve desired levels of cooperation and effort from employees with high levels of skills and expertise, just as they have to do in the case of managers. Employees with high levels of expertise, therefore, are able to appropriate surplus both because of their strategic location within the organization of production (as controllers of knowledge), and because of their strategic location in the organization of labor markets (as controllers of a scarce form of labor power).

The possession of skills and expertise defines a distinctive location within class relations because of a specific kind of power they confer on

---

[5] Credentials would not constitute a restriction on the supply of a particular kind of skill if there were no obstacles for individuals acquiring the credentials. A variety of such obstacles exist: restrictions on the number of slots in the training programs; restrictions in credit markets to get loans to obtain the training; inequality in the distribution of "cultural capital" (including such things as manners, accent, appearance, etc.) and "social capital" (especially such things as access to networks and information); and, of course, inequalities in genetic endowments.

employees – power in labor markets to capture skill rents and power within production to capture loyalty rents. It may also be the case that expertise, skills and knowledge are associated with various kinds of "symbolic capital" and distinctive life-styles, as Bourdieu (1984) and others have noted. While these cultural correlates of class may be of considerable explanatory importance for a variety of sociological questions, they do not constitute the essential rationale for treating skills and expertise as a dimension of class location within a materialist class analysis (except in so far as symbolic capital plays a role in acquiring skills and credentials). That rationale rests on the claim that experts, like managers, occupy a *privileged appropriation location within exploitation relations* that differentiates them from ordinary workers.

Throughout this book I will frequently use "skills and expertise" as a couplet. The term "skill" by itself sometimes is taken to refer simply to manual skills, rather than the more general idea of enhanced or complex labor power, contrasted to "raw" or undeveloped labor power. This enhancement can take many forms, both physical and cognitive. It may provide great flexibility to engage in a variety of work settings, or it may be highly specialized and vulnerable to obsolescence. Enhanced labor power is often legally certified in the form of official credentials, but in some circumstances skills and expertise may function effectively without such certification. The important theoretical idea is that skills and expertise designate an *asset embodied in the labor power* of people which enhances their power in labor markets and labor processes.

Incorporating skills in this way into class analysis somewhat blurs the sharp distinction between a *relational* class analysis and a *gradational* stratification analysis. Skills, after all, vary in more or less a continual manner – one can have greater or lesser skills. "Levels" of skills thus suggest *strata* within a structure of inequality rather than *locations* within a structure of class relations. The class analysis being proposed here, therefore, tries to combine an account of the social relations which constitute the classness of class structures with an account of processes which generate strata within class locations.

This way of specifying the distinctiveness of the class location of managers and experts is similar in certain respects to John Goldthorpe's (1982) treatment of the concept of the "service class." Goldthorpe draws a distinction between two kinds of employment relations: one based on a labor contract, characteristic of the working classes; and one based on what he terms a "service relationship," characteristic of managers and experts. In the latter, employees enter a career structure, not simply a job, and their rewards are in significant ways prospective, rather than simply payments for labor performed. Such a service relation, Goldthorpe argues, is "likely to be found where it is required of employees that they exercise delegated authority or specialized knowledge and expertise in the interests of their employing organization. In the nature of the case . . . their performance will depend upon the degree of moral commitment that they feel towards the organization rather than on the efficacy of external sanctions." (Erickson and Goldthorpe 1993: 42). This characterization is closely related to the idea that, because of their strategic power within organizations, the cooperation of middle-class employees is achieved in part through the payment of loyalty rents embodied in their earnings. The main difference between Goldthorpe's conceptual analysis and the one adopted here is, first, that Goldthorpe does not link his analysis of service-class jobs to the problem of exploitation and antagonistic interests; second, that he treats the authority dimension of managerial positions simply in terms of heightened responsibilities, not domination; and, third, he combines large capitalists, high-level professionals and upper-level corporate managers into a single class location in spite of their different location within capitalist property relations. Nevertheless, Goldthorpe's conceptualization of class structure taps many of the same relational properties of managerial and expert positions as the conceptualization adopted in this book.

A map of middle-class class locations

Adding position within authority hierarchies and possession of scarce skills and expertise to the fundamental dimension of capitalist property relations generates the map of class locations presented in Figure 1.1. With appropriate modifications depending upon our specific empirical objectives, this is the basic schema that underlies the investigations of this book.

It is important to stress that this is a map of class *locations*. The cells in the typology are not "classes" as such; they are locations within class relations. Some of these are contradictory locations within class relations, others are privileged appropriation locations within exploitation relations, and still others are polarized locations within capitalist property relations. By convention the polarized locations – "capitalists" and "workers" in capitalism – are often called "classes," but the more precise terminology would be to describe these as "the fundamental locations within the capitalist class structure." The typology is thus not a proposal for a six-class model of the class structure of capitalism, but rather a

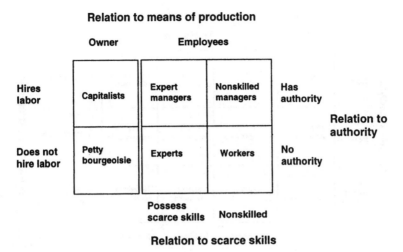

Figure 1.1 *Basic class typology.*

model of a class structure which differentiates six locations within class relations.

In some of the empirical analyses in this book, we combine some of the locations in this typology, typically to generate a four-category typology consisting of capitalists, petty bourgeois, "middle class" locations (contradictory locations and privileged appropriation locations among employees) and workers. In other analyses we will modify the typology by adding intermediary categories along each of the dimensions. On the ownership of means of production dimension this involves distinguishing between proper capitalists, small employers who only have a few employees, and the petty bourgeoisie (self-employed people with no employees). On the authority dimension this means differentiating between proper managers – people who are involved in organizational decision-making – and mere supervisors, who have power over subordinates but are not involved in policy-making decisions. And, on the skill dimension, this involves distinguishing between occupations which typically require advanced academic degrees, and other skilled occupations which require lower levels of specialized training. The result will be the twelve-location class structure matrix presented in Figure 1.2.

2 People not in the paid labor force

Many people in capitalist societies – probably the majority – do not fill jobs in the paid labor force. The most obvious case is children. How

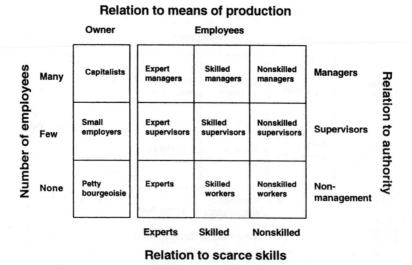

Relation to means of production

		Owner	Employees			
	Many	Capitalists	Expert managers	Skilled managers	Nonskilled managers	Managers
	Few	Small employers	Expert supervisors	Skilled supervisors	Nonskilled supervisors	Supervisors
	None	Petty bourgeoisie	Experts	Skilled workers	Nonskilled workers	Non-management

Number of employees (left axis, labels: Many, Few, None)

Relation to authority (right axis, labels: Managers, Supervisors, Non-management)

Experts   Skilled   Nonskilled

Relation to scarce skills

Figure 1.2 *Elaborated class typology.*

should babies be located in the class structure? But there are many other categories as well: retirees, permanently disabled people, students, people on welfare, the unemployed and full-time homemakers.[6] Each of these categories of people poses special problems for class structure analysis.

As a first approximation we can divide this heterogeneous set of situations into two broad categories: people who are tied to the class structure through interpersonal relations (especially within families),

[6] The claim that the people in these categories do not participate directly in production is simple enough for the unemployed, retirees and children, but it is problematic for housewives, since housewives obviously work and produce things in the home. This has led some theorists (e.g. Delphy 1984) to argue that the work of housewives should be treated as domestic labor performed within a domestic mode of production in which housewives occupy a distinctive class location, the domestic worker. Others have argued that household production is a subsidiary part of the capitalist mode of production. It has even been argued (Fraad, Resnick and Wolfe 1994) that household production is a special form of feudal production in which housewives are feudally exploited by their husbands since the husbands directly "appropriate" use-values from their wives. All of these views in one way or another attempt to treat the gender and kinship relations within a family as if they were a form of class relations. This amalgamation of class and gender undercuts the explanatory specificity of both class and gender and does not, I believe, enhance our capacity to explain the processes in question. In any case, since the empirical analysis in this book is restricted to people in the paid labor force, we will bracket these issues.

and people who are not. To be in a "location" within class structure is to have one's material interests shaped by one's relationship to the process of exploitation. One way such linkages to exploitation are generated by class structures is through jobs. This is the kind of class location we have been exploring so far. I will refer to these as *direct class locations*. But there are other mechanisms by which people's lives are linked to the process of exploitation. Of particular importance are the ways in which family structures and kinship relations link an individual's material interests to the process of exploitation. Being born into a wealthy capitalist family links the child to the material interests of the capitalist class via family relations. It makes sense, then, to say that this child is "in" the capitalist class. If that child, as a young adult, works in a factory but stands to inherit millions of dollars of capitalist wealth and can rely on family resources for various needs, then that person would simultaneously be in two class locations: the capitalist class by virtue of family ties and the working class by virtue of the job.

I will refer to these situations as *mediated class locations*. Family ties are probably the most important basis for mediated class locations, but membership in certain kinds of communities or the relationship to the state may also provide such linkages. In each case the question one asks is "how do the social relations in which a person's life is embedded link that person to the various mechanisms of class exploitation and thus shape that person's material interests?" Many people, of course, have both direct and mediated class locations. This is of particular importance in developed capitalist economies for households in which both spouses are in the labor force, for this creates the possibility that husbands and wives will have different direct class locations, and thus each of them will have different direct and mediated locations. Understanding such "cross-class families" is the core problem of chapter 7.

There are, however, people for whom family ties provide at most extremely tenuous linkages to the class structure. Most notably, this is the situation of many people in the so-called "underclass." This expression is used in a variety of ways in contemporary policy discussions. Sometimes it is meant to be a pejorative term rather like the old Marxist concept of "lumpenproletariat"; other times it is used more descriptively to designate a segment of the poor whose conditions of life are especially desperate and whose prospects for improvement are particularly dismal. In terms of the analysis of this chapter, one way of giving this concept a more precise theoretical status is to link it to the concepts of exploitation and oppression: an "underclass" can be defined as a category of social agents who are economically oppressed but not consistently exploited within a given class system.[7]

Different kinds of class structures will generate different forms of an "underclass." In many parts of the world today and throughout much of human history, the pivotal resource which defines the underclass is land. Landlords, agrarian capitalists, peasants and exploited agrarian producers all have access to land; people who are excluded from such access constitute the underclass of agrarian societies. In these terms, many Native Americans were transformed into an underclass in the nineteenth century when they were pushed off the land onto the reservations.

In contemporary advanced capitalism, the key resource which defines the predicament of the underclass is labor power itself. This might seem like an odd statement since in capitalism, at least since the abolition of slavery, everyone supposedly owns one "unit" of labor power, him- or herself. The point is that some people do not in fact own productively saleable labor power. The situation is similar to a capitalist owning outmoded machines. While the capitalist physically controls these pieces of machinery, they cease to be "capital" – a capitalistically productive asset – if they cannot be deployed within a capitalist production process profitably. In the case of labor power, a person can physically control his or her own laboring capacity, but that capacity can cease to have economic value in capitalism if it cannot be sold on a labor market and deployed productively. This is the essential condition of the "underclass." They are oppressed because they are denied access to various kinds of productive resources, above all the necessary means to acquire the skills needed to make their labor power saleable. As a result, they are not consistently exploited.

Understood in this way, the underclass consists of human beings who are largely expendable from the point of view of the logic of capitalism. Like Native Americans who became a landless underclass in the nineteenth century, repression rather than incorporation is the central

---

[7] Although he does not explicitly elaborate the term "underclass" in terms of a theory of exploitation and economic oppression, the definition proposed here is consistent with the more structural aspects of the way the term is used by William Julius Wilson (1982, 1987) in his analysis of the interconnection between race and class in American society. Wilson argues that, as legal barriers to racial equality have disappeared and as class differentiation within the black population has increased, the central determining structure of the lives of many African-Americans is no longer race as such, but class. More specifically, he argues that there has been a substantial growth of an urban underclass of people without marketable skills and with very weak attachments to the labor force, living in crumbling central cities isolated from the mainstream of American life and institutions.

mode of social control directed towards them. Capitalism does not need the labor power of unemployed inner city youth. The material interests of the wealthy and privileged segments of American society would be better served if these people simply disappeared. However, unlike in the nineteenth century, the moral and political forces are such that direct genocide is no longer a viable strategy. The alternative, then, is to build prisons and to cordon off the zones of cities in which the underclass lives.

3 Employee investments

In developed capitalist countries, many people are both owners of capitalist investments (and accordingly receive some of their income as returns on those investments) and paid employees in a job. This situation is most notoriously the case for high-level executives in large corporations whose income comes both from direct salaries as employees and from stockholding in the corporation. The latter often dwarfs the former. But, more generally, there is a fairly wide spectrum of people who are in jobs with sufficiently high pay that they are able to convert some of their employment earnings into capitalist property through personal investment, and others who work in firms which offer a variety of incentive schemes involving stock ownership for ordinary employees. And, of course, there is an even broader range of people who have no direct control of investments, but who nevertheless have vested rights in pensions which are invested in capitalist firms. In many cases, the investment portfolios of employees are trivial and only marginally shape their material interests. The United States is certainly very far from the fantasy of a "People's Capitalism" in which share ownership is so widespread that the distinction between owners and workers begins to wither away. Nevertheless, for certain segments of the employee population, particularly managers and professionals, the ability to turn surplus earnings into capital can become a significant part of their class situation. These kinds of situations define a specific kind of complexity in the class structure, a new kind of "contradictory class location" in which a person's job class and their property class become partially uncoupled.

4 Temporality

The final complexity to be added to the concept of class structure concerns the temporal character of class locations. So far we have treated class "locations" in a basically static matter, as slots within relations filled by persons. This can give a quite misleading picture of how people's lives are organized within class structures. Two individuals in identical working-class jobs in terms of statically defined relational characteristics would have very different class interests if one was certain to be promoted into a managerial position and one was certain to remain for life in a working-class position.

Typically, analyses of the temporal dimension of class structures treat this problem as one of *intra*generational "mobility." The suggestion in such a characterization is that individuals "move" from one location to another and thus the locations are definable independently of the movement. If, however, specific jobs are embedded in temporally organized careers, and certain kinds of careers cross class lines, then such movement are not properly considered class "mobility" at all. The class location itself has a temporal character.

In most real world situations, of course, it is not the case that people occupy class-careers with complete certainty about future states. The temporal dimension of class location, therefore, generally implies a degree of temporal *indeterminacy* in the class location of people.

This issue of the temporality of class locations applies to mediated class locations as well as direct class locations. In particular, it may be useful to understand the class location of married women as partially determined by what might be called their "shadow class" – the class location that they would occupy in the case of the dissolution of their marriage, either through divorce or widowhood. Since the shadow class for married women is frequently different from their current mediated class, this suggests that there is at least some temporal indeterminacy in the mediated class locations of many women, particularly given the high rates of divorce.

Adding these four sources of complexity to the concept of class – contradictory class locations, privileged relations to exploitation, mediated class locations, disjunctures between job class and property class, and the temporal dimension of locations – moves us very far from the simple, polarized class concept with which we began this discussion. Some sociologists, in fact, have argued that the existence of these kinds of complexities signal the "death of class," to quote Pakulski and Waters (1996). In this view, incorporating these complexities cannot enrich the explanatory power of class; rather, they compromise the basic relevance of class for sociological analysis. One of the main objectives of this book is to show that class remains a relevant and powerful concept, not in spite of these complexities but in part because of the way these complexities can be incorporated into class analysis.

1.5 Marxist versus Weberian class analysis

As a set of empirical categories, the class structure matrix in Figures 1.1 and 1.2 could be deployed within either a Weberian or Marxist framework. The control over economic resources is central to both Marxist and Weberian class analysis, and both frameworks could be massaged to allow for the array of categories I am using. Indeed, a good argument could be made that the proposed class structure concept incorporates significant Weberian elements, since the explicit inclusion of skills as a criterion for class division and the importance accorded income privileges for both managers and credentialed experts are hallmarks of Weberian class analysis. In a real sense, therefore, the empirical categories in this book can be seen as a hybrid of the categories conventionally found in Marxist and Weberian class analysis. In what sense, therefore, does this class structure analysis remain "Marxist"?

To answer this question we need to compare the theoretical foundations of the concept of class in the Marxist and Weberian traditions. The contrast between Marx and Weber has been one of the grand themes in the history of Sociology as a discipline. Most graduate school programs have a sociological theory course within which Marx versus Weber figures as a central motif. However, in terms of class analysis, posing Marx and Weber as polar opposites is a bit misleading because in many ways Weber is speaking in his most Marxian voice when he talks about class. The concept of class within these two streams of thought share a number of important features:

- Both Marxist and Weberian approaches differ from what might be called simple *gradational* notions of class in which classes are differentiated strictly on the basis of inequalities in the material conditions of life. This conceptualization of class underwrites the common inventory of classes found in popular discourse and the mass media: upper class, upper middle class, middle class, lower middle class, lower class, underclass. Both Marxist and Weberian class analysis define classes *relationally*, i.e. a given class location is defined by virtue of the social relations which link it to other class locations.

- Both traditions identify the concept of class with the relationship between people and economically relevant assets or resources. Marxists call this relation to the means of production; Weberians refer to "Market capacities." But they are both really talking about very similar empirical phenomena.

- Both traditions see the causal relevance of class as operating, at least in part, via the ways in which these relations shape the material interests of actors. Ownership of the means of production and ownership of one's own labor power are explanatory of social action because these property rights shape the strategic alternatives people face in pursuing their material well-being: *what you have determines what you get*, and *what you have determines what you have to do to get what you get*. To be sure, Marxists tend to put more weight on the objective character of these "material interests" by highlighting the fact that these constraints are imposed on individuals, whereas Weberians tend to focus on the subjective conditions, by emphasizing the relative contingency in what people want. Nevertheless, it is still the case that at their core, both class concepts involve the causal connection between (a) social relations to resources and (b) material interests via (c) the way resources shape strategies for acquiring income.

How then do they differ? The pivotal contrast is captured by the favorite buzz-words of each theoretical tradition: *life chances* for Weberians, and *exploitation* for Marxists. The reason why production is more central to Marxist than to Weberian class analysis is because of its salience for the problem of exploitation; the reason why Weberians give greater emphasis to the market is because it so directly shapes life chances.

The intuition behind the idea of life chances is straightforward. "In our terminology," Weber (in Gerth and Mills 1958: 181–182) writes:

"classes" are not communities; they merely represent possible, and frequent, bases for communal action. We may speak of a "class" when (1) a number of people have in common a specific causal component of their life chances, in so far as (2) this component is represented exclusively by economic interests in the possession of goods and opportunities for income, and (3) is represented under conditions of the commodity or labor markets . . . These points refer to "class situation," which we may express more briefly as the typical chance for a supply of goods, external living conditions and life experiences, in so far as this chance is determined by the amount and kind of power, or lack of such, to dispose of goods or skills for the sake of income in a given economic order. The term "class" refers to any group of people that is found in the same class situation . . . But always this is the generic connotation of the concept of class: that the kind of chance in the market is the decisive moment which presents a common condition for the individual's fate. "Class situation" is, in this sense, ultimately "market situation."

In short, the kind and quantity of resources you own affects your opportunities for income in market exchanges. "Opportunity" is a description of the feasible set individuals face, the trade-offs they encounter in deciding what to do. Owning means of production gives a person different alternatives from owning credentials, and both of these are different from simply owning unskilled labor power. Furthermore, in a market economy, access to market-derived income affects the broader array of life experiences and opportunities for oneself and one's children. The study of the life chances of children, based on parents' market capacity, is thus an integral part of the Weberian agenda of class analysis.

Within a Weberian perspective, therefore, the salient issue in the linkage of people to different kinds of economic resources is the way this confers on them different kinds of economic opportunities and disadvantages and thereby shapes their material interests. One way of representing this idea in a stylized way is by examining the income–leisure trade-offs faced by people in different classes as pictured in Figure 1.3. In this figure, everyone faces some trade-off between leisure and income: less leisure yields more income. However, for the propertied class it is possible to have high income with no work (thus the expressions "the leisure class" or the "idle rich"), whereas, for both the middle class and the working class in this stylized drawing, zero work corresponds to zero income. The middle class has "greater" opportunities (life chances) in the market than workers because the slope they face (i.e. the wage rate) is steeper. Some workers in fact might actually have a higher standard of living than some people in the middle class, but the trade-offs they face are nevertheless less desirable. These common trade-offs, then, are the basis for a potential commonality of interests among members of a class, and thus constitute the basis for potential common action.

Within a Marxist framework, the feature of the relationship of people to economic resources which is at the core of class analysis is "exploitation." Both "exploitation" and "life chances" identify inequalities in material well-being that are generated by inequalities in access to resources of various sorts. Thus both of these concepts point to conflicts of interest over the *distribution* of the assets themselves. What exploitation adds to this is a claim that conflicts of interest between classes are generated not simply by what people have, but also by what people do with what they have. The concept of exploitation, therefore, points our attention to conflicts within *production*, not simply conflicts in the *market*.

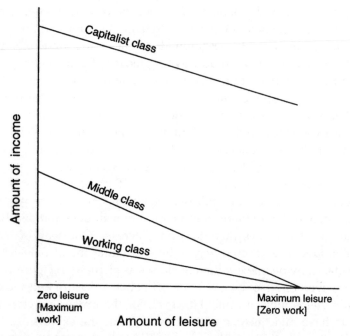

Figure 1.3 *Leisure vs. consumption trade-offs faced by people in different economic classes.*

This conceptual contrast between Marxist and Weberian perspectives on class is reflected in an interesting way in the *Li'l Abner* story about the shmoo. In commenting on the shmoo, the Dogpatch resident proclaims, "But nobody whut's got shmoos has t'work any more," whereas the manager declares, "Nobody'll have to *work hard* any more." The manager understands that the issue is the extraction of labor effort – exploitation – not simply getting people to show up for "work." The Dogpatchian only identifies an effect in the labor market; the manager identifies an effect in the labor process. To state the matter sociologically, the Dogpatchian provides a Weberian analysis, the manager a Marxist one.

Figure 1.4 summarizes this analysis of the differences between the Marxist and Weberian traditions of class analysis. Weberian class analysis revolves around a single causal nexus that works through market exchanges. Marxist class analysis includes the Weberian causal processes, but adds to them a causal structure within production itself as well as an account of the interactions of production and exchange. Part of our analysis, the class location of managers, for example, concerns the "loyalty rent" which managers receive by virtue of their position within

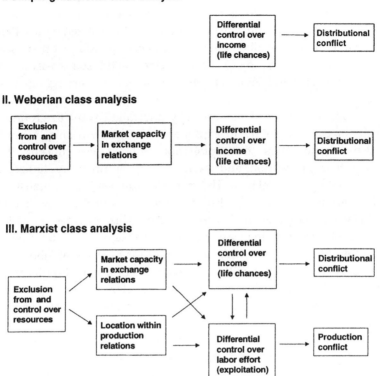

Figure 1.4 *Three models of class analysis.*

the authority structure of production. This reflects the way in which location within the relations of production and not simply within market relations affects the "life chances" of managers. Our analysis of the shmoo – and more broadly, the analysis of such things as the way transfer payments of the welfare state affect the market capacity of workers – illustrates how market capacity has an impact on the extraction of labor effort within production. The Marxist concept of class directs our attention both theoretically and empirically towards these interactions.

A Weberian might reply that there is nothing in the Weberian idea of market-based life chances that would prevent the analysis of the extraction of labor effort within production. A good and subtle Weberian class analyst could certainly link the analysis of market capacities within exchange relations to power relations within the labor process, and thus explore the causal structures at the center of Marxist class analysis. In systematically joining production and exchange in this way, however, the Weberian concept would in effect become Marxianized. Frank Parkin (1979: 25), in a famous gibe, said "Inside every neo-Marxist there seems to be a Weberian struggling to get out." One could just as easily say that inside every left-wing Weberian there is a Marxist struggling to stay hidden.

There are a number of reasons why one might want to ground the concept of class explicitly in exploitation rather than simply market-based life chances. First, the exploitation-centered class concept affirms the fact that production and exchange are intrinsically linked, not merely contingently related. The material interests of capitalists and workers are inherently shaped by the interaction of these two facets of the social relations that bind them together. This provides us with the way of understanding the class location of managers as determined not simply by their position within the market for managerial labor power, but also by their position within the relations of domination in produc-tion. More broadly, the exploitation-based class concept points our attention to the fact that class relations are relations of power, not merely privilege.

Second, theorizing the interests linked to classes as grounded in inherently antagonistic and interdependent practices facilitates the analysis of social conflict. Explanations of conflict always require at least two elements: an account of the opposing interests at stake in the conflict and an account of the capacity of the actors to pursue those interests. A simple opposition of interests is not enough to explain active conflict between groups. Exploitation is a powerful concept precisely because it brings together an account of opposing interests with an account of the rudimentary capacity for resistance. Exploiters not only have a positive interest in limiting the life chances of the exploited, but also are dependent upon the exploited for the realization of their own interests. This dependency of the exploiter on the exploited gives the exploited an inherent capacity to resist. Exploitation, therefore, does not simply predict an opposition of interests, but a tendency for this antagonism of interests to generate manifest conflicts between classes. This understanding of the inherent power of exploited classes is marginalized when class is defined strictly in terms of market relations.

Third, the exploitation-centered concept of class provides the founda-tions for what can be termed an endogenous theory of politics and ideology.[8] Exploitative relations are inherently unstable because of the way they meld intense conflict of interests – one group having positive interests in the deprivations of another – with deep interdependency – the exploiter needs the exploited. This implies a specific prediction: for relations of exploitation to be stably reproduced, there will be a tendency for social institutions to be developed which in one way or another neutralize or contain these conflicts. More specifically, it is predicted that there is a tendency for political institutions to emerge which coercively defend the interests of exploiters and ideological practices to emerge which evoke at least limited consent from the exploited. While this does not imply a smooth, functional correspondence of class relations and political and ideological institutions (as in the "base" and "superstructure" model of classical Marxism), it does suggest systematic endogenous pressures for such correspondence.

Finally, the exploitation-centered class analysis provides a rich menu of concepts for comparative historical analysis in which societies are analyzed in terms of the specific ways in which they vary in forms of exploitation and associated class structures. This generates the familiar typology of forms of society in the Marxist tradition: communalism, slavery, feudalism, capitalism. In classical Marxism these forms of society were seen as constituting the central stages within a broad theory of history. But even if one rejects the theoretical ambitions of historical materialism, this typology still constitutes a compelling menu for historical comparative analyses. Of course, this is not the only coherent conceptual typology of historical variations in forms of society. The Weberian typology of societies in terms of forms of legitimate authority is a notable alternative, and for some purposes it might be more useful than the class-centered typology. The class-centered typology, however, provides an especially rich agenda of research questions and analytical possibilities because of the ways in which it is so closely tied to problems of social conflict and the development of political and ideological institutions.

There is no metatheoretical rule of sociology which says that every sociologist must chose between these two ways of grounding class analysis. It certainly might be possible to construct an eclectic hybrid between Marxist and Weberian class analysis. Nevertheless, throughout this book I will interpret the class structure matrix we will be using

---

[8] "Endogenous" means that the theory in question is generated by elements that are *internal* to the system in question – in this case, class relations – rather than simply by external factors.

within a neo-Marxist class analysis framework. In the end, the decision to do this rather than adopt a more eclectic stance comes at least in part from political commitments, not simply dispassionate scientific principles. This does not mean that Marxist class analysis is pure ideology or that it is rigidly dictated by radical egalitarian values. My choice of analytical framework is also based on my beliefs in the theoretical coherence of this approach – which I have argued for in this chapter – and in its capacity to illuminate empirical problems – which I hope to demonstrate in the rest of this book. But this choice remains crucially bound up with commitments to the socialist tradition and its aspirations for an emancipatory, egalitarian alternative to capitalism.

Readers who are highly skeptical of the Marxist tradition for whatever reasons might feel that there is no point in struggling through the numbers and graphs in the rest of this book. If the conceptual justifications for the categories are unredeemably flawed, it might be thought, the empirical results generated with those categories will be worthless. This would be, I think, a mistake. The empirical categories themselves can be interpreted in a Weberian or hybrid manner. Indeed, as a practical set of operational categories, the class structure matrix used in this book does not dramatically differ from the class typology used by Goldthorpe (1980) and Erickson and Goldthorpe (1993). As is usually the case in sociology, the empirical categories of analysis are *under*determined by the theoretical frameworks within which they are generated or interpreted. This means that readers who are resolutely unconvinced about the virtues of understanding classes in terms of exploitation can still engage with the empirical analyses of this book as investigations of classes differentially situated with respect to life chances in the market.

1.6 The empirical agenda of the book

Broadly speaking, the empirical studies in this book explore three interconnected problems in class analysis: 1. Characteristics of and variations in class structure itself; 2. The relationship between class and gender as aspects of social structure; 3. The linkage between class structure and class consciousness.

Class structure

The research in Part I concerns various problems in the analysis of class structure itself. Chapter 2 sets the stage for the rest of the book by presenting basic descriptive data on the overall shape of the class structure in a number of advanced capitalist societies. Here we are not so much interested in testing specific hypotheses about cross-national variations than in carefully describing various aspects of these variations. As a result, in some ways this chapter may be less interesting theoretically than the empirical chapters which follow.

Chapter 3 examines changes in the distribution of people in the American class structure between 1960 and 1990 and decomposes these changes into a part that can be attributed to shifts in class distributions within economic sectors and a part to shifts in the distribution of people across economic sectors. The basic results are quite striking. The working class expanded slightly in the 1960s, but has declined at an accelerating pace since then, especially because of a decline in the working class within sectors. Supervisors increased significantly in the 1960s and modestly in the 1970s, but declined in the 1980s. In contrast, managers, experts and expert managers have all increased throughout this period. The petty bourgeoisie and small employer class categories declined both within and across sectors in the 1960s, but since then have had a more complex trajectory, leading in the 1980s to a quite significant expansion of the petty bourgeoisie and a nearly steady state for small employers. While our data do not allow us to test alternative explanations for these changes, I offer a tentative explanation in terms of the combination of technological change and the ramifications of long-term economic stagnation in an increasingly competitive international capitalist economic system.

Chapter 4 examines in much greater detail one of the trends in chapter 3, the initial decline and then steady expansion of self-employment. Two different strategies of data analysis are presented: first, a time series analysis of annual changes in the rate of self-employment in which we test whether or not changes in self-employment can be attributed to changes in the rate of unemployment; and second, an examination of the sectoral patterns of changes in self-employment in which we document that the upsurge in self-employment which began in the mid-1970s is a broad trend throughout the economy, not simply in the service sector.

Chapter 5 explores the degree of permeability of class boundaries in four countries, the United States, Canada, Norway and Sweden. Class structures vary not simply in the distribution of people into class locations, but in the extent to which the lives of people are narrowly confined to specific class locations or involve social contacts and experiences across class boundaries. In this chapter we explore three forms of permeability: the permeability of class boundaries to intergenerational mobility, the permeability of boundaries to friendships, and the permeability of boundaries to cross-class marriages. To somewhat oversimplify the main punchlines of the research, for each of these forms of permeability in all four countries, the authority boundary is the most permeable and, generally, the property boundary is the least permeable.

Class and gender

Since the late 1970s, one of the main challenges to class analysis has come from feminist scholars who have argued for the centrality of gender as an explanatory principle in social theory and research. Many feminists have been especially critical of claims to "class primacy," which are often attributed to Marxist scholarship (in spite of the fact that few Marxists today actually defend class primacy as a general principle).

In more recent years there has been something of a truce on the issue of class and gender as most people recognize that there is no point in arguing for all-encompassing abstract claims about the "primacy" of particular causal factors in social explanations. Primacy is a tractable issue only with respect to specific explananda, and even then it is often more fruitful to explore the forms of interaction of different causal processes than to focus on which is "more important."[9] Rather than seek any kind of metatheoretical priority to class analysis over gender analysis (or vice versa) it is more important to understand the interconnections of class and gender in specific explanatory problems.

This dialogue between Marxism and certain strands of feminism constitutes the backdrop to the analyses of class and gender in chapters 6–9. Chapter 6 defends a conceptualization of class and gender in which they are treated as analytically distinct relations which interact in various social settings. The chapter then frames the empirical agenda by discussing a menu of five different forms in which this interaction takes place.

Chapter 7 examines the conceptual and empirical problem of the class location of married women. In chapter 5, where we explore the permeability of class boundaries to cross-class marriages, the class character of households is defined in terms of the individual job classes of both husbands and wives. Some scholars have challenged this way

---

[9] For a general discussion of the problem of explanatory primacy, see Wright, Levine and Sober (1992).

of understanding the class location of married women in the labor force. They have argued that families, not individuals, occupy locations in class structures, and thus all members of a family must share the same class position. Since the class interests of families are most decisively shaped by the class character of the husband's job, the argument goes, all members of the family, including married women with paid jobs, should be seen in the husband's class. This chapter explores the conceptual foundations of this argument and various other approaches, and then proposes a strategy for empirically comparing the alternatives.

Chapter 8 examines an explanatory problem that is of considerable importance within gender analysis: the gender division of labor in the home. Many feminists have argued that the sexual division of labor within families is at the very core of the social practices which produce and reproduce gender hierarchy in the society at large. In this chapter we examine the relationship between the class composition of households and the amount of housework husbands perform in Sweden and the United States. The results are quite simple: class has almost no effect on husbands' performance of housework in either country.

Chapter 9 explores a specific aspect of gender distributions within class structures – the differential probabilities of men and women having workplace authority. It is hardly news that men are more likely to have authority within the workplace. What we explore in this chapter is first, the extent to which there are cross-national variations in this "gender gap" in authority; second, the extent to which this gender gap can be accounted for by a range of individual attributes of men and women (such as job experience, age, education, part-time employment, sector, occupation and a few other variables); and, third, the extent to which there is evidence of a "glass ceiling" within authority hierarchies (i.e. the gender gap in authority increases as you move up hierarchies). The basic answer to the first question is that there are quite substantial cross-national variations, with the United States and Australia having the smallest gender gaps, followed by Canada and the UK, then the two Scandinavian countries in the analysis, Norway and Sweden, and finally Japan, which has by far the largest gender gap in authority of all of these countries. The answer to the second question is that very little of the gender gap in authority or the cross-national differences in the gap can be explained by the distribution of attributes of men and women. The gaps thus appear to be largely due to direct discrimination within employment. The answer to the third question is perhaps the most surprising: there is virtually no evidence that a genuine glass ceiling exists, at least into the middle ranges of authority hierarchies.

Class structure and class consciousness

One of the main reasons for studying class structure is because of its importance in explaining other elements of class analysis, especially class formation, class consciousness and class struggle. Chapter 10 lays out a general model of the interconnection of these elements of class analysis. More specifically, the chapter tries to clarify the relationship between the micro- and macro-levels of class analysis. This involves first discussing in general metatheoretical terms the distinction between micro- and macro-analysis, and then elaborating a micro-model of the relationship between class *location*, individual class *practices* and class *consciousness*, and a macro-model of the relationship between class *structure*, class *struggle* and class *formation*.

Chapter 11 applies the framework in chapter 10 to a study of class consciousness and class formation in the United States, Sweden and Japan. These three countries are striking contrasts in the patterns of what we will call "ideological class formation." Sweden is quite ideologically polarized between a working-class coalition and a bour-geois coalition with a relatively large and distinct middle-class coalition in between. Ideological differentiation is sharpest along the property dimension of the class structure matrix, but is systematic and marked along the authority and skill dimensions as well. In the United States, the bourgeois coalition penetrates much more broadly into the class locations among employees, and the overall pattern of class formation is less ideologically polarized than in Sweden, but the basic shape of ideological differentiation across the class structure matrix is still quite similar in the two countries. In Japan, the patterns are drastically different: the degree of polarization is much more muted than in either the US or Sweden, and among employees the ideological cleavages occur mainly along the skill–expertise dimension rather than the authority dimension.

Chapter 12 concludes the book by reflecting on the ways in which the empirical analyses generate a variety of surprises which in turn provoke efforts at rethinking various theoretical formulations.

This is a highly heterogeneous set of empirical problems. What emerges cumulatively from the research is not a simple punchline about the superiority of Marxist approaches to class over its rivals, or the universal explanatory power of class relative to other social causes. Rather, the bottom-line message of the research is twofold: first, within the family of developed capitalist societies there is considerable variation in both the structural properties of the system of class relations and the effects of class, and, second, in spite of these variations, the fundamental class division based on ownership of the means of production remains a consistently important division within nearly all of the analyses of the book.

Part I

Structural analyses of classes

2. Class structure

The starting-point for class analysis is the problem of class structure. The investigation of class structure provides us with the way both of situating the lives of individuals for micro-class analysis and of describing variations in societies across time and place for macro-class analysis. In the previous chapter we explored the theoretical foundations for this concept. In this chapter we will descriptively map out the broad contours of the class structure in several developed capitalist countries and examine how it has changed over time in the United States.

In practical terms, this task involves pigeon-holing people into specific categories on the basis of responses they give to a questionnaire about their work. It is not possible to directly observe a "class structure" as such. What one observes are individuals who occupy specific places in a social structure. By asking them appropriate questions and aggregating their responses, we generate descriptions of the class structure as a whole. To some readers this may seem like a fairly sterile scholastic exercise. Taxonomy, classification, pigeon-holing – these are surely the tedious preoccupations of narrow academic specialists. What is worse, squeezing individuals into simple categories seems to obliterate the richness and complexity of their lives. Class becomes a static set of simple boxes rather than a complex, dynamic process. Would not it be better to pursue qualitative field research with relatively loose and flexible concepts capable of adapting to the complexity of the situation?

There is some truth in these criticisms. The categories we will be using are highly simplified representations of the complexity of class relations. The categories do become "fixed" in that once a set of criteria are adopted they are applied to all people in the same way in different countries. As a result, there will inevitably be many cases in which individuals are being squeezed uncomfortably into slots. The appropriate question, however, is not "do the categories we develop faithfully mirror the complexity of the world?" but rather, "are these categories capable of advancing our knowledge of specific problems in class analysis?" Do these categories, however crude they might be, enable us to identify interesting puzzles? Do they help to reveal places where existing theories run into trouble, and provide at least some relevant evidence for the reconstruction of those theories? In the end, as Engels once said, "the proof of the pudding is in the eating."

This chapter will be primarily concerned with describing the overall appearance of the pudding. In the rest of the book we will eat it and see how well it tastes.

2.1 The basic contours of the class structure

Figure 2.1 presents the distribution of the employed labor force into the twelve class locations described in chapter 1 for six countries: the United States, Canada, the United Kingdom, Sweden, Norway and Japan.[1] We will first look at the patterns across the property dimensions of the class structure and then turn to class distributions among employees.

The property dimension

The capitalist class, defined as self-employed people who employ ten or more employees, comprises no more than about 2% of the labor force in any of these countries, and less than 1% in two of them (Sweden and Norway). Of course, this figure does not include those capitalists who are not technically "employers." Many people who own significant amounts of capitalist wealth may be employed as top executives of corporations, others are employed in jobs completely unrelated to their capitalist wealth, and some are formally out of the labor force altogether, living as pure rentiers off the income from their wealth. A few are even professors. Unfortunately, with the comparative data in this project it is not possible to estimate the proportion of the population who would fall into the segment of the capitalist class which is not self-employed. In any case, this would probably only add at most a few percentage points to these figures.[2]

---

[1] The details of the measures and operationalizations of class structure used in this chapter can be found in Wright (1997: 74–90).

[2] According to Lawrence Mishel and David Frankel (1991: 162), in the richest 1% of US households defined by the income distribution, 47.8% of household income came from

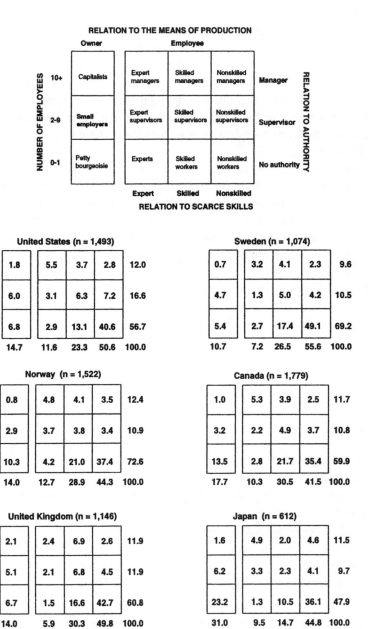

Figure 2.1 *Class distributions in six countries.*

As would be expected, there are considerably more small employers, defined here as self-employed individuals employing 2–9 employees, than proper capitalists. The range is between about 3% of the labor force in Canada and Norway to about 6% in the United States and Japan. Putting these two class locations together, between roughly 4% and 8% of the labor forces of these six developed capitalist countries are in class locations which are, to a greater or lesser extent, directly connected to the capitalist class.

There is much more variation across these countries in the size of the petty bourgeoisie (self-employed people with no more than one employee), which ranges from about 5% of the labor force in Sweden to over 23% in Japan. Japan is clearly the outlier. This high proportion of the labor force in the petty bourgeoisie in Japan compared to the other five countries occurs within nearly every major economic sector; it is not just a question of there being many small farmers or small shop keepers in Japan.[3] The persistence of economic activity not directly organized by capitalist firms is thus considerably stronger in Japan than in the other advanced capitalist countries we are studying.

Employees

At first glance it appears in Figure 2.1 that there is a fair amount of variation in the class distributions among employees across these six countries. The expert manager category is more than twice as large in Japan, Canada and the United States than in the United Kingdom, and the working class is more than 30% larger in Sweden than in Norway, Japan and Canada. These cross-national differences, however, may be somewhat misleading because of the variation across countries in self-employment (especially the high self-employment rate in Japan) and because of possible measurement problems for some of the intermediary categories in the class map. To get a clearer picture of variations across countries within the employee part of the class structure, it is useful to look at class distributions among employees taken separately rather than

capital assets in 1988. For the next richest 4%, this figure drops to 23.2%. The average assets per household for the richest 0.5% of American households in 1989 was over $8 million, and of the next 0.5% over $2.5 million. These data suggest that the wealthy capitalist class defined strictly in terms of holdings of financial assets – i.e. individuals whose livelihood is substantially dependent upon income derived from capital holdings – constitutes probably no more than 2–3% of the population.

[3] See Wright (1997: 50, Table 2.1).

for the entire labor force and to combine the two polarized categories among employees with the intermediary categories immediately adjacent to them by creating an "extended expert-manager" category (expert-managers, expert supervisors and skilled managers combined) and an "extended working-class" category (workers, skilled workers and nonskilled supervisors combined). In this modified class map of employees, the cross-national variability is considerably attenuated. In five of the six countries – the United States, Norway, Canada, the United Kingdom and Japan – 13–15% of all employees are in the extended expert-manager class location, and 71–74% are in the extended working class category. The one country which does differ modestly from these figures is Sweden, in which 79.2% of the employee labor force is in the extended working-class location and only 9.6% is in the extended expert-manager class location.[4] Still, given how different are the work organizations and historical experiences of these countries, it is really quite striking that their class distributions among employees are so similar. The working class and the class locations closest to the working class constitute around three-quarters of the employee labor force in these countries, and the privileged segments of the "middle class" – the extended expert-manager category – constitute about 10–15%.

2.2 Class and gender

Any analysis of the linkage between class and gender must confront the problem of the appropriate unit of analysis for analyzing class distributions. As we will discuss in detail in chapter 7, one view, advanced forcefully by John Goldthorpe (1983), holds that families, not individuals, occupy locations in class structures. Since families are units of shared consumption, all members of a family, Goldthorpe argues, share a common interest in the family's command of economically relevant resources, and therefore it does not make sense to say that different members of a family household are "in" different classes. Goldthorpe therefore argues in favor of what he calls the "conventional" practice of assigning the class location of the "head of household," typically the male breadwinner, to all members of the family including married women in the labor force.

An alternative approach is to treat individuals as the incumbents of

---

[4] For detailed results, see Wright (1997: 54, Figure 2.2). For an extended discussion of why Sweden has a somewhat larger working class and a smaller extended expert-manager class location, see Wright (1997: 53–58).

Table 2.1 *Class distributions of men and women in the United States and Sweden using individual job-class and family-class criteria*

	Job-class			Family-class	
	Men	Women	Total	Women	Total
United States					
1 Capitalists and small employers	10.2	5.2	7.9	5.8	8.2
2 Petty bourgeoisie	6.4	7.5	6.9	6.8	6.6
3 Expert and skilled with authority	24.9	9.6	17.8	18.0	21.8
4 Nonskilled with authority	5.3	12.7	8.7	8.7	6.8
5 Experts with authority	3.3	2.7	3.0	3.7	3.5
6 Skilled employees without authority	18.0	8.6	13.9	10.7	15.0
7 Nonskilled without authority (workers)	31.5	53.7	41.6	46.2	38.2
Sweden					
1 Capitalists and small employers	7.8	1.6	5.2	2.1	5.5
2 Petty bourgeoisie	7.0	2.9	5.3	6.0	6.6
3 Expert and skilled with authority	9.7	10.0	15.7	18.5	19.2
4 Nonskilled with authority	9.4	5.3	7.7	7.2	8.5
5 Experts without authority	2.3	2.7	2.5	4.4	3.2
6 Skilled employees without authority	17.8	14.0	16.3	19.0	18.3
7 Nonskilled without authority (workers)	35.9	63.5	47.3	42.8	38.7

class locations. In this view, class locations are constructed within the social relations of production, not consumption, and, since jobs are typically filled by individuals in capitalist society, individuals are the appropriate unit of analysis. The class location of married women in the labor force, therefore, is not derived from that of her husband, and families can be internally heterogeneous in terms of class location.

These two ways of thinking about the class location of married women generate quite different pictures of the class structure, as illustrated in Table 2.1 for the United States and Sweden. (The job–class distributions in this table are not exactly the same as elsewhere in this chapter because different operational criteria had to be used for the comparison with family-class). Following the "conventional wisdom" announced by Goldthorpe, for men family-class is identical to job–class, while for women, family-class is defined by their own individual job–class if they are single or if their spouse is not in the labor force but by their husband's job–class if their husband is in the labor force.

As one would expect, the class distributions for men and women are much more similar when class location is defined by family-class than when it is defined by job–class. For example, in the United States 31.5%

of men and 53.7% of women are in the working class when this is defined by individual job–classes, but the figure for women drops to 46.2% when we use the family-class specification of class location. The contrast is even sharper in Sweden: 35.9% of men and 63.5% of women are in the working class defined in terms of job–classes, whereas only 42.8% of women are in the working class defined in terms of family-class. The result is that the comparison of the overall class structures in these two countries is decisively different depending upon which conception of class structure is used: in terms of *job*-classes we would conclude that the working class is significantly larger in Sweden than in the United States – 47.3% of the employed labor force in Sweden compared to 41.6% in the United States – whereas if we used the family-class criterion, we would conclude that the working class was essentially the same size in the two countries – 38.7% in Sweden compared to 38.2% in the United States. Sweden thus has more proletarianized *jobs*, but not more proletarianized *households*, than the United States.

We will systematically engage the theoretical and empirical issues raised by these alternative views in chapter 7. In the rest of the present chapter we will stick with practice of treating individuals as the relevant unit of analysis. The class-by-gender distributions we examine in Table 2.2, therefore, should be interpreted as the class distributions of jobs held by men and by women in the labor force.

When individuals rather than families are taken as the unit of analysis within class structures, the class distributions among women and men are sharply different in all six countries:

1 A much smaller proportion of women than of men in all six countries are in the extended expert-manager category, the most privileged segments of the employee class categories. A minimum of 77% of all people in the extended expert-manager category are males, and in several countries this figure is well over 90%.

2 In all countries except for Japan, men are much more likely to be capitalists or small employers than are women. In Sweden, for example, 1.5% of women are small employers or capitalists compared to 8% of men, and in the United States the figures are 5.1% and 10.1. The result is that 70–85% of all employers and capitalists are men in these countries. Japan is the only exception to this, with 7.5% of the women in the sample being small employers or capitalists compared to 8.0% of men.

3 There is much less gender inequality within the petty bourgeoisie than

Table 2.2 *Class-by-gender distributions*

Class distributions within genders	Employers	Petty bourgeois	Extended expert-managers	Other "middle class"	Extended working class
US: Women	5.1	7.4	6.2	10.6	70.6
US: Men	10.1	6.4	17.5	13.2	52.8
Sweden: Women	1.5	2.9	2.2	10.9	82.5
Sweden: Men	8.0	7.2	13.2	9.5	62.1
Norway: Women	1.7	7.4	4.4	7.0	79.5
Norway: Men	5.0	12.2	18.0	14.5	50.3
Canada: Women	2.0	7.9	6.2	8.2	75.6
Canada: Men	5.6	17.5	15.2	11.5	50.4
UK: Women	2.5	5.4	5.6	9.4	77.1
UK: Men	10.5	7.7	15.3	11.9	54.6
Japan: Women	7.5	28.2	0.8	0.8	62.8
Japan: Men	8.0	19.4	17.5	17.9	41.3
% women within each class category					
United States	29.3	49.8	23.2	40.9	53.2
Sweden	12.3	22.4	10.9	45.5	49.1
Norway	17.9	28.0	13.5	23.9	50.4
Canada	20.3	24.2	22.1	33.3	51.1
United Kingdom	14.4	32.5	20.0	35.2	49.2
Japan	41.7	52.8	3.2	3.1	53.9

Definitions: "extended expert-managers" = expert-managers, expert supervisors and skilled managers; "extended working class" = workers, skilled workers and nonskilled supervisors.

within the two employer categories of the self-employed. While in four of the six countries (Sweden, Norway, Canada and the UK) there is still a higher percentage of men than women who are petty bourgeois, the differences are smaller than for employers and capitalists, and in the United States and Japan the proportion of women who are petty bourgeois is actually higher than the proportion of men.

4 In all countries, women are much more concentrated in the working class than are men. Across the six countries, roughly 60–80% of women are in the extended working class compared to about 40–60% of men. The result is that, while women are generally only about 40–45% of the employed labor force in these countries, they constitute about half of the extended of the extended working class (and 55–60% of the narrowly defined working class).

Men, unsurprisingly, are thus generally much more likely to be in privileged and powerful class locations than are women in all six countries.

There are two significant variations in these gender patterns across countries:

1 As we will explore in detail in chapter 9, gender differences on the authority dimension of the class structure vary considerably across these countries. The gender gap in authority is much greater in Japan than in any of the other countries, and greater in the two Scandinavian countries than in the three English-speaking countries. Only 3.2% of the extended expert-manager category in Japan are women, compared to 11–13% in the two Scandinavian countries and 20–23% in the three English-speaking countries. While males dominate the extended expert-managerial category in all countries, women have made greater inroads in some countries than in others.

2 The gender patterns in self-employment also vary significantly across the six countries. In Sweden, Norway, Canada and the United Kingdom, 17–25% of self-employed people are women, compared to 39% in the United States and 50% in Japan. This same configuration occurs when we look more restrictively at capitalists and small employers: 50% of all capitalists (defined as self-employed people employing more than 9 people) in Japan are women, about 20% in the United States, 12.5% in the UK and 6% or less in the other three countries.

At first glance, these results for Japan seem quite contradictory: Japan has by far the greatest gender inequality among expert managers but the least among capitalists and small employers. This anomaly is reduced, however, when we look more closely at the nature of self-employment in Japan compared to the other countries. Many more women than men in all countries define themselves as "unpaid workers in a family business or farm." I treat such women as self-employed and place them in a specific class location depending upon the number of paid employees in the family firm. Most unpaid family workers work in traditional, family enterprises which are often organized in a highly patriarchal manner. Furthermore, some women who identify themselves as employers rather than "unpaid" family workers nevertheless still work in traditional family enterprises in which their husbands are also employers. In our Japanese sample, a much higher proportion of women classified as employers or petty bourgeoisie worked in such traditional family enterprises than in any other country.[5]

2.3 Class and race

Of the six countries included in this chapter, race is a salient feature of the social structure only in the United States. Table 2.3 presents the class by race and gender distributions for the US. The results in the table indicate quite complex interactions between race and gender. For the various categories of self-employment, the racial differences are generally much bigger than the gender differences. In our sample, at least, there are no black capitalists, only 1 black small employer (a woman) and only a handful of black petty bourgeois (all men). Among white women, in contrast, 5.6% are either capitalists or small employers and nearly 9% are petty bourgeois. In terms of access to property ownership, racial inequality appears to make a much bigger difference than gender inequality.

The situation is quite different when we look at the extended expert-manager class location. In this case it appears that black men are somewhat advantaged relative to white women: 8.4% of all black men (in the employed labor force) are in the extended expert-manager positions compared to only 6.9% of white women and 1.7% of black women. White men, of course, are unambiguously the most privileged, with 18.5% being in the extended expert-manager category.

---

[5] For details of the situation of these self-employed women in Japan, see Wright (1997: 64–67).

Table 2.3 *Class by race by gender distributions in the United States*

Class distributions *within* race and gender categories (distributions sum horizontally)	Employers	Petty bourgeois	Extended expert-managers	Other "middle class"	Extended working class
White men	11.2	6.4	18.5	13.4	50.6
White women	5.6	8.8	6.9	11.7	67.0
Black men	0.0	3.6	8.4	11.4	76.6
Black women	1.3	0.0	1.7	10.1	86.9
Race-by-gender distributions *within* class categories (distributions sum vertically)					
White men	69.9	45.5	73.0	53.4	40.9
White women	29.1	51.1	22.7	36.8	43.8
Black men	0.0	3.3	3.7	4.9	6.6
Black women	1.0	0.0	0.6	4.9	8.7

See Table 2.2 for definitions of "extended expert-managers" and "extended working class."

If we combine these findings by defining a category of "privileged class locations" that includes capitalists, small employers and the extended expert-manager category, then just under 30% of white men occupy privileged class locations, compared to 12.5% of white women, 8.4% of black men and 3% of black women. In terms of proletarianization, nearly 87% of black women, 77% of black men and 67% of white women in the employed labor force are in the extended working class, compared to only about 51% of white men. Even excluding the problem of the so-called "underclass" – the chronically poor segment of the population outside of the formal labor force – race therefore seems to have a bigger overall effect on access to privileged class locations than does gender.[6]

When most people think of "the working class," the image that comes to mind is the white male industrial worker. When we define the working class in terms of individuals occupying positions within the social relations of production, this image is clearly grossly inaccurate. Only 33% of the people in the working class and 39% in the extended working class are white males. By a large margin, the American working class now predominantly consists of women and racial minorities.

2.4 Class structure: a summing up

This chapter has descriptively explored a wide range of properties of the class structures of advanced capitalist societies. Several broad generalizations stand out.

The working class, even if defined narrowly, remains the largest class location in the class structure of developed capitalist countries, and, if it is extended to include those contradictory locations closest to it, then it constitutes a substantial majority of the labor force. While, as we will see in the next chapter, the working class has declined somewhat in recent years, if the working class is defined in relational terms it is hardly the case that the working class has largely disappeared, as some commentators have suggested.

Not only is the working class the largest class location in all of the countries we have examined, among employees taken separately there is relatively little variation in class distributions across these countries. The

[6] If anything, these results understate the contrast between racial and gender differences in access to privileged class locations, since many white women will have indirect access to privileged class locations via their husbands (i.e. their "mediated" class location will be to a relatively privileged class even if their direct class location is not).

only partial exception to this is Sweden, which has a somewhat larger working class and smaller expert-manager category than the other countries. This difference in Sweden may be due to the political specificity of the Swedish "class compromise" which may have somewhat reduced the need for intensive supervision and surveillance in the labor process, thus reducing the need for supervisors and managers. Still, even including Sweden, the variations in class distributions among employees across these countries is fairly muted.

In contrast to the relatively small variation across countries in class distributions among employees, there is significant variation in the size of the petty bourgeoisie. With the exception of the Japanese case, the differences in the size of the petty bourgeoisie across these countries is mainly due to properties of the sectoral structure of their economies: having a large state sector depresses the size of the petty bourgeoisie; having a large agricultural sector expands it. In the case of Japan, there is higher self-employment in all sectors. This indicates the stronger persistence of traditional, very small family businesses in Japanese society.

Compared to the relatively modest differences across countries in overall class distributions, there are very sharp differences between genders in class distributions within countries. In all countries, women are much more proletarianized than men and are particularly excluded from the expert-manager class locations. While these gender differences are considerably more exaggerated in Japan than in the other countries, the basic pattern is the same across all countries. In other words, in terms of the probabilities of a person being in a given class location, one's gender matters more than one's country.

3. The transformation of the American class structure, 1960–1990

Two opposed images have dominated discussions of the transformation of class structures in developed capitalist societies. The first of these is associated with the idea that contemporary technological changes are producing a massive transformation of social and economic structures that are moving us towards what is variously called a "post-industrial society" (Bell 1973), a "programmed society" (Touraine 1971), a "service society" (Singelmann 1978; Fuchs 1968) or some similar designation. The second image, rooted in classical Marxist visions of social change, argues that in spite of these transformations of the "forces of production," we remain a capitalist society and the changes in that class structure thus continue to be driven by the fundamental "laws of motion" of capitalism.

The post-industrial scenario of social change generally envisions the class structure becoming increasingly less proletarianized, requiring higher and higher proportions of workers with technical expertise and demanding less mindless routine and more responsibility and knowledge. For some of these theorists, the central process underwriting this tendency is the shift from an economy centered on industrial production to one based on services. Other theorists have placed greater stress on the emancipatory effects of the technical–scientific revolution within material production itself. In either case the result is a trajectory of changes that undermines the material basis of alienation within production by giving employees progressively greater control over their conditions of work and freedom within work. In class terms, this augurs a decline in the working class and an expansion of various kinds of expert and managerial class locations.

The classical Marxist image of transformation of class relations in capitalism is almost the negative of post-industrial theory: work is becoming more proletarianized; technical expertise is being confined to a smaller and smaller proportion of the labor force; routinization of activity is becoming more and more pervasive, spreading to technical and even professional occupations; and responsibilities within work are becoming less meaningful. This argument was most clearly laid out in Braverman's (1974) influential book, *Labor and Monopoly Capital*. The basic argument runs something like this: because the capitalist labor process is a process of exploitation and domination and not simply a technical process of production, capital is always faced with the problem of extracting labor effort from workers. In the arsenal of strategies of social control available to the capitalist class, one of the key weapons is the degradation of work, that is, the removal of skills and discretion from direct producers. The result is a general tendency for the proletarianzed character of the labor process to intensify over time. In terms of class structure, this implies that the working class will tend to expand, skilled employees and experts decline, and supervisory labor to increase as the demands of social control intensify.

This chapter attempts to use quantitative data on the changes in distributions of people in the American class structure from 1960 to 1990 as a way of intervening in this debate. In section 3.1 I will lay out a series of alternative hypotheses about the expected changes in different class locations based on the arguments of post-industrial theory and traditional Marxist theory. Section 3.2 will explain the empirical strategy we will adopt. Section 3.3 will then present the basic results.

3.1 Contrasting expectations of post-industrial and Marxist theory

The debate between post-industrial and Marxist conceptions of social change can be seen as a set of competing claims about the relative expansion and contraction of different locations within the class structure.

The classical Marxist theory of capitalist development posits three trends which directly affect the class distribution of the labor force. First, the expansion of capitalism tends to destroy independent, self-employed producers. In the nineteenth century and the first half of the twentieth century this process massively affected self-employed farmers in the agricultural sector, but the process is a general one affecting all sectors of the economy. This yields the prediction of a steadily declining petty bourgeoisie. Second, the dynamics of capital accumulation tend to generate increasing concentration and centralization of capital as small capitalist firms are destroyed and larger firms grow. This trend yields the prediction of a decline in small employers and an expansion of managers, especially expert managers, to staff the administrative bureaucracies of corporations. Third, as noted above, in order to increase control over the labor force and the extraction of labor effort, capitalists have an incentive to reduce the autonomy of skilled labor and, where possible, replace skilled with unskilled labor. This, in turn, requires an expansion of the social control apparatus within production to monitor and supervise workers increasingly deprived of a knowledge about production. The appropriation by management of knowledge from skilled workers should also lead to the expansion of the expert-manager category. These trends of intensified proletarianization in the labor process generate the prediction of an expansion of the working class, an expansion of supervisors, managers and expert-managers, and a decline of (nonmanagerial) experts and skilled workers.

Post-industrial theory does not contain a systematic a set of hypotheses about transformations of the petty bourgeoisie and small employers, and therefore I will not impute formal predictions for these categories. The expectations for the changes in various categories of employees can be more clearly derived from the logic of post-industrialism. The expectation in post-industrial theory of a world of work with much more self-direction and autonomy than industrial capitalism suggests the prediction of a relative decline in purely supervisory labor (i.e. positions of social control within work which are not part of the managerial decision-making apparatus). On the other hand, managerial positions would be expected to increase as the complexity of organizations and decision-making increases.

Where post-industrial theory differs most sharply from the Marxist arguments outlined above is in the predictions about experts, skilled workers and workers. As a concomitant of the move to a knowledge- and service-based economy, post-industrial theorists would generally expect a pervasive expansion of jobs requiring high levels of expertise and autonomy. This implies a process of gradual *de*proletarianization of labor in which there was steady expansion of the expert and expert-manager class location and a corresponding decline of the core working class. Insofar as manual labor is still required, it would have an increasingly skilled and technical character to it, and thus highly skilled workers should also expand. The basic hypotheses of Marxist and post-industrial perspectives are summarized in Table 3.1.

Table 3.1 *Hypotheses for transformations of the American class structure*

	Predicted changes in class distributions	
Class location	Traditional Marxist prediction	Post-industrial theory prediction
Class locations for which the two theories make different predictions		
Workers	increase	decrease
Skilled workers	decrease	increase
Supervisors	increase	decrease
Experts (nonmanager)	small decrease	big increase
Class locations for which the two theories have similar predictions		
Managers	increase	increase
Expert-managers	increase	big increase
Class locations for which there is not a clear divergence of predictions		
Petty bourgeoisie	decrease	no prediction
Small employers	decrease	no prediction

3.2 Methodological strategy

The analytical technique used in this chapter is sometimes referred to as "shift/share" analysis (Wright 1997: 97). This procedure divides overall changes (shifts) over time in the class composition of the labor force into three components: a "sector shift" component, a "class shift" component and an interaction component. The first of these identifies the contribution to changes in the class structure that comes from the changing distribution of the labor force *across* economic sectors. For example, historically the agricultural sector has had an especially high concentration of the petty bourgeoisie in the form of small farmers. A decline in the relative size of the agricultural sector would thus, all other things being equal, have an adverse effect on the relative size of the petty bourgeoisie. In our analysis this would appear as a "negative sector shift" for the petty bourgeoisie. The "class shift" refers to changes in the class structure that result from a changing class composition *within* economic sectors, independent of changes in the relative size of these sectors. For example, the gradual replacement of Mom and Pop grocery stores by chain supermarkets would be reflected in a negative class shift for the petty bourgeosie and small employers within the retail trade sector and a positive class shift for managers and supervisors within that sector. Finally, some changes in the class structure cannot be uniquely attributed either to changes within sectors or to changes in the sectoral composition of the labor force. Rather, they result from the interaction of these two forces. This contribution to the overall change in class distributions is thus referred to as the interaction component.

Because of limitations of sample size, for the analyses of this chapter the 12 categories of the class structure matrix in Figure 1.3 have been collapsed into a simpler, eight-category model: employers (combining capitalists and small employers); petty bourgeoisie; expert-managers; managers (combining skilled and nonskilled managers); supervisors (combining skilled and nonskilled supervisors); experts (combining expert supervisors and nonsupervisory experts); skilled workers; and workers. We will also examine the results for workers and skilled workers combined. This eight-category typology drops the distinction between nonskilled and skilled within the two categories in the authority hierarchy, and the distinction between nonmanagers and supervisors within the expert category.[1]

Throughout the analysis which follows our focus will be primarily on the various class categories among wage-earners rather than on employers and the petty bourgeoisie. The problem of the historical trajectory of self-employment in the United States will be examined in the next chapter.

3.3 Results

The basic time series data for class distributions between 1960 and 1990 appear in Table 3.2.[2] The results of the shift-share analysis for the class shift components for selected class locations appear in Figure 3.2.[3] The

---

[1] The method for estimating these class distributions within economic sectors for the period 1960–90 is discussed in Wright (1997: 112–113).

[2] The estimates for the class distributions in this chapter differ somewhat from other chapters in this book because here we are combining census data with the data from the class structure project. For a discussion of the method for measuring class structure used here, see Wright (1997: 112–113).

[3] The detailed results of the shift share analysis can be found in Wright (1997: 100).

Table 3.2 *Class distributions in the United States, 1960–1990*

Class location	1960	1970	1980	1990
Nonowners				
1 Managers	7.50	7.57	7.95	8.25
2 Supervisors	13.66	14.86	15.23	14.82
3 Expert-managers	3.87	4.41	5.06	5.99
4 Experts	3.53	4.53	5.49	6.90
5 Skilled workers	13.46	14.08	12.92	12.77
6 Workers	44.59	45.13	44.05	41.38
All workers (5, 6)	58.05	59.21	56.97	54.15
Owners				
7 Petty bourgeoisie	5.54	4.09	4.53	5.19
8 Employers	7.86	5.33	4.77	4.71

numbers in this figure indicate the rate of change of the labor force in a particular class location that can be attributed to the changes in the number of people in that class *within* economic sectors. For example, consider the expert-manager category in the 1970s. This category increased from 4.41% of the labor force to 5.06% of the labor force in this decade (see Table 3.2). This represents a 14.7% increase in the relative size of this class location during the 1970s. Some of this change was due to the movement of people into sectors that already had a higher proportion of expert-managers than in other sectors, but most of it (in fact, nearly 14% of the total rate of expansion of 14.7%) was due to the expansion of expert managers within sectors, or what we are calling the "class shift component."

The results of the shift-share analysis in Figure 3.1 are much more consistent with the predictions of the post-industrial society thesis than the traditional Marxist view of changes in class structures. While in the 1960s, as predicted by Marxist theory, there was a small expansion of the working class within sectors (i.e. a small positive class-shift component), this expansion was reversed in the 1970s. By the 1980s, the class shift for the working class was -5%, meaning that the proportion of the labor force in the working class declined by an average 5% within sectors during that decade. There was also a small negative *sector* shift for the working class in all three decades (indicating that the sectors with relatively high concentrations of workers were declining in relative importance). In contrast, the class-shift component for expert

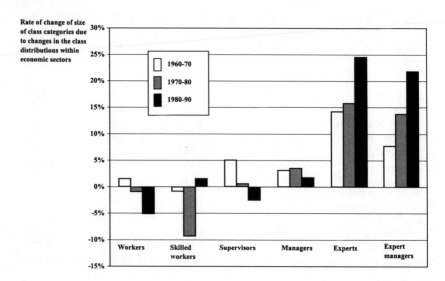

Figure 3.1 *Class-shift components of decade rates of change in class distributions for class locations among employees.*

managers and nonmanagerial experts was increasingly large and positive across the three decades. This is in keeping with the predictions of the post-industrial theory, especially those versions that emphasize technological change rather than sectoral change (since the class-shift components are much bigger and more consistent than the sector-shift components).

Overall, then, the main thrust of these results runs directly counter to the principal expectations of classical Marxism and formalized as hypotheses in Table 3.1. What is more, given that the 1970s and 1980s were a period of relative economic stagnation compared to the 1960s, classical Marxism would have predicted that the pressures towards degradation of labor would have intensified. The evidence in these results indicates that, if anything, there was an acceleration in the trend of *de*proletarianization in the 1970s and 1980s. While these results hardly indicate that the working class is in the process of dissolution – the core working class in the United States remains over 40% of the labor force in 1990, and, when combined with skilled workers, the extended working class is 54% of the labor force – nevertheless, the trajectory of change is more in keeping with the expectations of post-industrial theory than traditional Marxism.

Refined sectoral analysis

One final step in the data analysis is needed, however, to add force to this conclusion. It is important to know whether or not the class-shift components in Figure 3.1 are largely contained within particular sectors or are diffused throughout the economy, since this might affect the overall interpretation of the results. To check this out, I therefore disaggregated the class-shift components in Figure 3.1 into six sectors: extractive, transformative (mainly manufacturing and related sectors), distributive services (mainly retail and wholesale trade), business services, personal services and social-political services (see Wright 1997: 105–107 for detailed results).

For the working class, the negative class-shift component in the 1970s and 1980s – the deproletarianization process within economic sectors – is not simply a result of a massive change in one sector, but is present in 4 of the 6 aggregated sectors. In both decades, the biggest contributor to the negative class shift for the working class is the transformative sector (manufacturing and processing). This is also the one sector in the 1960s within which there was a negative class shift for workers. Thus, while overall the direction of the class shift component for the working-class changes from the from positive (proletarianization) in the 1960s to negative (deproletarianization) in the 1970s and 1980s, in the case of the transformative sector the 1970s and 1980s represent a continuation and acceleration of a deproletarianization process already in place in the 1960s.

In this more refined analysis, the positive class-shift component for experts and for expert-managers occurs within nearly all of these broad sectors. The only consistent exception is for the distributive services sector in which there is a negative component for expert-managers in all three decades. The expansion of class locations involving significant credentials and expertise, therefore, is pervasive across sectors in keeping with post-industrial theory.

Not only are the patterns of class-shift components fairly consistent with the expectations of post-industrial theory, so also are the broad patterns of sectoral shifts: the expansion of managers, experts, and expert-managers is most closely linked to the expansion of social and political services in the 1960s and the expansion of business services in the 1970s and 1980s, while the decline of the working class, skilled workers and supervisors throughout these decades is most linked to the decline of employment in the transformative sector.

Finally, the specific pattern of sectoral and class shifts for experts and expert-managers is consistent with the expectations of those post-industrial theorists who emphasize the increasing importance of knowledge and information in post-industrial economies. In the 1960s, the expansion of experts and expert-managers in the class structure was driven almost equally by sectoral shifts in the employment structure centered on the expansion of social-political services (especially medical services) and the expansion of these class locations within sectors. In contrast, by the 1980s the relative expansion of these class locations was almost entirely a product of changes in the class composition within sectors, especially in the transformative sector and the social political service sector. This is in keeping with the idea of the increasing centrality of knowledge and information within the production processes of post-industrial society, even within the manufacturing sectors of the economy.

3.4 Interpretations and implications

The results presented in this chapter pose a real challenge to traditional Marxist expectations about the trajectory of development of the class structure of advanced capitalist societies in general and particularly about the process of intensive proletarianization. Contrary to the traditional Marxist expectation, the working class in the United States modestly declined in the period 1960–1990, and this decline appears if anything to be accelerating. What is especially noteworthy is that this decline is not simply a question of the shift of employment from manufacturing to services; the decline is accelerating *within the transformative sector itself*. While it may also be true in recent decades that within the working class itself working conditions may have deteriorated and exploitation may have increased as real wages have declined, nevertheless within the class structure as a whole the evidence does not support the prediction of increasing and deepening proletarianization.

One response to this challenge is to question the validity of the results themselves by arguing that they are artifacts of the measurements employed. The procedure for estimating class structures in 1960 and 1970 is certainly open to question (see Wright 1997: 109). These could conceivably have lead to systematic over- or under-estimation of changes in working class in the period under study. Nevertheless, in the absence of specific evidence that measurement biases exist in sufficient magnitude to alter significantly our estimates, the results remain a sharp challenge to traditional Marxist expectations of continuing proletarianization.

A second line of response is to accept the results, but to argue that the transnational character of capitalism in the world today makes it inappropriate to study transformations of class distributions within single national units. The last twenty-five years have certainly witnessed a significant growth of multinational corporate industrial investment in the Third World and an accompanying expansion of the industrial working class in Third World countries. The Marxist theory of proletarianization is a theory about the trajectory of changes in class structures in capitalism as such, not in national units of capitalism. In a period of rapid internationalization of capital, therefore, national statistics are likely to give a distorted image of transformations of capitalist class structures.

If these arguments are correct, then one would expect that changes in the class structure of world capitalism would be unevenly distributed globally. In particular, there should be at least some tendency for managerial class locations and expert class locations to expand more rapidly in the core capitalist countries and proletarian positions to expand more rapidly in the Third World. It is hard to get meaningful data directly on this hypothesis. There are some indirect data in our results, however, which are at least suggestive. The economic sector within which globalization is likely to have the biggest impact on class structure is the transformative sector (principally manufacturing), since this is the sector within which, many people argue, multinational corporations are shifting large numbers of working-class jobs to less developed regions of the world. If this is true, then one would expect to find a large, positive class shift within this sector for manager experts (i.e. they should very substantially increase as a proportion of the labor force within this sector), combined with a large negative sector shift (as overall employment in this sector declines). This is in fact what we find in the disaggregated decompositions for the 1960s and 1980s (see Wright 1997: Table 3.4): the largest positive class-shift component for manager experts is in the transformative sector. It could thus be the case that, if it were possible to measure the global class structure of multinational capitalism, the decades of the 1970s and 1980s would have been a period of proletarianization worldwide.

A final line of response to these results is to acknowledge that capitalist class relations are changing in ways unexpected by the traditional Marxist theory of deepening proletarianization. While the problem of extracting labor effort from workers remains an issue within class relations, under conditions of highly developed forces of production this no longer generates an inherent tendency towards the degradation of labor. Instead, as Piore and Sabel (1984) have argued, we may be in the midst of a "second industrial divide" which requires labor with much higher levels of technical training and work autonomy than characterized "Fordist" production, training which makes workers capable of flexibly adapting to rapid changes in technology and the organization of work. The positive class shift for skilled workers within the transformative sector in the 1980s (+2.17), reversing the considerable negative class shift (-5.41) in that sector for this category in the 1970s, is consistent with this account.

These trends do not imply that "post-Fordist" capitalism is any less capitalistic than its predecessors – surplus is still appropriated by capitalists; investments are still allocated on the basis of profit-maximizing in capitalist markets; workers are still excluded from control over the overall process of production. And they also do not imply the immanent demise of the working class. In spite of the decline we have observed, the working class remains around 40% of the labor force in 1990, and when skilled workers are added, the extended working class is still over 50%. What these results do suggest, however, is a trajectory of change within developed capitalist societies towards an expansion, rather than a decline, of contradictory locations within class relations. Unless these trends are a temporary detour, it thus appears that the class structure of capitalism continues to become increasingly complex rather than simplified around a single, polarized class antagonism.

4. The fall and rise of the American petty bourgeoisie

200 years ago Thomas Jefferson (1786 [1984: 580]) argued that the prospect of self-employment justified whatever depredations accompanied indentured service and wage labor: "So desirous are the poor of Europe to get to America, where they may better their condition, that, being unable to pay their passage, they will agree to serve two or three years on their arrival there, rather than not go. During the time of that service they are better fed, better clothed, and have lighter labour than while in Europe. Continuing to work for hire a few years longer, they buy a farm, marry, and enjoy all the sweets of a domestic society of their own." In the middle of the nineteenth century Abraham Lincoln (1865 [1907: 50]) also saw self-employment as the natural route to individual prosperity: "The prudent penniless beginner in the world labors for wages awhile, saves a surplus with which to buy tools or land for himself, then labors on his own account another while, and at length hires a new beginner to help him." And even in the waning years of the twentieth century, in an era of large corporations and powerful governments, Ronald Reagan (Public Papers of the Presidents of the United States. Ronald Reagan 1983: 689) extols the virtues of self-employment. Speaking at the awards ceremony for the National Small Business Person of the Year, Reagan remarked: "I am vividly reminded that those shopkeepers and the druggist and the feed store owner and all of those small town business men and women made our town work, building our community, and were also building our nation. In so many ways, you here today and your colleagues across the country represent America's pioneer spirit . . . You also hold the promise of America's future. It's in your dreams, your aspirations that our future will be molded and shaped."

Being one's own boss, being self-employed, is a deeply held ideal in

American culture. In the 1980 US class analysis project data, 54% of people in the American working class, and two-thirds of male workers say that they would like to be self-employed some day (for detailed results, see Wright 1997: 115–117). What is more, this ideal is not a complete fantasy: while, depending upon precise definitions and data sources, only about 8–14% of the labor force in the United States was self-employed in 1980, 16% of current employees have been self-employed at some time during their work lives (almost 20% for men), which means that at least a quarter of the labor force and a third of the male labor force either is or has been self-employed. If we go back one generation, about 31% of Americans currently in the labor force come from families within which the head of the household was mainly self-employed when they were growing up, and 46% came from families within which the head of household was self-employed at least part of the time while they were growing up. Finally, if we ask Americans to describe the jobs of their three best friends, 31% indicate that at least one of their friends is self-employed, and 7% are married to someone who is self-employed. Taking all of these data together, two-thirds of Americans in the labor force have some direct personal linkage to self-employment, by being or having been self-employed themselves, by coming from a family of origin in which the head of household was self-employed, by having a close friend who is self-employed, or by being married to someone who is self-employed. What is more, this density of ties to self-employment varies hardly at all across the different class locations among employees.

This intermeshing of the lives of the petty bourgeoisie and employees is not a unique feature of the United States. Roughly comparable figures are found in the other countries in the Comparative Class Analysis Project. In Sweden, Norway and Canada, about 55% of the labor force has some direct personal tie to self-employment, while in Japan the figure is 68% (mainly because of a much higher level of people who are currently self-employed). Where the United States does seem to differ markedly from the other countries is in the aspiration of employees to become self-employed: nearly 58% of US employees say that they would like to be self-employed someday, compared to 49% in Canada, 40% in Sweden, 31% in Japan and only 20% in Norway.

Self-employment is thus a central part of both the ideological and social fabric of American life. Yet, remarkably, self-employment has received almost no systematic empirical study by sociologists. When sociologists study stratification, it is rare that self-employment is treated as a distinct problem. With limited exceptions, the typical class schema for sociological studies goes from upper white collar to lower blue collar and farm occupations, with the self-employed being fused with these categories according to their occupational activities. And, while there are many studies of small business and of specific categories of self-employment, especially farmers and various kinds of professionals, there is very little quantitative research on the general problem of self-employment.

The basic objective of this chapter is to analyze the historical trajectory of self-employment in the United States, particularly in the post-World War II period. The chapter will revolve around a striking feature of the time trend in rates of self-employment in the labor force: on the basis of the best available time series it appears that from the nineteenth century to the early 1970s there was a virtually monotonic annual decline in the rate of self-employment in the United States, dropping from around 40% at the end of the nineteenth century to about 20% in the 1940s and to under 10% in the early 1970s; from 1973 to 1976 the self-employment rate was basically stable, but since then there has been a gradual increase in the rate of self-employment (for detailed time series, see Wright 1997: 119). By the early 1990s, that rate was a full 25% higher than it had been in the mid-1970s. Similar trends are found in a number of European countries (Bechhofer and Elliott 1985). What is the explanation for this dramatic change? Does it reflect a response to the relative stagnation in the American economy from the early 1970s to the early 1990s? Is it an aspect of the transition to a "post-industrial" economy in which a variety of new kinds of services, often involving relatively little physical capital, is growing?

These questions are particularly relevant for the concerns of this book since the rise of self-employment in the last quarter of the twentieth century runs *counter* to traditional Marxist expectations of the demise of the petty bourgeoisie as a result of capitalist development. As noted in chapter 3, traditional Marxism identified two long-term causal processes which shape the historical trajectories of the petty bourgeoisie and small employers. First, there is the inherent tendency for the expansion of capitalism to destroy all precapitalist forms of economic relations, including subsistence producers and simple commodity producers. Second, as capitalism develops, there is a tendency for capitalist units of accumulation to become larger both relatively and absolutely which reduces the proportion of small employers in the population.

Taken together, these two causal processes lead Marx and subsequent Marxists to predict that the Petty Bourgeoisie (understood as small employers and the pure petty bourgeoisie combined) would gradually wither away. Certainly on a broad historical scale, this has been one of the most robust of Marx's predictions. While rates of change may have varied, in all developed capitalist countries, there was a steady decline in self-employment from 40–50% at the end of the nineteenth century to 10–15% or so at the end of the twentieth. Yet, in more recent decades, this longstanding decline seems to have been arrested and possibly even reversed. The task of this chapter is to explore why this may have occurred.

4.1 Self-employment and economic stagnation

One possible explanation for the recent increase in self-employment is that it is a direct response to cyclical patterns of unemployment. A certain amount of self-employment is plausibly a response to a lack of good wage labor employment opportunities. While unemployment insurance and welfare programs may reduce the incentives for the unemployed to seek self-employment, one would nevertheless expect increases in the unemployment rate to generate increases in self-employment. Given the relative economic stagnation in the American economy from the early 1970s into the 1980s, it might be the case that the apparent reversal of the long-term trend in self-employment simply reflects increases in unemployment in the period.

The best way to test this possibility is to estimate time series regression equations predicting the rate of self-employment and then see if the effect of time on self-employment changes when we control for the annual rate of unemployment in the equation. I calculated these regressions in a variety of different ways to be sure that the results were robust. The results were quite unambiguous: the positive time trend in self-employment since the early 1970s is significant even when we control for rate of unemployment (for details see Wright (1997: 127–130)). While long-term stagnation might be a contributing factor, it seems unlikely to provide the main explanation for this reversal of the historic decline of the petty bourgeosie.

4.2 Sectoral decomposition of changes in self-employment

Another possible explanation for the reversal of the historical trajectory of the petty bourgeoisie is that expanding opportunities for self-employment are in one way or another bound up with the transition to a "post-

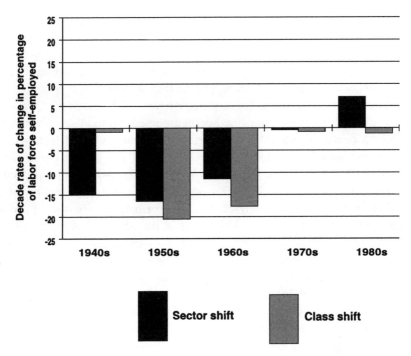

Figure 4.1 *Decomposition of decennial rates of change of self-employment, 1940–1990.*

industrial" society as discussed in chapter 3. One might hypothesize that the expansion of various kinds of high-tech services opens up greater possibilities for self-employment, since in many instances these services require relatively little physical capital.

We will explore in a preliminary way the plausibility of the post-industrial hypothesis by examining the relationship between changes in the sectoral composition of the labor force and self-employment using the same kind of sectoral shift-share decomposition procedure we adopted in chapter 3.

Figure 4.1 presents the sector-shift components and the class-shift components for the rates of change of self-employment in each decade between 1940 and 1990. Two things are especially striking in this figure. First, the sharp, negative class-shift component for self-employment – indicating a steep decline of self-employment *within* sectors – is heavily concentrated in the 1950s and 1960s. In the 1940s, virtually all of the decline in self-employment was attributable to sectoral changes in the composition of economy (especially away from agriculture), and, in both the 1970s and 1980s, the class-shift component is negligible. Second, the expansion of self-employment in the 1980s is entirely the result of changes in the distribution of the labor force across sectors. The decline in rates of self-employment may have been reversed in the mid-1970s, but this is not because it is increasing within sectors.

In order to get a more fine-grained picture of the economic processes that underwrite these changes, I disaggregated the total sector and class shifts for each decade into the contribution of the six broad sectors of the economy we examined in chapter 3. Selected results are presented in Figure 4.2 (for complete details see Wright,1997: 134). First let us look at the sector-shifts. From the 1950s on, there is a steady reduction of the effect of declines in the extractive sector (primarily agriculture) on self-employment. Agriculture is the sector of the economy with the highest levels of self-employment. Declines in the agricultural sector, therefore, have historically contributed heavily to the sectoral effects on the decline of self-employment. In the 1950s, the decline in the extractive sector reduced self-employment by roughly 22%. This dropped to about 16% in the 1960s, about 4% in the 1970s and less than 2% in the 1980s. As the agricultural sector becomes smaller and smaller, its continuing decline has less impact on the overall class structure of American society. In a complementary manner, the expansion of certain service sectors, especially business services, has an increasingly significant positive effect on self-employment.

The class-shift components also show interesting variations across sectors over time. In the 1940s there was a small *expansion* of self-employment in the transformative sector which partially countered the decline in self-employment in most other sectors. The result is that the overall class shift was a modest −4.2%. In the 1950s, self-employment declined in all but one of the six broad sectors of the economy, generating a considerably larger total negative class shift. The decline of self-employment within sectors accelerated in the 1960s. During that decade, the sectoral contributions to the negative class-shift component were large and fairly evenly distributed across the economy, indicating a very broad pattern of destruction of self-employment within every economic sector of the economy.

The decade of the 1970s represents a sharp break in the pattern of the previous two decades. In those sectors which still contributed a negative class-shift component during the 1970s, the negative effects are always much smaller than in the 1960s. And in two sectors – the transformative sector and business services – the negative class-shift effect is actually

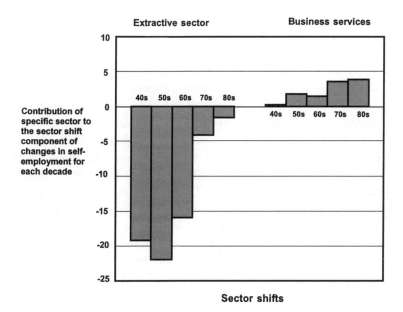

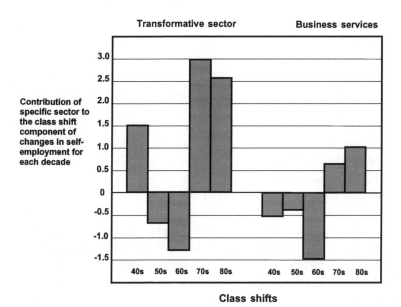

Figure 4.2 *Decomposition of changes in self-employment for selected sectors, 1940–1990.*

reversed: self-employment increased as a proportion of the labor force in these sectors over the decade. This basic trend in the transformative sector and business services continued in the 1980s.

How do these sector-specific results bear on the question of whether or not self-employment is largely a "post-industrial" phenomenon? In order to get a more nuanced picture of the changes in the 1970s and 1980s, I further disaggregated the sectoral results into a much more fine-grained 32–sector typology (examples of detailed sectors in this 32-category typology include entertainment; textiles; machine tools; education; insurance; and repair services). This makes it possible to identify the specific sectors which contributed most to the expansion of self-employment in the 1970s and 1980s. (The results are reported in Tables 4.10 and 4.11, in Wright 1997: 136–138.)

In the 1980s, 6 of the 10 sectors which contributed most to the overall expansion of self-employment are dominated by post-industrial activities: business services, medical and health services, professional services (law, engineering, etc.), banking, education and insurance. A seventh sector, childcare services, while not itself an instance of a post-industrial service (since it does not involve high levels of codified knowledge), is nevertheless closely linked to the expansion of the post-industrial sectors of the economy since those sectors have contributed heavily to the expansion of female labor-force participation. All of these, except for professional services, contributed positively both to the sectoral shift in self-employment and the class shift. At the other end of the spectrum, 11 of the 12 sectors whose total contribution to self-employment was negative are sectors within which post-industrial activities are generally marginal. This includes traditional services like lodging or retail, core sectors in the industrial economy like metalworking and food processing, and agriculture. These results thus seem to confirm the centrality of post-industrial tendencies in the expansion of self-employment.

However, if we look a little closer at the decomposition of these effects on self-employment, the picture becomes somewhat more complex. In both the 1970s and the 1980s, the detailed sectors of the economy within which there was the largest, positive *class shift* in self-employment were traditional transformative sectors (manufacturing, machine tools, mining, utilities, food, textiles, chemical and transportation). Indeed, in the 1970s, the rate of self-employment *within* post-industrial services actually declined, thus contributing a negative class shift to the overall self-employment rate, and, while the class shift was positive within post-industrial services in the 1980s, it was still smaller than in the transformative sector. What is more, this positive class-shift component within the traditional transformative sectors in the 1980s is generated by some of the core subsectors of the traditional industrial economy: miscellaneous manufacturing, machine tools and metal working. The reason why the overall contribution of the transformative sector to the expansion of self-employment is smaller than the contribution of post-industrial services is thus entirely due to the negative *sector* effects of the transformative sector (i.e. due to the shift of employment out of these activities).

Taking these results together, it appears that, while the sectoral shift towards post-industrial services contributed substantially to the expansion of self-employment in the 1980s, increasing self-employment within specific lines of economic activity was more concentrated within manufacturing and other traditional transformative sectors. If this class-shift within the transformative sector had not occurred (and everything else remained the same), the expansion of self-employment would have been roughly 40% less.

It thus appears that while more than half of the expansion of self-employment in the 1980s can be attributed to sectoral change in the economy towards post-industrial services, the expansion of self-employment within manufacturing and other transformative sectors is also a significant factor. Expanding self-employment is thus not simply a post-industrial phenomenon; it also reflects changes in class distributions within the traditional industrial economy.

4.3 Conclusions and unresolved issues

Four general conclusions stand out among the results of the various data analyses presented here:

First, there is strong evidence that the numerical decline of the petty bourgeoisie which has marked the long-term history of American capitalism has at least temporarily stopped and perhaps been modestly reversed.

Second, this reversal of the historical decline of the petty bourgeoisie is not a direct consequence of countercyclical movements of people from unemployment to self-employment. While there is an effect of the rate of unemployment on self-employment, this effect has been declining in the post-war period, and in any case does not account for the increase in self-employment since the mid-1970s.

Third, the growth of post-industrial services does appear to have significantly contributed to the expansion of self-employment, but this is largely through a direct sectoral change effect, not because self-employment is generally increasing rapidly within post-industrial sectors.

Fourth, within many of the older, more traditional industrial sectors of the economy, there appears to be a growth in self-employment in recent years. This is especially noticeable in construction and miscellaneous manufacturing, but is also true in machinery, transportation and even metal working. The expansion of self-employment within particular branches of economic activity, therefore, is not exclusively a post-industrial process but a structural feature of more traditional segments of the economy as well.

The data in this chapter do not provide a basis for exploring alternative possible explanations for this expansion of self-employment within these traditional sectors of the industrial economy. Five possibilities seem particularly important. First, it could turn out that the apparent expansion of self-employment is an illusion, that it represents changes in the systems of classification of particular jobs but not a genuine expansion of self-employment properly understood. Dale (1986) has argued, for example, that much apparent "self-employment" is really simply a new way for employers to hire workers under schemes of homework, freelancing, subcontracting, out-working and the like. Marsh, Heady and Matheson (1981) found that a third of the formally self-employed workers in the construction industry worked exclusively for contractors and provided only their own labor. In such cases, there is really very little to distinguish them from wage-workers. While for tax purposes and purposes of labor relations it may be advantageous for employers to reclassify part of their labor force as "self-employed," this does not reflect a sociologically meaningful expansion of the "petty bourgeoisie." The fact that in the 1980s, as we saw in the previous chapter, the class-shift component of the changing class distributions for small employers was negative in the 1970s and 1980s, whereas it was positive for the petty bourgeoisie, is consistent with the view that a significant part of the overall expansion of self-employment could be linked to such contract devices within labor markets.

Second, the increase in self-employment within certain traditional sectors of the industrial economy could be at least partially a demographic phenomenon, reflecting the entry of the baby-boom generation into the age range of maximum likelihood of self-employment. Self-employment is generally highest in mid- to late-career stages, after a certain amount of savings have been accumulated. As the baby-boom generation enters mid-career, therefore, one might expect a temporary increase in self-employment. If this demographic explanation is correct, then the rate of self-employment should decline again as this generation ages further.

Third, it might be argued that increasing self-employment could be partially an effect of the increasing participation of married women in the labor force. Self-employment generally brings with it more risks than wage labor employment. If those risks were to decline, one might expect more people to start their own businesses. One mechanism that could reduce risks to a family would be for one member to hold a stable wage-earner job while another attempts self-employment. The increasing prevalence of two-earner households, therefore, could be partially underwriting the expansion of self-employment.

Fourth, the increase of self-employment within traditional sectors of the industrial economy could reflect the long-term stagnation of the economy. While we have shown that the increase in self-employment in the 1970s and 1980s cannot be attributed to a direct countercyclical response to unemployment rates, it could nevertheless be a structural response to declining opportunities for good jobs in the industrial economy. As many commentators have noted, much of the job expansion in the wage labor force in the 1980s has centered on low-paying service sector jobs, while much of the decline has been in well-paying core industrial jobs. Many people may therefore enter self-employment because of the absence of good job alternatives, not simply because of the absence of jobs as such. If this explanation is correct, then it would be expected that very little of the expansion of self-employment would be among small employers, but rather would be concentrated in the individual self-employed petty bourgeoisie. The patterns of class shifts in the previous chapter lend some support to this interpretation.

Finally, the introduction of information technologies and improvements in transportation and communication may have lowered the barriers to entry in many areas of light manufacturing, thus facilitating the growth in the numbers of smaller businesses. In recent years there has been much talk about the virtues of decentralization, and many larger corporations have both downsized and increased their reliance on a variety of forms of subcontracting to small employers. The expansion of self-employment in the more traditional manufacturing sectors of the economy may partially reflect these technological and organizational developments.

The American class structure appears to be in a period of significant structural reorganization. As we noted in the previous chapter, the rate of decline of the working class appears to have accelerated in recent decades, and, in the 1980s, the proportion of the labor force that is supervisors also appears to be declining. We also now see that the decline of the petty bourgeoisie that persisted since the nineteenth century has been halted, at least temporarily. Explaining the mechanisms which are generating these changes is essential if we are to understand the trajectory of the American class structure into the next century.

5. The permeability of class boundaries

Class structures differ not only in the distribution of people across the various locations in that structure, but also in the extent to which people's lives are bounded by specific class locations. At the micro-level, class is explanatory because it shapes the interests, strategic capacities and experiences of people, and each of these effects depends not simply on the static location of individuals in a job-class structure, but also on the complex ways in which their lives are linked to various classes through careers, mobility, voluntary associations and social ties. In some class structures, friendships, marriages, churches and sports clubs are largely homogeneous with respect to class. In such cases, class boundaries can be thought of as highly impermeable. In other class structures, these social processes frequently bring together people from different class locations. When this happens, class boundaries become relatively permeable.

In this chapter, I will begin by giving some precision to the concept of the permeability of class boundaries and then propose a general empirical strategy for analyzing permeability. This will be followed by an empirical examination of three kinds of permeability: the formation of friendship ties across class locations, the class composition of families, and intergenerational class mobility.

5.1 Theoretical issues

Permeability in the Marxist and Weberian traditions

The two primary sociological traditions of class analysis – Marxist and Weberian – have given different priorities to class structure and boundary permeability as objects of analysis. In a variety of ways,

Marxists generally put the analysis of class structure (or a closely related concept like "relations of production") at center stage and pay relatively little attention to the permeability of class boundaries. In contrast, the permeability of class boundaries looms large in the Weberian tradition, whether termed "class structuration" (Giddens 1973) or "closure" (Parkin 1974, 1979). This is especially clear in the analysis of social mobility, which is largely inspired (if in a somewhat diffuse way) by Weberian conceptions of class rooted in a concern with "life chances." Weberians tend to devote much less attention to the rigorous elaboration of the concept of class structure itself. As Burris (1987) and Wright (1989: 313–323) have argued, sociologists working in the Weberian tradition typically treat locations within class structures as soft categories requiring only loose definitions and relatively casual theoretical defense.

The analysis of class boundary permeability in this chapter, therefore, combines the conceptual apparatus of the Marxist tradition with the substantive focus of the Weberian tradition on the intersection of people's lives with class structures. This marriage of Marxist categories with Weberian questions is motivated by a desire to deepen the micro-analysis of class within the Marxist tradition. My assumption is that the complex ways in which individual lives traverse class boundaries is one of the important factors that shape the ways in which people experience class structures. For example, political coalitions across specific class boundaries should be facilitated to the extent that friendship and family ties cross these boundaries. On the other hand, higher levels of class consciousness would be expected in societies in which friendship ties and biographical trajectories were overwhelmingly confined within the same class rather than diffused across a variety of class locations.

Static and dynamic permeability

The permeability of class boundaries can be usefully divided into two general forms which we will refer to as *static* permeability and *dynamic* permeability. The static permeability of class boundaries refers to the patterns of active social ties between people situated in different locations within a class structure. Examples would include such things as the cross-boundary patterns of neighborhood composition, household composition, memberships in voluntary associations and friendship networks. Dynamic permeability, on the other hand, refers to the ways in which biographical trajectories traverse different locations within class structures over time. Inter- and intra-generational class mobility would, of course, be prime examples, but life-course patterns of participation in various social networks would also be relevant to the dynamic permeability of class boundaries. For example, different levels of the education system might vary a lot in the extent to which they bring people from very different classes together in the classroom. Pre-school might be more class homogeneous than elementary school, and elementary school classrooms less class segregated than high schools (because of tracking in high school), and high schools less than universities. The biographical trajectory of people through the education system, therefore, can involve moving through a series of settings with more or less permeable class boundaries.

Defined in these terms, the problem of the permeability of social boundaries is by no means restricted to class analysis. International migration, for example, constitutes an aspect of the dynamic permeability of national boundaries, while patterns of membership and participation in international professional associations are an aspect of the static permeability of those boundaries. Interethnic marriages and friendships are aspects of the static permeability of ethnic boundaries, while the problem of "salad-bar ethnicity" and the intergenerational transmission of ethnicity are aspects of the dynamic permeability of those boundaries. Interdisciplinary research institutes and faculty seminars are instances of the static permeability of the boundaries of academic disciplines, while the pattern of career trajectories through academic specialities is an example of dynamic permeability.

The problem of permeability of social boundaries is sociologically important because it may help us to understand the extent to which various kinds of social cleavages are reinforced or undermined by the social ties and experiences of people within social structures. It is often argued, for example, that a regime of very high social mobility will tend to generate less bitter interclass conflict than a regime of rigid class boundaries. It would be expected that situations in which there are high degrees of interracial, interethnic or interreligious marriage and friendships will contribute to (and be fostered by) low levels of conflict across these boundaries. Interlocking directorates among firms are generally thought to facilitate cooperation among corporations. Career trajectories that involve movement from private business to government and back to business probably reduce conflict between the state and private enterprises. In these and other ways, the variable permeability of different kinds of social boundaries can play an important role in bridging or intensifying the fault lines of social structures.

In what follows we will explore two aspects of the static permeability of class boundaries – friendships and cross-class families – and one aspect of dynamic permeability – inter-generational mobility.

5.2 Methodological strategy

Operationalizing class structure[1]

In the analysis of class-boundary permeability we ideally would want to examine the patterns of social ties that people in each of the categories of the 12-category class structure matrix in Figure 1.2 have with friends, spouses and parents, also classified into this same 12-category matrix. That would mean examining 144 possible combinations. Unfortunately, the samples available in this project are simply not large enough to reliably study such a large number of combinations. We have therefore had to collapse a number of the categories in the class structure matrix. For the friendship and family analyses we can operationalize eight class locations: employers (capitalists and small employers), petty bourgeoisie, expert-managers, managers, supervisors, experts, skilled employees, and workers[2]. In the mobility analysis, managers and supervisors are combined, yielding a total of seven categories.[3]

The permeability-event matrix

On the basis of these class location categories we can construct an 8×8 matrix of "permeability events" (a 7×7 matrix in the case of mobility). In the analysis of mobility, one axis of this matrix represents class origins, the other class destinations. In the analysis of friendship ties, one axis represents the class locations of respondents and the other the class location of respondents' friends. And, in the analysis of the cross-class

---

[1] The details of the operationalization of the class structure variable are somewhat different for this chapter from other chapters. See Wright 1997: 152–154.

[2] The relationship between the class location categories we are using here and those in Figure 1.2 are as follows: employers = small employers and capitalists combined; petty bourgeoisie = petty bourgeoisie; expert-managers = expert-managers, skilled managers, expert supervisors and skilled supervisors; managers = nonskilled managers; supervisors = nonskilled supervisors; experts = experts; skilled worker = skilled worker; and worker = workers.

[3] Managers and supervisors had to be combined in the mobility analysis because we were unable to distinguish managers from supervisors for the head of household in the respondents' family of origin.

families, one axis represents the class location of husbands and the other of wives in two-earner households. The cells in the matrix thus constitute types of permeability and impermeability events: the off-diagonal cells represent events that cross class locations; the diagonal cells represent events contained within a given class location. Thus, for example, in the mobility analysis, the diagonal cells are different types of *im*mobility and the off-diagonal cells different types of mobility, say from a worker origin to an expert destination.

Our analytical task is to analyze the relative likelihood of different types of permeability events in this matrix. If, for example, the likelihood of friendship ties linking an employer with an employee is much lower than the likelihood of friendship ties linking an expert with a nonexpert, then we will say that the property boundary is less permeable than the expertise boundary. The statistical strategy for modeling differential relative odds of such events is standard log-linear analysis. It is not necessary, however, to understand the technical details of this methodology to understand the empirical research in this chapter (see Wright 1997: 165–168 for a brief technical introduction).

Alternative approaches to analyzing permeability

There are two ways to conceptualize the problem of "boundary permeability" in the class structure. The first strategy sees the class structure as an array of categorically defined locations (cells in a matrix). A permeability-event, therefore, is anything in the life of an individual which links that person to two or more of these locations. Thus, for workers in the eight-category class structure variable we are using here, there would be seven possible boundary-crossing events: WORKER I EMPLOYER, WORKER I PETTY BOURGEOIS, WORKER I EXPERT-MANAGER, etc.[4] For expert-managers, there are six additional boundary-crossing events (since the WORKER I EXPERT-MANAGER boundary has already been counted). Among the eight class locations we are using, there are thus 28 boundaries across which permeability events can occur. We will refer to this as *locational* permeability. One approach to studying the permeability of class boundaries, then, would be to measure the relative permeability of each of

---

[4] Throughout our analyses we will generally treat permeability-events as "symmetrical" (e.g. we will treat a friendship tie between a respondent who is a worker and a manager–friend as the same as a tie between a respondent who is a manager and a worker–friend).

these 28 location-boundaries and rank order them from highest to lowest degree of permeability.

The second strategy analyzes directly the three underlying mechanisms that generate the locations in the class structure: property, authority, and skills/expertise. These mechanisms might be thought of as more fundamental than class location as such, since the concept of class structure is constructed by combining these mechanisms in different ways.[5] Data analysis would then involve assessing the relative densities of permeability events which span the categories defined by these three underlying mechanisms rather than studying the permeability events between pairs of cells of the class structure matrix. We will refer to this as *dimensional* permeability.

To measure dimensional permeability, we will trichotomize each of the three dimensions of the class structure matrix: the property dimension is trichotomized into employers, petty bourgeoisie and employees; the authority dimension into managers, supervisors and workers; and the skill dimension into experts, skilled and nonskilled.[6] In order to insure that we are measuring significant incidents of class-boundary crossing permeability, we will define a "permeability event" as an event that spans the *extreme* categories in these trichotomies. For example a friendship between an employer and an employee will be treated as a permeability event across the property boundary, whereas friendships between employers and petty bourgeois or between petty bourgeois and employees will not. Similarly, a friendship between an expert and a worker will be treated as crossing the expert boundary, and a friendship between a manager and a worker will be viewed as crossing the authority boundary.

In the empirical investigations of friendships, mobility and family structure in this book we will examine both locational and dimensional permeability, although the emphasis will be on dimensional permeability. The bulk of the analysis thus investigates the relative likelihood of permeability events across the property, authority and expertise boundaries. Once the basic pattern of dimensional permeability is

---

[5] Halaby and Weakliem (1993) argue that the concept of class structure used in the class analysis project should be decomposed into these three "primitive" dimensions and that nothing is gained by the theoretical gestalt class "structure." For a critique of Halaby and Weakliem's argument, see Wright (1993).

[6] Employers are treated as managers on the authority dimension in this analysis and treated as being in the intermediary category – skilled – on the skill dimension. See Wright (1977: 160–161).

mapped in terms of these three class boundaries, we will then analyze in a more fine-grained manner the locational permeability between the working class and other specific class locations.

How to read the results

The results of the data analyses in this chapter will be presented as graphical comparisons of values on what I will call the "permeability coefficient" for different kinds of permeability events.[7] A value of 0 on this coefficient would mean that there were no events that crossed the class boundary at all – no friendship ties, no mobility, no marriages. The boundary in question would thus be perfectly *im*permeable. A value of 1 for this coefficient means that the event in question occurred at the frequency that would be expected if boundary-crossing events were strictly random. If, for example, the permeability coefficient for a friendship tie across the authority boundary was 1, this means that the probability of a friendship tie between a person with authority and a person without authority is the same as between any two randomly selected persons. A permeability index value of greater than 1 thus indicates that the boundary in question is positively permeable: more events occur across such a boundary than would be predicted randomly.

5.3 Intergenerational class mobility

It is perhaps not surprising that most research on social mobility has been at least loosely linked to a Weberian framework of class analysis. The Weberian concept of class revolves around the problem of common life chances of people within market exchanges. This naturally leads to a concern with the intergenerational transmission of life chances – i.e., the extent to which one's own class location is determined by the class into which one is born and raised.

Marxist class analysis has paid much less systematic attention to the problem of mobility. Although Marxists engaged in qualitative and historical research on problems of class consciousness and class formation frequently allude to the issue of mobility in the context of discussing the development and transmission of class cultures and community solidarities, there are virtually no systematic quantitative investigations

---

[7] Technically, the values on the permeability index are the antilogs of the coefficients in log-linear models of permeability events. For a more technical discussion, see Wright (1997: 163–168)

of class mobility within a specifically Marxist framework. Thus, while we know a great deal about social mobility between categories defined in *occupational* terms, we know little about the specific patterns of mobility across *class* boundaries defined explicitly in terms of social relations of production. Exploring such patterns is the basic objective of this analysis.

Theoretical expectations

The relative permeability of class boundaries

There are two basic reasons why one might expect different class boundaries to have different degrees of permeability to intergenerational mobility. First, the extent to which the parental generation is able to appropriate surplus income through mechanisms of exploitation shapes the material advantages and disadvantages experienced by their children. It would therefore be predicted that the more exploitation is linked to a class boundary, the more that class boundary should be impermeable to mobility. Second, insofar as the cultural resources of the parental generation are linked to different class locations, children from different class origins will have different occupational aspirations and cultural advantages. It would therefore be predicted that the more divergent is the "cultural capital" across class boundaries, the less permeable will be the boundary. The first of these mechanisms is the one most associated with Marxist understanding of class. The second is more closely associated with theorists such as Bourdieu (1984, 1985, 1987) who stress the cultural dimension of class relations. Goldthorpe (1987: p. 99) combines these arguments when he asserts that the class mobility regime depends on the different material opportunities parents have to shape their children's economic welfare, and the likely preferences of offspring for some jobs rather than others.

Taken together, these arguments imply relatively impermeable boundaries associated with both property and skills, and a more permeable boundary associated with authority. Mobility across the property boundary is likely to be limited because, first, financial and physical capital are potentially transferable to the offspring of property owners, and, second, capitalist parents are able to finance their children's businesses out of profits or borrowings. Parental property ownership is therefore "insurance" against downward mobility into wage labor for the offspring of capitalists, and the requirement of capital ownership is a barrier to entry to the children of most employees. The rigidity of the property boundary may be further compounded by the preferences of children of property owners for self-employment rather than wage labor. In small businesses, the experience of unpaid family labor may lead the offspring of the self-employed to value self-employment especially strongly. At the very least, the experience of growing up in a capitalist family of origin presents children with an example of property owner-ship as a viable form of economic activity that children whose parents are not capitalists may lack.

The material circumstances and lived experiences associated with high levels of skill assets also make for a relatively impermeable mobility boundary on the expert dimension of the class typology. Like financial capital, skills and expertise are potentially transferable to children, and this generates a barrier to entry into expert labor markets. Because of the rent components of their wages, parents in expert class locations have significant economic resources to invest in their children's education. In addition, given that the economic welfare of experts depends on the mobilization of institutionalized skills, expert parents may have an especially strong commitment to education as a mechanism of social attainment. Such preferences form part of the cultural capital expert parents are uniquely placed to pass on to their children through familial socialization.

Unlike the property and expertise boundaries, the mechanisms of inheritance associated with managerial authority are much weaker, and thus our expectation is that the mobility boundary between managers and nonmanagers would be much more permeable. Organizational control is an attribute of a position in a formal authority hierarchy, and as such is not individually transferable to offspring in the manner of physical capital or expertise.

Our first expectation, then, is that the property and skill boundaries will be less permeable than the authority boundary to intergenerational mobility. It is less clear what should be the expectations about the relative mobility permeability of the property boundary compared to the skill boundary. Marxist class analysis assumes that private property in the means of production is fundamental to the distribution of material welfare and control over the surplus product in capitalist societies and thus capitalist property ownership should generate bigger divisions in financial resources available to offspring than either of the other class boundaries. On the other hand, non-Marxists such as Bourdieu (1987: 733) have argued that the most important source of social power in advanced capitalist societies is the symbolic mobilization of cultural capital, rather than the ownership of means of production. In Bourdieu's account, generalized cultural competencies are symbolically legitimated in formal academic qualifications, and reproduced intergenerationally through class-specific differential educational attainment (Bourdieu and Passeron 1990: 153–164). This view suggests that the skill boundary should be most impermeable to intergenerational mobility.

The above arguments imply two rankings from the least to most permeable class boundaries to intergenerational mobility: property, skill, authority for Marxist class analysis; skill, property, authority for Bourdieu's culturally-grounded class analysis. Both of these hypotheses rest on assumptions that the capacity to transmit assets to offspring is an integral aspect of property rights in productive resources, and that the impermeability of mobility boundaries associated with these resources is a function of the relative importance of such resources in the distribution of social power.

Cross-national variations

The reasoning in both the Marxist and Bourdieu approaches to class have implications for expected cross-national variations in patterns of class-boundary permeability. Both approaches would argue that the more purely capitalistic is an economy, the more impermeable would be the property boundary relative to other boundaries. To use Bourdieu's formulation, the more central to a system of power and privilege is a specific "form of capital," the greater will be the concern of those who hold such capital to safeguard its reproduction. In terms of permeability of class boundaries, this means that the more a class structure is dominated by capitalist relations, the greater will be barriers to acquiring capitalist property. In a purely capitalist economy, therefore, Bourdieu would agree with Marxists that the property boundary should be less permeable than the expertise boundary. This runs counter to popular mythologies of capitalism, where it is believed that the more open and unfettered is the "free market," the greater will be the opportunity for propertyless individuals to accumulate wealth and thus traverse the class boundary between wage earners and capitalists.

In this analysis we will study four countries: the United States, Canada, Sweden and Norway. While all four of these countries have capitalist economies, they differ significantly in terms of the extent to which their economies are dominated by capitalist principles. Within the family of economically developed capitalist economies, the United States is generally considered the most purely capitalistic, both in its institutional structure and in its popular culture, while Sweden is the paradigm of social democratic capitalism, a capitalism in which the state plays a systematic role in countering the inequalities generated by capitalist markets. According to figures cited in Currie and Skolnick (1983: 41–43), next to Japan, the United States has the lowest rate of taxation (29% in 1984), and the lowest rate of Government expenditure (38% in 1983) as a proportion of GDP among developed capitalist countries, while Sweden has the highest rate for both of these (taxes are 50.5% and spending is 66% of GDP). Sweden also has the highest level of government expenditure on social welfare of all capitalist countries (Ginsburg 1992: 33). Canada is generally closer to the United States, and Norway closer to Sweden on these and other indicators.

This leads to the following two comparative hypotheses for the four countries in the study: first, the property boundary should be less permeable in the North American countries (especially the United States) than in the Scandinavian countries (especially Sweden), and, second, the difference in permeability between the property boundary and the skill boundary should be greater in the North American countries than in the Scandinavian countries.

Hypotheses
Taking all of these arguments together yields five general hypotheses about the relative permeability of class boundaries to intergenerational mobility:

> *Hypothesis 1*: The authority boundary should be the most permeable of the three class boundaries.
>
> *Hypothesis 2*: *Marxist hypothesis*. The rank ordering of class boundaries from least permeable to most permeable will be property, skill, authority.
>
> *Hypothesis 3*: *Cultural Capital hypothesis*. The rank ordering of class boundaries from least permeable to most permeable will be skill, property, authority.
>
> *Hypothesis 4*: The property boundary should be less permeable in North America than in Scandinavia.
>
> *Hypothesis 5*: The difference in permeability between the property and skill boundaries should be greater in North America than in Scandinavia.

A note on gender and class boundary permeability to mobility
In a manner similar to most research on social mobility, the analyses of class boundary permeability to intergenerational mobility in this chapter will be restricted to men. The analysis of boundary permeability to intergenerational mobility for women raises a number of special complexities that would take us too far afield for present purposes. Readers interested in this topic can find systematic analysis of gender differences in boundary permeability in Wright (1997: 176–178, 192–195).

Results

The relative permeability of class boundaries
Figure 5.1 presents the permeability coefficients for the *dimensional* permeability of class boundaries to intergenerational mobility for men in the sample for all four countries combined. Several things are worth noting. First, the authority boundary has a permeability coefficient of 0.92, quite close to 1.0. This means that the chances of mobility across the authority boundary are almost what one would predict if such mobility was random. Although in terms of formal statistical tests, this value on the permeability coefficient is still "statistically significant" (i.e. we can be confident at a 5% level of certainty that it is less than 1.0) for all practical intents and purposes, the authority dimension of the class structure does not constitute much of a barrier to intergenerational class mobility. Second, in contrast to the authority boundary, both the property boundary and the skill boundary do generate substantial barriers to intergenerational mobility: the permeability coefficient for property is 0.33 and for skill, 0.55. This means that there are one-third as many instances of intergenerational class mobility across the property boundary than one would predict if such mobility were random, and about half as many instances of mobility across the skill boundary. Finally, when a formal statistical test is done of the *difference* between the permeability coefficients for these boundaries, the property boundary is significantly less permeable than the skill boundary and both are significantly less permeable than the authority boundary. These results are broadly in keeping with the expectations of a neo-Marxist approach (Hypotheses 1 and 2).

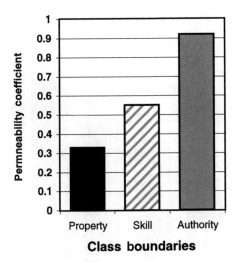

Figure 5.1 *The relative permeability of class boundaries to intergenerational mobility among men, four countries combined.*

Mobility across the working-class boundary

In analyzing what we are calling *locational* permeability (the permeability across the boundaries of specific *locations* within the class structure) we are particularly interested in discovering whether or not the patterns of permeability barriers between working-class locations and other class locations can be considered simply the sum of the permeability barriers across the relevant dimensions of class structure, or, alternatively, whether there may be special barriers attached to specific boundaries between class locations. For example, consider mobility between the working class and expert-managers. This mobility crosses two "boundaries" – the authority boundary and the skill boundary. The question in this case, then, is this: is the permeability of mobility between workers and expert-managers simply the sum of the permeability of the authority boundary and the skill boundary, or is there also an *interaction* between these two dimensions which affects the permeability of the specific boundary between workers and expert-managers?

To answer this question, a mobility model needs to be studied in which the effects of the three dimensions of class boundaries – property, authority, and skill – are first examined and then a variable which measures all of the specific pairs of mobility events connecting the working class to other locations is added. The technical statistical issue in this model is whether the "fit of the model" – how well it captures all

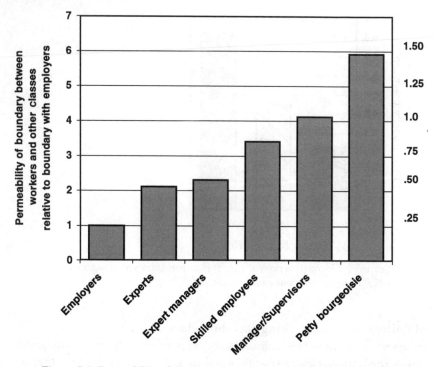

Figure 5.2 *Permeability of class boundaries between workers and other class locations, four countries combined.*

of the patterns in the data – is improved when these "locational permeability" variables were added. As is shown in Wright (1997: 185–186), the fit of the model was substantially increased.

Figure 5.2 presents the permeability coefficients for each of the specific class boundaries between the working class and the other class locations.[8] A number of things are striking in this figure. First, the class mobility permeability coefficient for the class boundary between the working class and the petty bourgeoisie is nearly 1.5, significantly greater than 1.0. This indicates that there are nearly 50% more mobility events between these two class locations than would be predicted if mobility was a random process. Second, the permeability coefficient between workers and employers is only 0.25. The permeability to mobility of the WORKER | EMPLOYER boundary is thus one sixth that of the

---

[8] The coefficients in this figure are derived from the sum of the relevant dimensional permeability coefficients and the location-specific coefficients for each category.

WORKER | PETTY BOURGEOIS boundary. Clearly, the socially significant barrier to mobility across the property boundary for people in the working class is not between workers and self-employment as such, but between workers and employers. Third, the permeability to intergenerational mobility of the boundary between workers and experts and between workers and expert-managers are virtually identical – just over 0.5. As in our earlier discussion of dimensional permeability, this indicates that the barrier to mobility is much more concentrated on the skill/expertise dimension than the managerial dimension.

This analysis of locational permeability has important implications for the broader concept of class structure itself. One way of thinking about locational permeability is that this represents *interactions* among the three underlying dimensions of the class structure. If there were no interactions of this sort, then the concept of "class structure," formed through the combination of the three "primitive terms" (property, authority and skill) would simply be a heuristic convenience. Nothing would be lost by simply talking serially about the effects of property ownership, the effects of skill, and the effects of authority, and ignoring the effects of specific locations in the class structure. "Location" gets its analytical bite from the synergetic consequences of the specific combinations of dimensions that generate a given location. To use a cliché, "the whole is greater than the sum of the parts," and the presence of significant locational permeability effects (i.e. interaction effects) captures this.

Cross-national variations

So far we have examined the mobility permeability of class boundaries for data which combines the samples for men from the United States, Canada, Norway and Sweden. Figure 5.3 presents the results for each of these countries taken separately. In the United States and Canada the property boundary is significantly less permeable than the skill boundary; in Norway, the property boundary appears less permeable than the skill boundary, but the difference between these two boundaries is not statistically significant (at the conventional 0.05 significance level); in Sweden the skill boundary is nominally (although not statistically significantly) *less* permeable than the property boundary. There therefore appears to be a significant difference in the class-boundary permeability patterns in the two North American countries and the two Scandinavian countries in our study: in North America, but not in Scandinavia, the property boundary is significantly less permeable than the skill

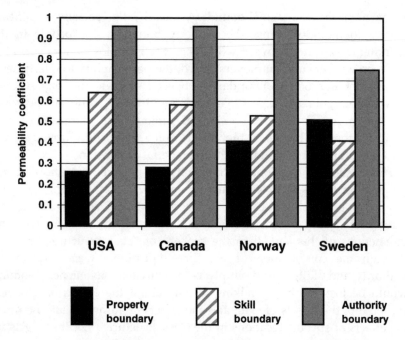

Figure 5.3 *Class-boundary permeability to intergenerational mobility among men, four countries compared.*

boundary to intergenerational class mobility. The basic source of this difference lies in the significantly greater permeability (at the 0.05 significance level) of the *property* boundary in Scandinavia. This coefficient is roughly 50% greater in the Scandinavian countries (0.41 in Norway and 0.51 in Sweden) compared to the two North American countries (0.26 in the US and 0.28 in Canada). The results are thus consistent with Hypotheses 4 and 5, suggesting that the property boundary is less permeable in societies within which capitalist economic relations are less constrained by state interventions.[9]

---

[9] A possible objection to all of these results involving the property boundary is that they might all be due to presence of farmers among the self-employed. Since it is well known that there is relatively little mobility from nonfarm to farm occupations, this might account for the relative impermeability of the property boundary. To check this, all of the analyses were also done excluding everyone in either a farmer origin or farmer destination. While this did affect somewhat the magnitudes of the coefficients, the basic patterns of results were unchanged. See Wright (1997: 174–175, 190–192)

Conclusions for mobility analyses

Three general conclusions stand out from these results.

First, in North America, the patterns of permeability of class boundaries to mobility among men are broadly consistent with the expectations of neo-Marxist conceptualizations of class: the property boundary is the least permeable, followed by the skill boundary and then the authority boundary. On the basis of these results, the material resources linked to capitalist property relations appear to constitute a more significant barrier to mobility in the USA and Canada than the cultural resources linked to skills.

Second, in Sweden and Norway, the property and skill boundaries do not differ significantly in their degree of permeability to intergenerational mobility among men. This difference from North America is primarily because the property boundary is more permeable in Norway and Sweden. The relative degree of permeability to mobility of different class boundaries, therefore, is not an invariant feature of capitalist class structures. Our results suggest that the more purely capitalistic is an economic structure, the less permeable will be the property boundary to intergenerational mobility.

Third, the permeability patterns suggest that the class structure should not be viewed simply as the "sum" of the three dimensions that underlie it. Halaby and Weakliem (1993) argued that combining these three dimensions into a "class structure" typology is simply a descriptive convenience; the analysis of classes can just as easily be carried out directly on the basis of the three "primitive" dimensions taken one by one. The results of the analysis of *locational permeability* (Figure 5.2) indicate that the additive effects of these three dimensions do not exhaust mobility patterns within this typology, and thus class structures are indeed "wholes" that are not reducible to the "sum of their parts" in the sense that there are distinctive effects of the gestalt as such.

5.4 Cross-class friendships

Class mobility is not the only issue involved in understanding the permeability of class boundaries. Patterns of intimate social interaction among people within marriages and friendships are also relevant aspects of the permeability of such boundaries. A rigid class structure in which people's lives are tightly bounded within particular class locations is not simply one in which there are few prospects for individual mobility but

Table 5.1 *Rank orderings of relative impermeability of class boundaries to friendship ites in different theoretical perspectives*

| | Ranking from most impermeable (1) to most permeable (3) | | |
Theoretical Perspective	PROPERTY	AUTHORITY	SKILL
Class interests (Marxian variant)[a]	1	2 or 3	3 or 2
Class interests (Dahrendorf variant)	2	1	3
Class habitus (Bourdieu)	2	3	1
Class as opportunity structure[b]	1 or 2	3	2 or 1

[a] The Marxian variant of the class interest perspective predicts the property boundary to be the most *im*permeable, but provides no clear basis for rank ordering the authority or skill boundaries.

[b] The "opportunity structure" perspective predicts the authority boundary to be the most permeable, but provides no clear basis for rank ordering the property or skill boundaries.

one in which social networks rarely cross class boundaries. In the popular consciousness, when people argue that social classes are not very important in the United States part of what they mean is that the social barriers that separate people in different classes are thought to be relatively weak. The extent of cross-class friendships would be one measure of the extent to which this is true.

Orienting hypotheses

A number of orienting hypotheses can be derived from class analysis and the sociology of friendships to guide our exploration of class boundary permeability to friendships. As in the mobility analysis, these hypotheses are organized around the rankings of the three class boundaries by degree of impermeability (see Table 5.1). These rankings are derived from arguments about three ways in which these class mechanisms might generate obstacles and facilitations to friendship formation: (1) by structuring the *interests* of actors; (2) by shaping actors' *life styles*; and (3) by creating differential *opportunities* for informal interpersonal contact. Each of these causal processes suggests different rankings of the three kinds of class boundaries by relative permeability.

Class interests (Marxian variant)
Marxism has relatively little to say about interpersonal relations. Nevertheless, the Marxist approach to class analysis would generally predict

that the more antagonistic are two peoples' class interests, the less likely it is that friendships will form between them, both because the antagonism of class interests would directly constitute a tension within interpersonal interactions and because class interests shape values and ideologies, which also affect the likelihood and durability of friendships. On these grounds, Marxists would predict that friendships crossing the property boundary are particularly unlikely. More tentatively, insofar as Marxists regard the interests of managers as generally more closely integrated with the interests of capitalists than are the interests of experts, they would rank the authority boundary as more impermeable than the skill boundary. This prediction, however, would be tempered by the realization that segmentation of labor markets by credentials is a deep source of conflict in contemporary capitalist societies.

Class interests (Dahrendorf variant)

Ralf Dahrendorf (1959) argued that in contemporary societies authority is the fundamental basis of class antagonism. In early periods of capitalist development, his argument goes, authority and property coincided, and thus social theorists like Marx mistakenly identified property as the fundamental axis of class conflict. In the twentieth century, however, the deepening separation of formal ownership of property from substantive command means that property ownership has declined as a basis for class relations. This perspective would therefore predict that the authority boundary should be the most impermeable. To the extent that property ownership still confers some authority, the property boundary would be expected to have intermediate permeability. Since skill without organizational authority confers little capacity to command, the skill boundary should be the most permeable of the three.

Class habitus (Bourdieu)

Virtually all research on friendship formation has argued that one of the primary mechanisms shaping friendship patterns is common values and life styles. As Pierre Bourdieu (1984, 1985, 1987) has argued in his analysis of "class habitus," a pivotal determinant of life style is cultural capital. This suggests that the odds of friendship ties between experts and nonexperts should be particularly low since people on either side of the skill boundary are likely to differ sharply in terms of cultural capital. Thus, class habitus theory would predict the skill dimension to be the most impermeable. Furthermore, because wealth and income are generally viewed as crucial bases of life style (although perhaps less important than cultural capital), the property boundary would be expected to be more impermeable than the authority boundary.

Interaction opportunity

Sociological analyses of friendships decompose the friendship formation process into two consecutive processes, meeting and mating. Meeting is the process of strangers being converted into acquaintances; mating is the conversion of acquaintances into friends. Although meeting can simply be a matter of chance, typically it is the result of people being in situations that systematically facilitate friendship formation. In part, this is a question of spatial proximity, as in the importance of neighborhood of residence as a factor influencing friendship formation – people often make friends with neighbors of dissimilar social position. More significant than sheer proximity for our present purposes, certain "foci" of social interaction, to use Feld's (1981) expression, generate sustained joint activities among people and thus enhance the probabilities of people getting to know each other in ways that could lead to friendship.

Worksites are an important instance of such interactional foci. Furthermore, many worksites involve joint activity among people in different class locations, thus creating opportunities for cross-class friendships, particularly between managers and nonmanagers. These opportunities are further enhanced by the fact that many supervisors and even some managers spend significant parts of their careers as nonmanagerial employees. Intra-career authority mobility is undoubtedly much higher than intra-career mobility across either the property or skill boundaries. To the extent that friendships survive promotions, then, this would also enhance the permeability of the authority boundary. The opportunity structure arguments, therefore, would suggest that the authority class boundary should be the most permeable. The opportunity structure perspective, however, makes no clear prediction about relative impermeability of the property or skill boundaries.

Results

Respondents in the class analysis survey were asked a battery of questions about the principal jobs of their three closest friends. If a friend was currently unemployed or out of the labor force, they were asked about that person's last job (see Wright 1997: 218–222 for details). On the basis of this information, we are able to classify friends into the same basic class structure matrix as respondents.

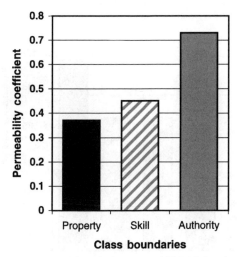

Figure 5.4 *The relative permeability of class boundaries to friendships, four countries combined.*

The relative permeability of the three exploitation boundaries

Figure 5.4 presents the basic permeability coefficients for the friendship ties across the three class-boundary dimensions for all four countries combined.

All three boundaries have statistically significant coefficients, indicating that these boundaries do in fact constitute obstacles to the formation of friendships. The coefficients for the property and expert boundaries are significantly smaller than that of the authority boundary: the odds of a friendship across the authority boundary are nearly 100 percent greater than the odds of a friendship across the property boundary and 60 percent greater than a friendship across the skill boundary. The coefficient of the property boundary is also significantly less than that of the skill boundary. These results are most in keeping with the expectations of the Marxist and opportunity structure perspectives on class-boundary permeability.

Friendship ties between the working class and other class locations

Figure 5.5 presents the results of the specific pattern of *locational* permeability of class boundaries to friendship ties between the working class and each of the other class locations. As in the class mobility results, the addition of locational permeability to the simpler dimensional permeability analysis significantly improves the "fit" of the model. Of the

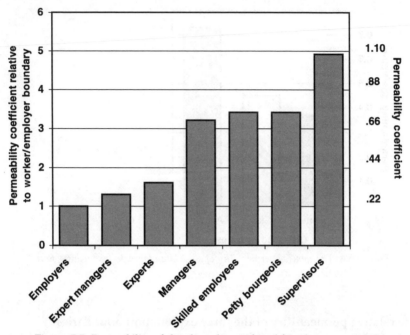

Figure 5.5 *Permeability of class boundary to friendships between workers and other class locations, four countries combined.*

seven boundaries between the working class and other class locations, the WORKER│EMPLOYER boundary is the least permeable, while the WORKER│SUPERVISOR boundary is the most permeable: workers have nearly five times the odds of a friendship with a supervisor than with an employer. The second and third ranks in impermeability are the WORKER│EXPERT-MANAGER and WORKER│EXPERT boundaries. The next three boundaries – WORKER│MANAGER, WORKER│SKILLED-EMPLOYEE, and WORKER│PETTY BOURGEOIS – are of roughly equal permeability. As in the previous results for mobility, the results for the WORKER│PETTY BOUR-GEOIS boundary indicate that the salient issue for the property boundary is not self-employment as such, but capitalist property relations. The odds of friendship ties between workers and petty bourgeois are over three times greater than those between workers and employers.

Variations across countries in permeability to friendships
Figure 5.6 presents the results of the dimensional permeability of class boundaries to friendships separately for each of the four countries. In

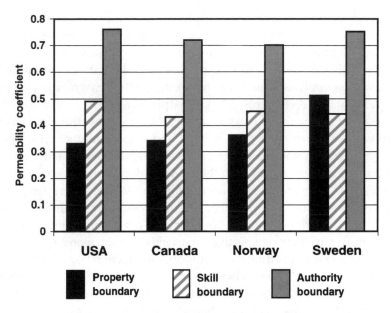

Figure 5.6 *Class-boundary permeability to friendships, four countries combined.*

formal statistical tests, none of the differences across countries were statistically significant. The only apparent difference across these countries is that in Sweden the property boundary and the skill boundary are not significantly different, whereas they are in the other three countries.

Conclusion for the friendship analysis

Overall, these results indicate that, with the exception of Sweden, the property boundary is the most impermeable to the formation of friendships, followed by the skill boundary, with the authority boundary being the most permeable. This rank order is most sharply inconsistent with Dahrendorf's class analysis. Not only is authority the most permeable of the three boundaries in relative terms, it is also quite permeable in absolute terms.

What about the three other theoretical perspectives outlined in Table 5.1? Marxist theory predicts that the property boundary should be the most impermeable, and this is generally supported by the analysis. The results for the skill and authority boundaries, however, are not entirely what most Marxists would expect: the skill boundary is less permeable and the authority boundary is more permeable than would be expected strictly on the basis of a theory of exploitation, domination and common class interests alone. While with a bit of a stretch the Marxist concern with exploitation and class interests may be consistent with the finding that the skill boundary is less permeable than the authority boundary, Marxist class analysis would not expect the relative magnitude of these two permeability coefficients to be so sharply different.

The findings for the skill and authority boundaries, therefore, seem more consistent with the class habitus and opportunity structure perspectives. On the one hand, the relatively high impermeability of the skill boundary is consistent with theories of cultural capital, even if such theories tend to minimize the continuing importance of property as a basis for structuring class practices. On the other hand, the high relative permeability of the authority boundary is most consistent with the opportunity structure perspective on friendships. In many workplaces there are diverse opportunities for informal interaction between workers and supervisors, and even between workers and managers. This density of interactional possibilities, combined with relatively high levels of career mobility across authority boundaries compared to the property and expert boundaries, may account for the relatively high permeability of the authority boundary.

The analysis thus suggests that the causal mechanisms identified by theories of class interests (at least the Marxist variant), class habitus and opportunity structure probably all operate to create obstacles and opportunities for friendship formation across class boundaries. The result of the joint operation of these three clusters of causes is that the boundary Marxists predict to be the least permeable is indeed the least permeable. This might imply that the property–exploitation–interest mechanism is a more powerful structuring mechanism than are the class habitus or opportunity mechanisms. Such a conclusion, however, is vulnerable to criticism on two scores. First, claims about the relative potency of causal processes are always vulnerable to measurement issues. Our conclusion about the relatively high permeability of the authority boundary might change if we adopted a more restrictive definition of authority, e.g., limiting "managers" to high-level executives. Also, if we distinguished among experts between highly credentialed professionals with advanced degrees and other experts, the skill boundary might become the "least" permeable. While such conjectured results could potentially be countered with a comparable respecification of the property-boundary, this would only reaffirm the sensitivity of claims about relative causal potency to measurement choices. Second, even if a more fine-grained inspection revealed that our core results were robust across alternative specifications of these boundaries, there is still the problem of ascribing this impermeability to "exploitation interests" rather than class habitus or opportunity structure. Employers certainly live different life styles from most nonproperty owners, and the physical opportunities for informal interaction between most employees and employers are few. Therefore, while our data are consistent with the claim that property-based interests have stronger effects on friendship formation than either opportunity structure or class habitus, they cannot effectively refute counterclaims.

5.5 Cross-class families

The third form of class-boundary permeability we will explore occurs when husbands and wives in dual-earner families occupy jobs in different classes. The patterns of homogeneity and heterogeneity of class compositions within families is the result of three interconnected processes:

1 The process of what sociologists call "assortative mating" by which men and women from different class origins and occupying different job-classes before marriage make marriage choices in the first place.
2 The process within marriages which determine if and when the wife enters the labor force.
3 The processes which determine the job-class occupied by husbands and wives given their class origins and the decisions about labor force participation.

With the available data we cannot even begin to sort out the separate contributions of these three processes. What we can do, in a manner parallel to the exploration of permeability of class boundaries to friendships and mobility, is map out the static patterns of class boundary permeability within families that result from the interactions of assortative mating, labor force participation decisions and job acquisition.

As in the case of the problem of friendship formation, the Marxist tradition of class analysis has little explicitly to say about the class structuring of marriage markets or labor market choices within families. Nevertheless, the arguments around class interests we explored in the contexts of friendship formation are broadly applicable to the present problem as well. We will therefore explore the same basic theoretical predictions as in the discussion of mobility and friendships. I will take the core predictions from a Marxist class analysis to be that the property boundary will be the least permeable to cross-class families, whereas a class analysis that emphasizes issues of cultural capital would predict that the skill boundary would be the least permeable.

Results

Patterns of cross-class families

Before looking at the results of our statistical models of class boundary permeability for cross-class families, it will be useful to get some sense of the overall distribution of cross-class families. Figure 5.7 distinguishes five kinds of two-earner households based on the eight class categories we have been using in this chapter: 1. households with a homogeneous class composition (the jobs of the husband and wife are in the same class location); 2. marginally heterogeneous households, in which the husband and wife are in different class locations, but they occupy adjacent locations in the class structure matrix (e.g workers and supervisors); 3. cross-class households in which there is no clear status difference between husband and wife (eg expert and expert manager); 4. cross-class households in which the class location of the wife is more privileged than that of her husband; 5. cross-class households in which the husband's class is more privileged than the wife's.[10]

Several things are worth noting in this figure. First of all, in all of these countries roughly two-thirds of all households in which both the husband and the wife are in the labor force are either class homogeneous or only marginally heterogeneous.

Second, cross-class families are not a rare occurrence. In roughly 30–35% of dual-earner families in these four countries, the husbands and wives occupy jobs in clearly different class locations. Virtually every possible form of cross-class household exists in all four of these countries (see Wright 1997: 227). In the United States, for example, in 1.2% of dual-earner households, the wife is an employer and the husband a worker and in 3.1% the wife is an expert-manager and the husband a worker. Roughly half of these cross-class families consist of one spouse in the

---

[10] The details of the data used in this and other figures in the analysis of cross-class families are given in Wright (1997: 235–236). The detailed description of the distribution of households across all combinations of husband's and wife's class locations can be found in Wright (1997: 226).

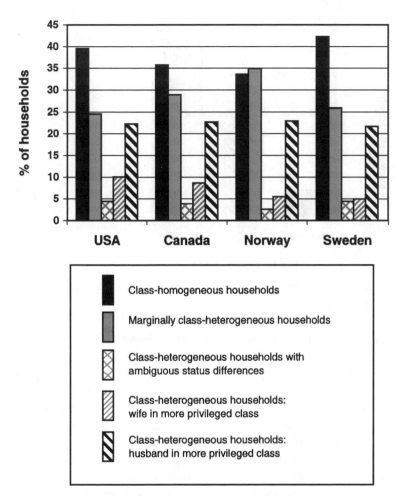

Figure 5.7 *Class composition of families, two-earner households.*

working class and one who is an employer, an expert-manager, a manager, or an expert. Since in the early 1980s when these data were gathered, roughly 40% of all people lived in dual-earner households in these countries, this means that about 12% or so of the population live in unambiguously cross-class families. While it is still the case that most people live in class-homogeneous households, cross-class families are a significant reality in developed capitalism.

Third, as would be expected, it is much more common in cross-class families for the husband to be in a more privileged class location than the wife. In the United States, for example, about 10% of all dual-earner

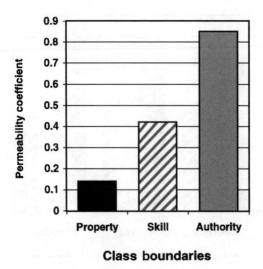

Class boundaries

Figure 5.8 *The relative permeability of class boundaries within dual-earner households, four countries combined.*

marriages consist of a manager or expert husband and a working-class wife, but only 5% consist of a manager or expert wife and a working-class husband. In Sweden and Norway this contrast is even greater: 10–12% of dual-earner households have manager/expert husbands and worker wives, but only 2–3% have manager/expert wives and working-class husbands. Overall in the United States and Canada women are about two-and-a-half times more likely to live in households with husbands whose jobs are in more privileged rather than less privileged class locations than their own jobs, whereas in Scandinavia they are four-and-a-half times more likely to live in such a household. Still, even though this expected gender difference occurs, there is a significant number of households, especially in the United States and Canada, in which the wife's job is in a more privileged class location than is their husband's.

The relative permeability of the three class boundaries

Figure 5.8 presents the permeability coefficients for household composition for the four countries combined. The coefficients for all three class boundaries indicate some degree of impermeability. The property boundary is clearly the least permeable and the authority boundary the most permeable for cross-class marriages: the odds of a cross-class family across the property boundary is less than one-sixth the odds of

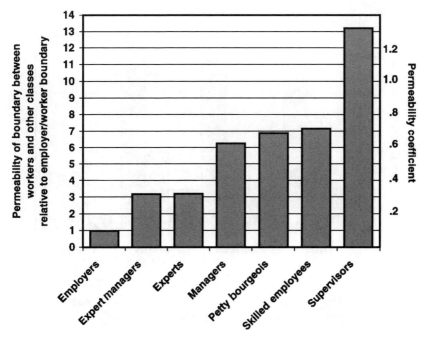

Figure 5.9 *Permeability of class boundary within two-earner households between workers and other class locations, four countries combined.*

one across the authority boundary and one-third the odds of one across the expertise boundary. These results are strongly consistent with expectations of Marxist class analysis.

The locational permeability of boundaries between working-class and other class locations

As in the prior analysis of mobility and friendships, the locational permeability analysis significantly improves the statistical fit of the models. This, again, indicates that the degree of permeability of class boundaries within households between working-class locations and other classes is not simply an additive effect of the three underlying dimensions of the class structure; interactions among these dimensions matter.

Figure 5.9 presents the relative locational permeability of the working class with other class locations within households. As in the prior analyses, the odds of a WORKER ǀ EMPLOYER cross-class family are much lower than any other combination. The odds ratio for a WORKER ǀ EXPERT-MANAGER family is three times greater than for a WORKER ǀ EMPLOYER

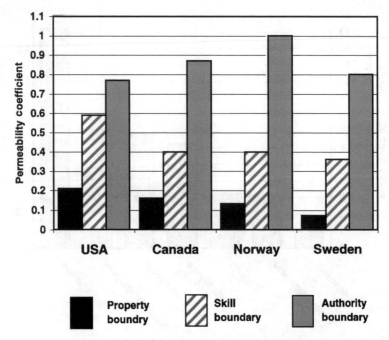

Figure 5.10 *Permeability of class boundaries within two-earner households, four countries compared.*

family, for a WORKER I PETTY BOURGEOIS family almost seven times greater, and for a WORKER I SUPERVISOR family thirteen times greater. These results again confirm the relatively high permeability of the authority boundary, the impermeability of the property boundary, and the fact that the salient aspect of the property boundary is not self-employment as such, but capitalist class relations.

Country interactions

Figure 5.10 presents the patterns of class-boundary permeability separately in each of the four countries. In this case the basic patterns are virtually identical in all four countries: the property boundary is the least permeable to the formation of cross-class families and the authority boundary the most permeable. While there are a number of nominal differences between the countries which might turn out to be significant if we had larger samples – the coefficient for skill seems larger in the US and the coefficient for property seems somewhat smaller in Sweden – nevertheless, with the present data none of these even approach the conventional levels of statistical significance. We can thus conclude that the patterns of permeability of class boundaries within cross-class families appear relatively invariant across countries.

5.6 Comparing the three forms of class-boundary permeability

Figure 5.11 compares the permeability coefficients for the three aspects of class-boundary permeability we have been exploring across the four countries. Considering how much friendships, family structure, and mobility differ as social phenomena, the patterns of boundary permeability within countries are quite similar across these three social phenomena. In all four countries, the authority boundary is the most permeable for all three of these social phenomena, although in the United States the authority and expertise boundaries are not significantly different for cross-class families. In the United States, Canada and Norway, the rank order of permeability for the three phenomena are the same, although in a few cases the coefficients for the property and skill boundaries do not differ significantly. Only Sweden exhibits clear differences in the basic patterns for the property boundary across the three phenomena: the property boundary is much less permeable than the expertise boundary for the class composition of marriages, while the two boundaries do not differ significantly for mobility or friendships. With the exception of Sweden, therefore, the patterns of boundary permeability are rather consistent across these qualitatively different social phenomena.

Taken together, these results support several general conclusions. First, they lend support to the general expectation in Marxist class analysis that the property dimension of the class structure remains the most fundamental in capitalist societies. While class structures in capitalism cannot adequately be described simply in terms of relationship to the means of production, nevertheless the property boundary appears to be the most rigid. What is more, this relative impermeability of the property boundary is not generated by the division between the self-employed and employees, but rather by capitalist property relations. As the analysis of the location-permeability between the working class and other class locations demonstrates in all three analyses, the boundary between the working class and employers is the least permeable of all boundaries, and much less permeable that the boundary between workers and the petty bourgeoisie.

Second, with the exception of some of the results for Sweden, the cross-national variations in the patterns of class boundary permeability

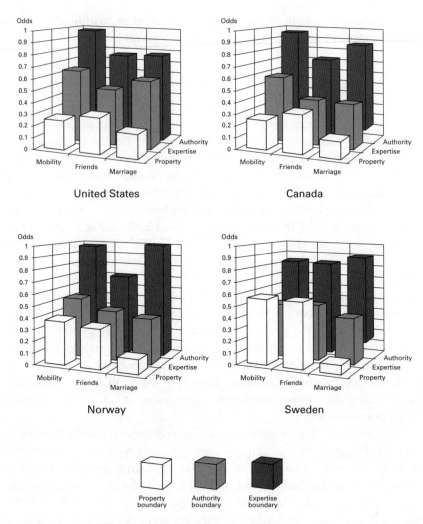

Figure 5.11 *The odds of class-boundary permeability to mobility, friendships and cross-class families in the United States, Canada, Norway and Sweden.*

are quite muted. While in the case of the mobility results, there was some basis for distinguishing the patterns in the social democratic Nordic countries from the more purely capitalistic North America, nevertheless these differences constitute variations on a theme rather than completely different patterns. This suggests that the relative permeability of different class boundaries is shaped more by properties of the class structure itself than by cultural or political processes.

Finally, the results from the analysis of the locational-permeability between the working class and other class locations support the view that the class structure is not simply the "sum" of its underlying dimensions. The probabilities that friendships, biographies and marriages cross specific class boundaries are the result of the interactions among these dimensions, not simply their separate effects. If this interpretation of the results is correct, then the concept of "class structure," should not be seen simply as a heuristic convenience for summarizing the three separate underlying dimensions.

Part II

Class and gender

6. Conceptualizing the interaction of class and gender

6.1 The debate over class primacy

In many ways, the most sustained challenge to class analysis as a central axis of critical social theory in recent years has come from feminists. Class analysts, especially in the Marxist tradition, have often implied that class was a "more important" or "more fundamental" dimension of social structure than gender.[1] While such claims to explanatory primacy have rarely been explicitly defended, the relative inattention to gender in the Marxist tradition is taken by many commentators as a *de facto* denigration of gender as a significant explanatory factor.

To some extent this suggestion that class is "more important" than gender is simply a by-product of a specific set of theoretical preoccupations. To focus on class as a causal mechanism in social explanations implies bracketing other concerns. Class analysis is an "independent variable" specialty, and of necessity this means focusing on class and its ramifications and giving relatively less attention to other causal factors. This does not absolve class analysts from the criticism of sometimes overstating the explanatory power of class for certain problems, but it does imply that the sheer fact of focusing on class and its effects is not a legitimate basis for indicting class analysis.

There are times, however, when the claim that class (or closely associated concepts like "mode of production" or "economic structure") is "more important" than other factors is a substantive thesis, not a heuristic device. Classical historical materialism is the most elaborated instance of such an argument. As G. A. Cohen (1978) has forcefully

[1] The idea that in a multicausal system one factor is "more important" than another is fraught with ambiguities and is very difficult to pin down. For an extended discussion of the problem of causal primacy, see Wright, Levine and Sober (1992: ch. 7).

demonstrated, the part of historical materialism that is built around the base/superstructure metaphor ascribes explanatory primacy to class through the use of functional explanations: the base (the economic structure conceptualized in class terms) "functionally explains" the superstructure. What does this mean? It means that superstructural phenomena take the form that they do because this form helps to reproduce the existing economic structure. This is quite akin to functional explanations in biology where a given trait of an animal is functionally explained by its effects in helping the animal survive and reproduce. Why are the bones in the wings of birds hollow? Because this helps them to fly. The beneficial effect of hollowness (lighter wings facilitate flight) explains the fact of hollowness. In the social case, the functional explanation embodied in historical materialism means that various social institutions – certain features of the state, certain aspects of ideology, certain kinds of laws and so forth – are explained by the fact that they generate effects which help reproduce the economic structure.[2] Since the economic structure is itself composed of social relations of production which collectively define the class structure, this is a form of class primacy.

At first glance it might seem like classical historical materialism makes extraordinarily strong and encompassing claims about the centrality of class. But as G. A. Cohen (1988: ch. 9) has also argued, even classical historical materialism does not make the grandiose claim that class is the most important cause of *everything* social. Historical materialism is not a theory of all social phenomena, but only of a specific set of *explananda* – the historical trajectory of economic structures and their accompanying superstructures.[3] The superstructure, in these terms, is not defined as all social relations and institutions that are not part of the economic base.

---

[2] It is important to note that in this kind of functional explanation there is no suggestion that the superstructure is "epiphenomenal" – a mere reflection of the base that has no consequences in its own right. To say that X functionally explains Y implies that Y has significant effects on X. If it is true that the class structure of capitalism functionally explains the form of the state, then this implies that the state must have significant consequences for reproducing the class structure. If the state had no consequences there would be no point to a functional explanation.

[3] There are Marxists, particularly those working within a strongly Hegelian tradition, who insist that Marxist concepts and theory do attempt to explain everything. Shelton and Agger (1993: 36), for example, write, "Marxism is *not* simply a theory of class but a theory of everything, including women." While I do not think that the aspiration for such a totalizing theoretical project should be rejected a priori, in practice Marxism has not been successful in accomplishing this ambition, and the prospects for doing so are not very promising.

Rather, the superstructure is limited to those noneconomic social phenomena which have effects on the reproduction of the base; these are the phenomena which are candidates for functional explanations of the sort historical materialism defends. What Cohen aptly calls "restrictive historical materialism" is agnostic about the relative explanatory importance of class for various phenomena which are not part of the economic structure or the superstructure, and this would potentially include many cultural phenomena and possibly significant aspects of gender relations.[4]

This kind of functionalist reasoning in historical materialism has played an important role in Marxist analyses of gender relations. Engels' (1968 [1884]) famous discussion of the origins of male domination, for example, explains the subordination of women in terms of its effects on stabilizing the inheritance of private property. This is an explanation of gender relations in terms of the functional requirements of maintaining a system of private property. In more recent discussions, the functional explanations have shifted to the beneficial effects of gender oppression for capital accumulation.[5] For example, a number of contributors to the "domestic labor debate" of the 1970s (e.g. Secombe 1974; Gardiner 1975) argued that the subordination of women is rooted in the sexual division of labor in the household, and this in turn is to be explained by the fact that the unpaid domestic labor of women raises the rate of profit by lowering the costs of reproducing labor power (since part of the consumption of workers takes the form of unpaid services of housewives). Others (e.g. Zaretsky 1976) have argued that the central basis for women's oppression in capitalism lies in the ways the gender division of labor helps to reproduce capitalism ideologically by strengthening a

---

[4] The contrast to "restrictive" historical materialism is "inclusive" historical materialism, in which the superstructure is defined as everything that is not in the base. Cohen shows that inclusive historical materialism is wildly implausible. Probably no one who really thought systematically about the issues seriously ever really held it.

[5] These arguments do not necessarily use the explicit language of functional explanation. Thus, for example, Gardiner (1975: 52) discusses domestic labor in terms of the "essential although changing role" it plays. She asks the question, "Why has domestic labour been maintained?" and answers it by saying: "capitalism developed out of feudalism through workers becoming dependent on the wage system, but has never provided totally for workers' needs through commodity production, instead retaining domestic labor to carry out an important part of the reproduction and maintenance of labor power." The suggestion here is that the explanation for the maintenance of unpaid domestic labor (and the gender relations associated with this labor) is the role played by this labor for capitalism. The word "role" in this context implies a functional explanation.

privatized, consumption-centered vision of family life. In all of these instances, class is accorded explanatory primacy through the use of functional explanations.

Relatively few class analysts, even those still explicitly identifying with the Marxist tradition, strictly adhere to the tenets of classical historical materialism any longer. Virtually no one defends strong functionalist versions of the base/superstructure image of society, even for the specific task of explaining historical trajectories of economic structures. Marxist class analysis is now generally closer to what might be loosely termed "sociological materialism" in which class, because of its linkage to exploitation and the control of economic resources, has a presumptive importance for a broad range of social problems, but is not invariably viewed as the most important determinant. While it remains the case that Marxists generally do try to place class analysis in an historical context, this usually has at best a tenuous relation to a materialist theory of the overall trajectory of human history as such. In practice, then, to be "historical" has generally come to mean "to be historically specific," rather than "to be embedded in a theory *of* history."[6] As a result, the debate over what was once called "class reductionism" or "economic determinism" has waned considerably in recent years.

If one accepts this way of understanding the explanatory project of class analysis, then the central task is to sort out for specific *explananda* the forms of interaction between class and gender as causal processes. Class may indeed turn out to be "more important" than gender for certain problems, but equally, gender may be more important than class for others. Advances in the class analysis of gender *and* the gender analysis of class depend upon research that will clarify these interactions.

6.2 Forms of interconnection of class and gender

As a preliminary task to empirical investigations of class and gender, it is useful to lay out a conceptual menu of the various ways that class and gender might be interconnected. This list is not meant to be exhaustive, and it certainly does not constitute a *theory* of class and gender. Rather, it is an agenda of issues that need to be considered within empirical

[6] For a discussion of the slide from historical materialism towards sociological materialism, see Wright, Levine and Sober (1992: ch. 5).

research and theory construction. Five forms of possible class/gender interconnections are particularly important: gender as a *form* of class relations; gender relations and class relations as *reciprocally affecting* each other; gender as a *sorting mechanism* into class locations; gender as a *mediated linkage* to class locations; and gender as a *causal interaction* with class in determining various outcomes. Let us briefly look at each of these.

1 Gender as a form of class relations

While the concepts of class and gender are analytically distinct, there are empirical situations in which gender relations themselves are a form of class relation (or, equivalently, that class relations are themselves directly organized through gender relations). Frederick Engels (1968 [1884]: 503), in his classic essay on the family and private property, formulates the relationship between class and gender in early civilizations this way: "The first class antagonism which appears in history coincides with the development of the antagonism between man and woman in monogamian marriage, and the first class oppression with the of the female sex by the male.." Gerda Lerner (1986) elaborates a rather different argument about the confluence of class and gender in early civilizations. She argues that one of the earliest forms of male domination consisted of men effectively *owning* women, and by virtue of this appropriating the surplus produced by women. The most important form of this surplus was new people – children – who were a valuable resource in early agrarian civilizations. Control over the capacity of women to produce new labor power was thus a pivotal form of property relations. If this account is correct, then this would constitute a specific form of gendered slavery in which gender and class are melded into a single relation.[7]

2 Gender relations and class relations as reciprocally affecting each other

Certain kinds of class positions may only exist by virtue of the fact that specific forms of gender relations are present. The classic example is domestic services: gender relations play a crucial role in making possible maid and childcare services (Glenn 1992). It is not just that gender sorts people into these jobs; if gender relations were dramatically more

[7] This would only strictly be true if it were the case that all women were slaves, which does not seem to be the case in the historical examples cited by Gerda Lerner. The dystopia portrayed by Margaret Atwood (1987) in *A Handmaid's Tale* comes closer to a society within which class and gender are fused into a single relation.

egalitarian, the jobs themselves might not exist. The availability of single, unmarried farm girls in nineteenth-century New England who were not needed on the farm and who were not in line to inherit the farm was important for the development of the textile industry and the accompanying emergence of the early industrial working class. In many parts of the Third World, gender plays a critical role in making available a supply of cheap, vulnerable labor employed in various kinds of manufacturing. Again, it is not just that gender distributes people into an independently created set of class positions; the structure of gender relations helps to explain why jobs with particular characteristics are available.

Equally, class relations can have an impact on gender. The physical demands of many blue-collar, industrial working-class jobs put a premium on toughness, which in turn may help to reinforce a macho gender culture among working-class men. The competitive, high-pressure career demands of many managerial and professional occupations help to reinforce a specific kind of domestic gender relations in which housewives are available for managing the personal affairs of their husbands. As it is often quipped by women in such careers, what they need is a wife.

One of the most important ways in which class relations and gender relations have shaped each other centers on the problem of the "family wage." Johanna Brenner and Maria Ramas (1984) have argued that the material constraints of working-class life in the nineteenth century were a major force in shaping the development of the working-class family form, and thus gender relations. Because of high infant mortality and the need for high rates of fertility among workers (since having adult, surviving children was crucial for old-age security for parents), it was in the interests of working-class families for the wife to stay at home and the husband to work in the paid labor force. This was not feasible, however, until the "family wage" was instituted. The family wage, in turn, became a powerful material force for keeping women in the home and reinforcing gender differences in pay. These gender differentials in pay, in turn, made it rational for families to orient their economic strategies around the class and job interests of the "male breadwinner," further marginalizing women's paid work. It is only in the last several decades as the male breadwinner family wage has begun to decline that this system has begun to erode.[8]

[8] There has been a lively debate over the explanation of the family wage (see, for example, Humphries 1977; Hartman 1979; Barrett 1984; Lewis 1985). In contrast to Brenner and Ramas's argument that the family wage was in the interests of both male

Particular class relations may also facilitate the transformation of gender relations in more egalitarian directions. As a professor, I occupy a quite privileged class location as a relatively affluent "expert" with high levels of control over my own work. Of particular importance to many professors is the way in which professorial work confers tremendous control over scheduling and time. Professors may work many hours per week, but they often have considerable discretion over when and where they put in the hours. Furthermore, at various times I have had grants which enabled me to buy off teaching and thus have even greater flexibility in organizing my time. This has made it possible within my family for me to play a major role in all aspects of parenting from the time when my children were infants. It has also changed the domestic terrain on which struggles over the domestic division of labor have been waged. The result is a relatively egalitarian division of labor around most domestic chores. This does not imply that class determines the gender division of labor. Far from it. As we shall see in chapter 8, class location does not have a powerful overall impact on the gender division of labor in the home. Nevertheless, the specific properties of class positions transform the *constraints* within which people struggle over gender relations in their own lives, and under certain conditions this facilitates forging more egalitarian gender relations.

3 Gender as a sorting mechanism into class locations[9]

The way gender sorts people into class locations is probably the most obvious aspect of the interconnection of class and gender. One does not need to do high-powered research to observe that men and women in

and female workers, many feminists have argued that the family wage should primarily be viewed as a victory of men over women, reflecting the strategic interests of men in keeping women in their place. Insofar as it was the gender interests of men that formed the basis for the struggle over the family wage, then this would be another instance of the way in which gender relations shape the class structure. In any case, once the family wage is in place as a specific feature of class relations, it becomes an important material condition constraining transformations of gender relations.

[9] It may also be possible to conceptualize the complementary causal relation: class as a sorting mechanism of people into "gender locations." At first glance this might seem like a bizarre claim since we tend to think of gender categories as dichotomous, polarized and isomorphic with sexual categories – male and female. This image reflects the tendency for most people (including most sociologists) to conflate gender categories with sex categories, in spite of the formal acknowledgement that gender is a social, not biological, category. Once we break from the biological specification of gender *relations*, however, then it is clear that men and women can occupy many different sorts of gender locations, and class may influence where people end up in such relations.

the labor force have very different occupational and class distributions, and most people would explain these differences by referring to gender in one way or another. It is less obvious, of course, precisely what gender mechanisms are at work here. Relatively few social scientists now believe that biological differences between men and women are the primary cause of occupational sex segregation, but such views are undoubtedly still common in the general population. Typically in social-science discussions of these issues two kinds of factors linked to gender relations are given center stage in explanations of gender differences in occupational and class distributions: (1) gendered socialization processes which shape the occupational aspirations and skills of men and women, and thus affect the kinds of jobs they are likely to get; (2) various forms of inequality, domination and discrimination which either directly affect the opportunities of men and women to pursue various kinds of jobs, or indirectly affect access by affecting their acquisition of relevant resources. As feminists have often noted, inequalities in the sexual division of labor in the household constrain the labor market strategies of many women and thus the kinds of jobs for which they can realistically compete. Discrimination in credit markets may make it more difficult for women to become capitalists. Traditionally, discrimination in admissions to certain kinds of professional schools made it more difficult for women to acquire the credentials necessary to occupy the expert locations within class structures. As we shall see in chapter 9, gender discrimination in promotions within authority hierarchies directly affects the probabilities of women becoming managers. In each of these instances, the distribution of power and resources within gender relations affects the likelihood of men and women occupying certain kinds of class locations.

4 Gender as mediated linkage to class location

As we discussed in chapters 1 and 2, individuals are linked to class structures through a variety of relations other than their direct location in the social relations of production. The class locations of children are derived from the social relations within families that tie them to the class of their parents, not their own "jobs." Gender relations constitute one of the pivotal ways in which such "mediated linkages" to the class structure are organized, especially through marriages. One of the ways in which class and gender are interconnected, then, is via the way gender relations within families and kinship networks link people to various locations within the class structure. These mediated class locations affect both the gender interests of men and women – the interests they have by virtue of the specific gender relations within which they live – and their class interests.

5 Gender as a causal interaction with class in determining outcomes

Gender and class are interconnected not merely through the various ways they affect each other, but also through their mutual effects on a wide range of social phenomena. Of particular interest are those situations in which class and gender have interactive effects, for the presence of interaction effects indicates that the causal processes represented by the concepts "class" and "gender" are intertwined rather than operating simply as independent mechanisms.

One way of formally representing the interaction of class and gender is with a simple equation of the sort used in multivariate regression analysis. Suppose we were studying the effects of class and gender on political consciousness. The interaction of class and gender could then be represented in the following equation:

$$\text{Consciousness} = a + B_1(\text{Class}) + B_2(\text{Gender}) + B_3(\text{Class} \times \text{Gender})$$

The coefficients B_1, B_2, and B_3 indicate something about the magnitude of the effects of each term in the equation on consciousness. The interaction term, B_3, indicates the extent to which the effects of class vary by gender or, equivalently, the effects of gender vary by class. An example would be a situation in which the ideological difference between capitalists and workers was greater among men than among women.

In a model of this sort, it could turn out that the additive terms were negligible (i.e. B_1 and B_2 would be zero). This would imply that both class and gender only have effects on this dependent variable when they are combined in a particular way. This would be the case, for example, if male and female capitalists and male workers all had indistinguishable attitudes, but female workers were significantly different. In such a situation, the two independent variables in our equation – class and gender – could in practice be replaced by a single variable which would have a value of 1 for female workers and 0 for everyone else. The effects of class and gender would thus function like hydrogen and oxygen in water. When the amount of water given to plants is varied, there is no "additive effect" of the amount of hydrogen and the amount of oxygen on plant growth; the effects are entirely a function of the amount of the "interaction" compound, H_2O. If class and gender behaved this way then perhaps it would be useful to introduce a new concept, "clender," to designate the interaction term itself. In general, however, the claim that class and gender "interact" in generating effects does not imply that there are no additive effects. This means that some of what is consequential about gender occurs independently of class and some of what is consequential about class occurs independently of gender. The task of class analysis, then, is to sort out these various kinds of effects.

In chapters 7, 8 and 9 we will explore several of these forms of interconnection of class and gender. Chapter 7 discusses the problem of the class location of married women in dual-earner families. It is thus an investigation of the ways in which gender mediates class locations. The chapter also includes an analysis of the effects of the interaction of the class composition of households and gender on class identity. Chapter 8 explores the ways in which class locations might shape one important facet of gender relations – the sexual division of labor in the home. Finally, chapter 9 looks in detail at one specific aspect of the way gender sorts people into class locations – the differential access to position of workplace authority of men and women.

7. Individuals, families and class analysis

Consider the following list of households in which family members are engaged in different kinds of jobs:

Employment composition of household

	Wife's job	*Husband's job*
1	Typist, full time	No husband
2	Typist, full time	Factory worker
3	Typist, full time	Lawyer
4	Typist, part time	Lawyer
5	Lawyer	Lawyer
6	Lawyer	Factory worker
7	Homemaker	Factory worker
8	Homemaker	Lawyer

What is the appropriate way of defining the social class of each of the individuals in this list? For some of the cases, there is no particular difficulty: the women in the first two households and the man in the second would usually be considered working class, while both people in the fifth household, "middle" class. Similarly, the class of the homemakers in cases 7 and 8 would generally be identified with the class of their husbands.[1] The other cases, however, have no uncontroversial

---

[1] Some feminists would object to deriving the class location of full-time housewives from the class of their husbands. Such critics insist that the social relations of domination within the household should also be treated as a "class relation." One rationale for this claim treats production in the household as a distinctive mode of production, sometimes called the "domestic mode of production." In capitalist societies, it is argued, this mode of production is systematically structured by gender relations of domination and subordination. As a result, within the domestic mode of production, the domestic laborer (the housewife) occupies a distinctive exploited and dominated class position in relation to the nonlaborer (the male "head of household"). This effectively places

solutions. In particular, how should we understand the class location of married women in the labor force when their jobs have a different class character from that of their husbands? Intuitively, it seems that a typist married to a factory worker is not in the same class as a typist married to a lawyer, even if the jobs of the two typists are indistinguishable. And yet, to simply say that the second typist is "middle" class seems to relegate her own job to irrelevance in class analysis. In class terms she would become indistinguishable from the woman lawyer in case 5. And what about the woman lawyer married to a worker? It seems very odd to say that she is in the same class as the typist married to a factory worker. Many feminists have strongly objected to equating a married woman's class with her husband's, arguing, to use Joan Acker's (1973) formulation, that this is an example of "intellectual sexism." And yet, to identify her class position strictly with her own job also poses serious conceptual problems. A typist married to a lawyer is likely to have a very different life style, and above all very different economic and political interests from a typist married to a factory worker.

Of course, if these kinds of "cross-class" household compositions were rare phenomena, then this issue of classification would not have great empirical importance, even if it still raised interesting theoretical issues. However, as we saw in chapter 5, the kinds of examples listed above are not rare events: in the United States (in 1980) 32% of all married women employed in expert manager jobs have husbands in working-class jobs, and 46% of men in such expert manager jobs whose wives work have wives employed in working-class jobs. Class heterogeneous families are sufficiently prevalent in contemporary capitalism that these problems of classification cannot be ignored in class analysis.

The central purpose of this chapter is to try to provide a coherent conceptual solution to this problem of identifying the class location of married women in the labor force and then to deploy this solution in an empirical analysis of the relationship between class location and sub-jective class identity in the United States and Sweden. There are two basic reasons why I think solving this problem of classification is important. First, as a practical matter, if one is doing any kind of research in which the class of individuals is viewed as consequential, one is forced to adopt a solution to this conceptual problem if only by default.

housewives in a distinctive class in relation to their husbands. A housewife of a working-class husband is thus not "in" the working class as such, but in what might be termed "proletarian domestic labor class." One of the best-known defenses of this view is by Christine Delphy (1984: 38–39).

Survey research on political attitudes, for example, frequently examines the relationship between an individual's class and attitudes. Typically, without providing a defense, attributes of the job of the respondent, whether male or female, are used to define class. Like it or not, this implies a commitment to the view that the class of individuals is appropriately measured by their own jobs regardless of the class composition of their households.

More substantively, this problem of classification raises important issues concerning the underlying explanatory logic of class analysis. By virtue of what is a person's class location explanatory of anything? Is it because class identifies a set of micro-experiences on the job which shape subjectivity? Even though they are not dealing with the problem of class and gender, this is essentially the argument of Melvin Kohn (1969) in his numerous studies of the effects of the complexity of work on cognitive functioning and of Michael Burawoy (1985) in his research on consent and conflict within work. If one adopts this job-centered view of the mechanisms through which class matters, then household class composition becomes a relatively secondary problem in class analysis. On the other hand, if one sees the central explanatory power of class as linked to the ways in which class positions shape material interests then household class composition becomes a more salient issue. Resolving this issue of classification, therefore, is bound up with clarifying the mechanisms through which class is explanatory.

In the next section of this chapter, I will briefly review the discussion in the 1980s of the problem of defining the class location of married women. In section 7.2, I will elaborate an alternative approach built on the distinction between direct and mediated class relations briefly discussed in chapter 1. Section 7.3 will then use this distinction to develop a concrete set of predictions about the linkage between class location and class identity in Sweden and the United States. Section 7.4 will present the results of the analysis.

7.1 The debate on women and class

These empirical and theoretical issues on the class analysis of women were crystallized in a debate launched in 1983 by John Goldthorpe's controversial essay, "Women and Class Analysis: in Defense of the Conventional View." Goldthorpe endorses the conventional view that the class of women is derived from the class of their husbands:

... the family is the unit of stratification primarily because only certain family members, predominently males, have, as a result of their labour market participation, what might be termed a directly determined position within the class structure. Other family members, including wives, do not typically have equal opportunity for such participation, and their class position is thus indirectly determined: that is to say, it is "derived" from that of the family "head" . . .

Moreover, the authors in question [traditional class analysts] would not regard their case as being basically affected by the increase in the numbers of married women engaged in paid employment. They would emphasize that although the degree of women's economic dependence on their husbands may in this way be somewhat mitigated, such employment typically forms part of a family strategy, or at all events, takes place within the possibilities and constraints of the class situation of the family as a whole, in which the husband's employment remains the dominant factor. (Goldthorpe 1983: 468–469)

Goldthorpe's paper sparked a lively, if sometimes overly polemical series of exchanges. Goldthorpe's critics (e.g. Heath and Brittain 1984; Stanworth 1984) argued that the class character of the jobs of married women in the labor force has significant effects independently of the class of their husbands, and, as a result, those families within which husbands and wives occupy different job-classes should be treated as having a dual-class character.

Goldthorpe (1984) replied by arguing that treating families as having a cross-class composition risks undermining the coherence of class analysis and subverts the explanatory capacity of the concept of class. Since class conflicts run between families, not through families, if families are treated as lacking a unitary class character, class structure will no longer provide a systematic basis for explaining class conflicts.

Goldthorpe's argument can be broken down into two primary theses:

1 *Unitary family-class thesis*: Families pool income as units of consumption. This means that all family members benefit from the income-generating capacity of any member. Consequentially, all family members have the same material – and thus class – interests. As a result, it is in general families, rather than atomized individuals, that are the effective units collectively organized into class formations. Class struggles occur *between* families, not *within* families.

2 *Husband's class derivation thesis*: Because of the gender division of labor in the household and male dominance in the society at large, the economic fate of most families depends much more heavily upon the class character of the husband's job than of the wife's. In family strategies of welfare maximization, therefore, in nearly all cases the class-imperatives of the husband's job will overwhelmingly *pre-empt*

strategic considerations involving the wife's job. As a result, the causally effective class of married women (i.e. the class that has any explanatory power) is in general derived from the class location of her husband.

Goldthorpe, of course, does not deny that by and large individuals rather than families fill *jobs* in capitalist economies. What he disputes is the claim that the class structure should be treated as a relational map of the job structure. Instead, classes should be defined as *groups of people who share common material interests*. While it may be the case that the basic material interests of people depend upon their relationship to the system of production, it need not be the case that those interests depend primarily upon their individual position within production (i.e. their "job"). Insofar as families are units of consumption in which incomes from all members are pooled, then all members of the family share the same material interests and thus are in the same class, regardless of their individual jobs. Individual family members would occupy different locations in the class structure only when it is the case that the family ceased to genuinely pool resources and act as a unit of consumption sharing a common fate.

A number of interconnected criticisms can be leveled against these theses. First, while it may be true that all family members benefit from income brought into the household, it does not follow from this that they all share a unitary, undifferentiated interest with respect to such income. To claim that wives and husbands have identical interests with respect to the gross income of the family is somewhat like saying that both workers and capitalists have an interest in maximizing the gross revenues of a business – which is frequently true – and therefore they are in the same class – which is false. Families may pool income, but there is evidence (e.g. Sorensen and McLanahan, 1987) that this does not mean that husbands and wives always share equally in the real consumption derived from that income.

Inequality in the consumption of family income by husbands and wives, of course, does not necessarily mean that married women in the labor force have material interests in their own individual earnings as such, and thus distinct individually based class interests in their jobs. It could be the case that they have *gender* interests in a redistribution of power within the household, but that they still lack any autonomous *class* interest in their own earnings independently of the family income as a whole. There are, however, two reasons why it is plausible to see married women as having individual class interests linked to their own earnings. First, the high rates of divorce in contemporary capitalist societies means that the jobs of many women in the labor force constitute for them a kind of "shadow class" – the class they would occupy in the face of marital dissolution. Given the relatively high probability of such events, married women have personal class interests in the earnings capacities they derive from their individual jobs. Secondly, there is evidence that the proportion of the family budget brought in by the wife affects her bargaining power within the family. Even if the family pools income, therefore, married women would have some autonomous personal interests in their own earning capacity in their paid jobs.

A second general criticism of Goldthorpe's argument concerns his very narrow understanding of class interests. The unitary family class thesis rests on the claim that since husbands and wives pool income, they have identical interests with respect to overall family earnings capacity and thus identical class interests. The interests that are tied to classes, however, are not simply income-based interests. At least if one adopts a broadly Marxist concept of class, issues of autonomy, the expenditure of effort and domination within work are also systematically linked to class. These kinds of interests are at the heart of what Burawoy (1985) has called the "politics of production" and center much more directly on individuals as job-holders than as members of household units of consumption. Even if married couples share a unitary family consumption class, the potential differences in their job-classes could still generate differences in their class interests.

Third, contrary to Goldthorpe's view, it is not inherently the case that families rather than individuals are mobilized into class struggles. While this may generally be the case, especially in situations where families are class-homogeneous, it is possible to imagine circumstances in which a wife is a union member engaged in union struggles of various sorts and her husband is a manager or petty bourgeois generally opposed to unions. Particularly if class interests are seen as broader than simply interests in income, one can imagine husbands and wives in different job-classes, involved in organizations supporting quite different kinds of class interests. To be sure, it would be extremely rare for husbands and wives to be actively on "opposite sides of the barricade" in a given class struggle – for the husband to be a top manager or employer in a firm in which his wife was on strike. But this does not imply that in other contexts they could not be involved in quite distinct and even opposing kinds of class formations.

Finally, Goldthorpe argues that because the economic fate of the family is *more dependent* upon income from the husband's job than the wife's, the class location of the family should be *exclusively* identified with his job. This assumes that in the strategic choices made within families over labor market participation and job choices there is minimal struggle, negotiation and bargaining, and as a result the interests linked to the husband's job always pre-empt those of the wife's job. Family strategy, in this view, is not some kind of negotiated weighted average of the class-based imperatives linked to each spouse's job, but uniquely determined by the class imperatives of the male breadwinner.

This claim by Goldthorpe is simply asserted on his part, unbacked by either theoretical argument or empirical evidence. Of course, there are many cases where a story of this sort has considerable face validity. There are undoubtedly families in which the husband is in a well-paying managerial or professional job with a systematic career structure while the wife holds part-time flexible work to which she has little commitment. In such situations it might well be the case that whenever there is a trade-off between interests tied to the wife's job and the husband's job, *both* parties agree to adopt a strategy supporting the husband's interests. In such a situation, it may be reasonable, at least as a first approximation, to identify the family-class exclusively with the husband's job. But there is no reason to assume that this particular situation is universal. It is much more plausible to suppose that there is systematic variation across families in such strategic balances of interests and power, and thus that the relative weight of different spouse's job-classes in shaping the class character of the family as a whole is a variable, not a constant.

In 1980, in roughly 10% of all two-earner families in the United States the wife earns 40–49% of the family income and in 25% of all two-earner married couples she contributes 50% or more of the total family income. In Sweden, the figure is even higher: 45% of respondents in two earner families report the wife contributes "about 50%" of the income and 10% report that she brings in 75% or more of the income. Certainly in such families, even from a narrow economic point of view, the family strategies should be affected by the class-character of both spouses' jobs. Furthermore, even when it is the case that in decisive zero-sum trade-off situations, interests derived from the husband's job usually pre-empt those of the wife's, it does not follow from this that in other situations the interests linked to the wife's job are irrelevant and do not shape family income maximization strategies. Even where the wife contributes less than the husband, therefore, the class character of her paid work could systematically shape family strategies, and thus the class character of the family unit.

If these criticisms are correct, then one is unjustified in simply equating the class location of married working women with the job-class of their husbands. But it also seems unsatisfactory to treat their class as simply based on their own immediate work. Some other conceptual solution to defining their class must be found.

7.2 An alternative approach: direct and mediated class locations

Most class concepts view class structures as a set of rooms in a hotel filled by guests. The dwellers may be individuals or families, and they may change rooms from time to time, but the image is of "empty places" being filled by people. There is, however, an alternative general way of understanding class structure: instead of a set of rooms, class structures can be understood as a particular kind of complex network of social relations. What defines this network of relations as a *class* structure is the way it determines the access of people to the basic productive resources of a society and the processes of exploitation, and thus shapes their material interests. A "location," then, is not a "room" in a building, but a node in a network of relations.

In a highly simplified model of the world we can reduce such a network of social relations to a single link between individuals and productive resources constituted by their direct, personal control or ownership of such resources. This is the abstraction characteristic of most Marxist class analysis. But there is no reason to restrict class analysis to such simplifications. The material interests of real, flesh-and-blood individuals are shaped not simply by such direct, personal relations to productive resources, but by a variety of other relations which link them to the system of production. In contemporary capitalist societies these include, above all, relations to other family members (both within a single generation and intergenerationally) and, perhaps, relations to the state. I will refer to these kinds of indirect links between individuals and productive resources as "mediated" relations, in contrast to the "direct" relations embodied in the individual's immediate job and personal ownership of productive resources.

For certain categories of people in contemporary capitalism, location in the class structure is entirely constituted by mediated relations. This is most clearly the case for children. To say that children in a working-class family are "in" the working class is to make a claim about the ways in which their class interests are shaped by their mediated relations (through their families) to the system of production. Mediated class relations also loom large in understanding the class interests of house-wives, the unemployed, pensioners, students. In each of these cases an adequate picture of their class interests cannot be derived simply from examining their direct participation in the relations of production.

The class structure, then, should be understood as consisting of the totality of direct and mediated class relations. This implies that two class structures with identical patterns of direct class relations but differing mediated relations should be considered as different kinds of structures. Consider the following rather extreme contrast for purposes of illustration:

> *Class Structure I.* In 66% of all households, both husband and wife are employed in working-class jobs and in 33% of households both husband and wife are co-owners of small businesses employing the workers from the other households.
>
> *Class structure II.* 33% of the households are pure working-class households, 33% have a working-class husband and a small employer wife and 33% have a small employer husband and a working-class wife.

For a strict adherent of the view that class structures are constituted by the individual's direct relation to the means of production, these two class structures are the same: 66% working class, 33% small employers. Also, ironically perhaps, for a strict adherent of Goldthorpe's husband-based family class approach, the two class structures are identical: 66% working class, 33% small employers. If, however, class structures are defined in terms of the *combination* of direct and mediated class locations, then the two structures look quite different: in the first structure, two-thirds of the population is fully proletarianized (i.e. both their direct and mediated class locations are working class); in the second structure, only one-third of the population is fully proletarianized.

Once the distinction between direct and mediated class locations is introduced into the conceptual repertoire of class analysis, it becomes possible to ask the question: what determines the relative weight of these two kinds of linkages to productive resources for particular categories of actors? There may be variations both within and across class structures in the relative importance of these different mechanisms that link people to productive resources. One can imagine a class structure in which mediated relations loom very large for certain people and not for others in shaping their material interests, and thus their overall location in the class structure.

The problem of married women (and of married men) in the class structure can now be recast in terms of the relative salience of direct and mediated class relations in determining their class interests. Goldthorpe takes a rather extreme position on this question for contemporary industrial capitalist societies: with few exceptions, the mediated class location of married women completely overrides any systematic relevance of their direct class location. Implicit in his argument, however, is the acknowledgment that under appropriate conditions, this would not be the case. If, for example, there was a dramatic erosion of the sexual division of labor in the household and gender differences in power and labor market opportunities, then the direct class location of married women would begin to matter more both for their class location and for that of their husbands.

The theoretical task, then, for understanding the location of women in the class structure, consists of trying to identify causal processes which shape the relative salience of direct and mediated class relations. We will explore this problem in the context of an empirical comparison of the relationship between the class composition of families and class identity in Sweden and the United States.

7.3 A strategy for studying the effects of direct and mediated class locations

There are two general empirical strategies that could be adopted to explore these arguments about direct and mediated class locations. If one had adequate longitudinal micro-level household data, one could actually measure the extent to which the material interests of married working women in the United States and in Sweden depend upon their own direct class location or the class location of their husbands, and one could assess the extent to which these direct and mediated class interests impact on individual and collective family strategies. Alternatively, we could consider something which an individual's class location is meant at least partially to explain – such as class consciousness, class identity, participation in class conflict, etc. – and examine the relative "explanatory power" of the direct and mediated class locations of individuals. The only reason for introducing the distinction between direct and mediated class locations is because we believe that an individual's location in a class structure is consequential and that this distinction provides a better specification of this consequence-producing process. Variations in the relative salience of direct and mediated class locations, therefore, should be reflected in the effects of these two dimensions of class location on whatever it is that class locations ought to explain.

In this chapter I will adopt this second strategy. More specifically, we will examine the relationship between class locations (direct and mediated) and the probability of having a working-class identity, i.e. subjectively considering oneself in the working class. Subjective class identity is not, perhaps, the most subtle indicator of the subjective effects of class location. However, of all dimensions of "class consciousness" it is probably the one most directly reflecting the subjective understanding of one's place in the class structure. Class identity is thus the indicator most closely tied to the theoretical questions of this chapter. The premise of the analysis is that to the extent direct class relations more powerfully determine a person's class location than do mediated relations they will also be more strongly associated with the probability of having a particular class identity.

Underlying the empirical investigation is the simple theoretical model presented in Figure 7.1. Direct and mediated class locations are associated with different causal pathways that affect class identity. Direct class locations affect class identity both because a person's job affects a range of class experiences within work and because direct class locations shape material interests. Mediated class locations, on the other hand, only affect class identity via material interests. The relative weight of direct and mediated class locations on class identity, therefore will depend upon two kinds of factors: (1) the relative weight of direct and mediated class locations on material interests, and (2) the relative salience of production-centered class experiences and consumption-centered class experiences in shaping class identity.

Hypotheses

Goldthorpe predicts that for both men and women the effect of husband's direct class on class identity will be substantially greater than the effects of the wife's class. Indeed, in the most extreme formulation of his position, controlling for her husband's class, the effects of the wife's own direct class should be zero even on her own class identity – the unitary class of the family is entirely derived from the husband's class and therefore the effects of the wife's job-class on class identity should be negligible.

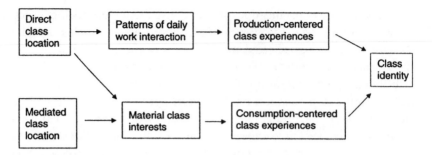

Figure 7.1 *A general model of the effects of direct and mediated class locations on class identity.*

In contrast, the view that a person's class location should be viewed as a combination of direct and mediated class relations suggests that the relative effects on class identity of the husband's direct class and of the wife's direct class should be variable across families, across economic conditions, and across countries depending upon the relative salience of the individual's direct class location and their mediated location via their family ties. Because of the economic dependency of married women on their husband's jobs, it would generally be expected that family mediated class locations would be more salient for women than for men. But, unlike in Goldthorpe's approach, there is no general expectation that the effects of the wife's direct class will generally be negligible.

We will examine the above expectations for married couples with two earners in the United States and Sweden. There is a variety of reasons why one might expect the relative salience of direct and mediated class locations for married women to vary between Sweden and the United States: greater parity in wages between men and women in Sweden means that Swedish wives are less economically dependent upon their husbands' jobs than American wives, and thus their economic welfare depends less upon their mediated class location; the strong redistributive policies of the state mean that Swedes in general – both men and women – are less dependent than Americans upon their family's earnings for their standard of living; the higher degree of class organization within work in Sweden means that an individual's own job is likely to be more salient in shaping their consciousness. This line of reasoning suggests that the salience for a wife's class identity of her own direct class location relative to her husband's class location should be greater in Sweden than in the United States.

The empirical analysis which follows, therefore, will revolve around the following contrasting hypotheses for predicting the probability of a subjective working-class identification:

Goldthorpe hypotheses

(1.1) *Weak version*: The husband's job-class is significantly more important than the wife's job-class in predicting the identity of both husbands and wives.

(1.2) *Strong version*: Controlling for husband's job-class, the wife's direct class will not affect either her own or her husband's class identity.

Mediated and direct class locations hypotheses

(2.1) The class identity of married women in the labor force will be affected by both their direct and mediated class locations.

(2.2) Mediated class locations will have greater salience for the class identity of wives than of husbands.

(2.3) The direct class location of married women will have greater salience relative to their mediated class location for their class identity in Sweden than in the United States.

7.4 Results

Because of limitations in sample size – there are only between 550 and 600 respondents in each country living in dual-earner families – it was impossible to make fine-grained distinctions among types of cross-class families. This has two important consequences for our analyses. First, there were too few people in cross-class families involving small employers and petty bourgeois to include in the study. We will therefore concentrate entirely on families in which both husbands and wives are employees.[2] Secondly, we could not make distinctions among the various categories of the "middle class." For present purposes, therefore, we have simplified our class structure concept into a two-class model: middle-class employees (anyone occupying managerial or supervisory positions or in professional, managerial or technical occupations) and working-class employees (both skilled and nonskilled nonsupervisory employees). Our task, then, is to examine the subjective class identity of

---

[2] For a discussion of the results for families with at least one self-employed member, see Wright (1997: 264–265).

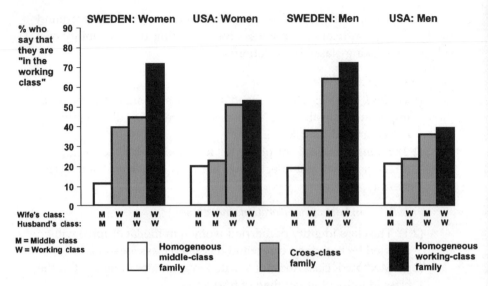

Figure 7.2 *Percentage of people who say they are "working class' in dual-earner families with different class compositions.*

men and women in four kinds of dual-earner families: homogeneous middle-class families; homogeneous working-class families; families with middle-class husbands and working-class wives; and families with working-class husbands and middle-class wives.

Figure 7.2 indicates the percentage of respondents who subjectively identify with the working class in each of these four types of families in the United States and Sweden. In the United States, among wage-earning families, the class character of the wife's job seems to have no effect on the class identification of either women or men. Roughly 20% of women wage-earners married to men with middle-class jobs and roughly 50% of women wage-earners married to men with working-class jobs subjectively identify with the working class, regardless of the class character of the woman's own job. Among men the pattern is essentially the same, although the percentages are somewhat different: 20% of men in middle-class jobs and just over 35% of men in working-class jobs subjectively identify with the working class, regardless of the class character of their wife's job. Mediated class locations, therefore, have a strong effect on the class identity of women, but none at all on the class identity of men. In short, in the United States, once you know the class position of husbands, your ability to predict class identification for either husbands or wives does not improve by adding information on the wife's class position.

When we turn to the Swedish data, however, we get a very different picture. In Sweden, for both men and women, there are consistent effects of both husband's and wife's job-class on the subjective class identification of respondents. For Swedish women, about 12% of the respondents in homogeneously middle-class families subjectively identify with the working class compared to nearly 72% in homogeneously working-class families. Women in class-heterogeneous families – women in middle-class jobs married to husbands in working-class jobs or women in working-class jobs married to husbands in middle-class jobs – have an intermediate likelihood of working-class identification, around 40%. A similar, if attenuated, pattern occurs for Swedish men: 19% of the men in homogeneous middle-class families and 72% of the men in homogeneous working-class families subjectively identify with the working class, compared to about 38% of middle-class men married to working-class wives and 64% of working-class men married to middle-class wives. Unlike in the United States, the class identity of both husbands and wives in Sweden is significantly affected by the class character of the wife's job as well as the husband's. None of these results for either country are substantively changed in more complex analyses in which a variety of other variables are included as controls.[3]

7.4 Implications

One simple way of characterizing the results we have been discussing is that the predictions from the "conventional wisdom" of Goldthorpe's model are reasonably accurate for the United States, but not for Sweden: the strong version of the Goldthorpe hypothesis is supported by the US data, while all three hypotheses about mediated and direct class locations are supported by the Swedish data. In the United States, therefore, no predictive power is lost by defining the class location of married women in the labor force by the class of their husbands, whereas in Sweden this is not the case.

How can these different causal structures in Sweden and the United States be explained? There are a range of interpretations which might be pursued. The different patterns we have observed could directly reflect

---

[3] Formal statistical tests using logistic regressions predicting class identity confirm all of these observations for both the United States and Sweden. See Wright (1997: 268–269) for details.

different cultural conventions for the meaning of class identity for men and women in the two countries. Alternatively, they could be effects of strategies by political parties or unions in treating men and women differently in the forging of collective solidarities. Or, perhaps, the results we have been discussing could be artifacts of measurement problems in one or more of the variables in the analysis. All of these arguments have some plausibility. In the present context, however, I will limit the discussion to two alternative class-centered explanations since these most directly bear on the theoretical agenda of direct and mediated class relations.

The first explanation centers on the causal pathway from class location through class interests to class identity in Figure 7.1. Along this causal path, the less dependent a wife's material welfare is on her husband's job, the less will her class interests be derived from his direct class, and thus the greater the relative weight of her own direct class location. In Sweden, a higher proportion of family income in two-earner families is contributed by wives than in the United States. It is also the case that the welfare and redistributive policies of the Swedish state make the individual economic interests of married women less dependent upon their husbands. In this line of reasoning, then, the greater *relative* impact of a married woman's own job on her class identity in Sweden than in the United States is seen as a consequence of the lower degree of economic dependence of wives on husbands in Sweden. In terms of the model in Figure 7.1, this implies that relative to women in Sweden, for women in the United States, the causal path between direct class location and material interests is much weaker than the path from mediated location and interests.

The second explanation emphasizes that class locations are explanatory not simply because they determine a set of material interests, but because they deeply shape patterns of daily lived experiences, above all within work. Michael Burawoy suggested, in an informal discussion of these results, that a central contrast between Sweden and the United States might be that between a society within which class has its effects primarily through work and a society within which class has its effects primarily through consumption. This general view of the effects of class emphasizes the production-centered causal path in Figure 7.1. In terms of this model, then, the United States would be characterized as a society within which the causal effects of class – both direct and mediated – work primarily through the material interests/consumption path, whereas Sweden is a society within which both causal paths play an important role.

A variety of historical and institutional factors might explain the greater weight of the production-centered class effects in Sweden than in the United States: the nature of the politics of production within the two societies, the forms of articulation between "global politics" and shop floor politics, the degree of collective organization of workers as workers through unions, etc. For example, it might be the case that the specific form of corporatist, centralized unionism in Sweden has the effect of reducing competition between workers in different labor markets (both external and internal). This, in turn, could mean that the daily experiences within work tend to reinforce class-based solidarities, which in turn strengthen working-class identity. But whatever the specific historical and institutional explanation might be, the result is that in Sweden subjective class identification is forged much more systematically through experiences within work than in the United States, whereas in the United States, class identity is formed primarily within consumption and community.

This line of argument, then, suggests that the reason the direct class of married women does not matter very much for predicting class identity in the United States is precisely because in the United States classes are primarily constituted within consumption on the basis of material interests alone, and in terms of consumption a married woman's mediated class location is generally much more causally important than her own direct class. *If* in Sweden classes were similarly constituted primarily in the realm of consumption, then in spite of the weaker economic dependency of women on their husbands, their direct class would still not have a particularly powerful impact on their identity. The greater predictive power of married Swedish women's direct class on their identity comes from the greater salience of class experiences within work on the lives of workers in general in Sweden. In this alternative approach to the issues, then, Goldthorpe's predictions about married women work reasonably well in the United States because the central presupposition of his conceptualization of class – that classes consist of families as units of common material interests/consumption – is much more appropriate for the class structure of the United States than of Sweden.

The data in the present analysis do not lend themselves to a direct assessment of these alternative explanations. To explore properly the issues we would need two other cases: one which was rather like Sweden in the degree of economic autonomy of women, but shared with the United States a consumption-based (family-based) constitution of classes, and one which shared with Sweden the production-centered salience of class, but had the American pattern of economic dependency. Parallel data for such cases are not available.

There are indirect pieces of evidence in the data, however, which are supportive of the interpretation of US/Sweden differences which emphasizes the workplace causal pathway in Figure 7.1. If the material interest dependency argument was correct, then it would be expected that the *greater the wife's relative economic contribution* to household income, the more her own direct class location should affect her class identity. In statistical tests of this hypothesis, there were no significant interactions of this sort (Wright 1997: 274). Thus, while it is the case that Swedish married women contribute proportionately more to the total family income than do American married women, there is no evidence that the class identity of either American or Swedish women is affected by the variation across households in such contributions.

A second piece of evidence consistent with the emphasis on workplace experience rather than simply material interests concerns the effects of hours worked in the paid labor force on class identity. This variable is very significant for Swedish women, but not for American women, indicating that the more hours a Swedish women works on the job, the higher the probability of a working-class identification. If we assume that class experiences at the workplace become more salient as one works longer hours, then this result for Swedish women is consistent with the view that what is distinctive in Sweden is the greater salience of workplace-centered class experiences in constituting classes.

These results, it should be stressed, do *not* indicate that it is incorrect to conceptualize classes in terms of common material interests. The consistent explanatory power of women's mediated class locations for their identity in both the United States and Sweden is consistent with the view that class structure is explanatory at least in part because of the material interests it generates. What the data do not support is the view that *differences* in the class-based configurations of material interests for women in the two countries explains the *differences* in the patterns we have observed. The evidence reported here suggests that the reason why direct class relations have greater salience relative to mediated class relations among Swedish women seems largely due to causal processes which intensify the importance of workplace class experiences in the constitution of class in Swedish society in general, rather than mechanisms which affect the relative contribution to material interests of direct and mediated relations.

7.5 Conclusion

At the core of much Marxian class analysis is the claim that class structure is a fundamental determinant of social conflict and social change. In trying to defend and deepen this intuition, contemporary Marxist theorists have been torn between two theoretical impulses. The first impulse is to keep the concept of class structure as simple as possible, perhaps even accepting a simple polarized vision of the class structure of capitalism, and then to remedy the explanatory deficiencies of such a simple concept by introducing into the analysis a range of other explanatory principles (e.g. divisions within classes or between sectors, the relationship between work and community, the role of the state or ideology in shaping the collective organization of classes, etc.). The second impulse is to gradually increase the complexity of the class structural concept itself in the hope that such complexity will more powerfully capture the explanatory mechanisms embedded in class relations. Basically, these alternative impulses place different bets on how much explanatory work the concept of class structure itself should do: the first strategy takes a minimalist position, seeing class structure as at most shaping broad constraints on action and change; the second takes a maximalist position, seeing class structure as a potent and systematic determinant of individual action and social development.

My work on class has pursued this second strategy. In my theoretical discussions of class structure I have been preoccupied with the problem of the "middle class," with elaborating a class structure concept that would give a coherent and systematic theoretical status to nonproletarian employees in the class structure. This led to the introduction of the concept of "contradictory locations within class relations" and subsequently, the reformulation of that concept in terms of a multidimensional view of exploitation.

In this chapter I have tried to elaborate a second kind of complexity in the problem of class structure, a complexity derived from the fact that people are tied to the class structure not simply through their own personal jobs and property but through a variety of other kinds of social relations. Above all, in the present context, social relations within families constitute an important mechanism through which people are indirectly linked to the class structure. Since families are units of consumption, the class interests of actors are derived in part from the total material resources controlled by the members of a family and not simply by themselves. Social relations within families thus constitute a crucial source of what I have termed "mediated class relations."

The risk in adding this kind of complexity to class analysis is that the concept of class structure becomes more and more unwieldy. The simple, polarized image of class structure contained in Marx's theoretical writings has enormous polemical power and conceptual clarity. A concept of class structure that posits contradictory class locations and complex combinations of direct and mediated class relations may, in the end, add more confusion than analytical power.

For the moment, however, I think that this is a line of theoretical elaboration that is worth pursuing. In particular, the couplet direct/mediated class relations offers a specific way of linking a Marxist class analysis to an analysis of gender relations without simply subsuming the latter under the former. When the concept of class structure is built exclusively around direct class locations it seems reasonable to treat class relations and gender relations as having a strictly *external* relationship to each other. Gender relations may help to explain how people are *sorted* into class positions, and they may even have specific effects on the overall distribution of class positions (i.e. particular gender patterns may shape the availability of certain kinds of labor power and thus potential for expansion of certain kinds of class positions), but the two kinds of relations – gender and class – do not combine to form a system of internal relations.[4]

When mediated class relations are added to a class structure analysis, this strict dualism of external relations becomes unsatisfactory. Gender mechanisms do not simply sort people into mediated class locations whose properties are definable independently of gender. Rather, gender relations are constitutive of mediated class relations as such. Such mediated class relations through the family are inherently gendered since the gender relations between husbands and wives are the very basis for their respective mediated class locations. The concept of

---

[4] The contrast between X and Y being linked by *external* relations and *internal* relations is rather similar to the distinction between a liquid in which two elements are in suspension and a liquid in which two elements have combined to form a compound. In the former case, X and Y act independently of each other producing effects; in the latter they constitute a gestalt formed by the internal relations, and some of their effects come from the operation of these internal relations.

mediated class relations, therefore, makes it possible to move away from a view of class and gender in which these two kinds of relations are treated as entirely distinct, separate structures. And yet it does not move all the way towards the view that class and gender constitute a unitary, undifferentiated system. Mediated class relations therefore provides a basis for conceptualizing one form of interaction of class and gender without collapsing the distinction itself.

We began this chapter by asking a question about the class location of husbands and wives in a number of "cross-class" families. The theoretical and empirical analyses of this chapter suggest that this question needs to be re-posed in a somewhat different way. Rather than asking "in what class is person X," we should ask, "what is the location of person X within a network of direct and mediated class relations." While the question is rather inelegant, nevertheless it identifies a critical dimension of complexity of the class structures of contemporary capitalism.

8. The noneffects of class on the gendered division of labor in the home

The central objective of this chapter is to explore systematically the empirical relationship between *the location of households in the class structure* and *gender inequalities in performance of housework*. Since the middle of the 1970s, class analysts interested in gender, particularly those rooted in the Marxist tradition, have placed domestic labor at the center of analysis. In a variety of different ways, they have argued that the linkage between the system of production, analyzed in class terms, and the domestic division of labor, analyzed in gender terms, was at the heart of understanding the social processes through which gender relations were themselves reproduced (or perhaps even generated) in capitalist societies. Sometimes this argument took a rather reductionist form, particularly when the performance of unpaid domestic labor by women in the home was explained by the functional requirements of capital accumulation.[1] In other cases, the argument was less reductionist, emphasizing the nature of the class-generated constraints imposed on strategies of men and women as they negotiated gender relations within the household rather than the functional fit between capitalism and patriarchy. And, in still other analyses, the possibilities of systematic contradictions between the logics of capitalist class domination and patriarchal male domination were entertained. In all of these analyses, in

---

[1] The debate over the functional relationship between capitalist exploitation and unpaid domestic labor by housewives came to be known as the "domestic labor debate" in the 1970s. The essential argument of the class-functionalist position was: (1) unpaid domestic labor had the effect of lowering the costs of producing labor power; (2) this increased the rate of capitalist exploitation since capitalists could pay lower wages; (3) in an indirect way, therefore, capitalists exploited housewives; (4) the basic explanation for the subordination of women – or at least, for the reproduction of that subordination – lay in the ways such domestic production served these functions for capitalism. For a review of this debate see Molyneux (1979).

146

spite of the differences in theoretical argument, the role of domestic labor in the linkage between class relations and gender relations was a central theme.

With this theoretical preoccupation, it might have been expected that there would have developed a substantial body of research exploring the empirical relationship between the domestic division of labor and classes. This has not happened. While there are historical and qualitative case studies which examine the domestic division of labor and a few of these attempt to explore the class variations in such patterns, there is almost no research that tries to map out in a systematic quantitative manner the relationship between class and the gender division of labor in the household.

The basic objective of this chapter, then, is to explore empirically the relationship between class and the gendered domestic division of labor. More specifically, we will examine how the proportionate contribution by husbands to housework in dual-earner families varies across households with different class compositions.

8.1 Theoretical expectations

As in chapter 7, because of limitations of available data for spouses' class and because of limitations in sample size, the empirical investigations of this chapter will rely on a stripped-down class concept. In this case we will distinguish three categories: the self-employed (consisting of employers and petty bourgeois), "middle class" (employees who occupy a managerial or supervisory position within authority structures and/or are employed in an professional, managerial or technical occupations) and working class (all other employees). This simple three-category class variable in principle yields nine family-class locations. Unfortunately, again because of the relatively small sample size, there were too few people in family-class locations involving the self-employed to be able to differentiate all five of these categories. As a result, for families involving self-employment we will not distinguish between the husband and wife being self-employed. We will thus analyze family-class composition and housework using the following seven family-class categories: 1. homogeneous self-employed households; 2. one spouse self-employed, one middle class; 3. one spouse self-employed, one working class; 4. homogeneous middle class household; 5. husband middle class, wife working class; 6. husband working class, wife middle class; 7. homogeneous working-class household. Our empirical task, then, is to explore how inequality between husbands and wives in housework varies across the categories of this family-class composition typology.

While neither Marxism nor Feminism has a well-developed body of theory about the *variability* of the domestic division of labor across households with different class compositions, nevertheless there are some general expectations within class analysis and feminism that point towards certain broad hypotheses about this relationship. We will explore four such hypotheses.

Proletarianization and gender equality

The most well-known discussion of the gender division of labor in classical Marxism is found in Frederick Engels' study, *The Origin of the Family, Private Property and the State* (Engels 1968 [1884]). Engels argued that male domination within the family was rooted in male control of private property. The pivot of this linkage was the desire by men to insure that their property was inherited by their children. To accomplish this, men needed to control the fertility of women. Given the power and status they had by virtue of controlling property, men were able to translate this desire into practice. The broad institutions of male domination, Engels argued, are built upon this foundation.

On the basis of this reasoning, Engels' argued that male domination would wither away in the households of propertyless proletarians:

> Here, there is a complete absence of all property, for the safeguarding and inheritance of which monogamy and male domination were established. Therefore, there is no stimulus whatever here to assert male domination . . . Moreover, since large-scale industry has transferred the woman from house to the labour market and the factory, and makes her, often enough, the breadwinner of the family, the last remnants of male domination in the proletarian home have lost all foundation. (Engels, 1968 [1884]: 508).

Engels' reasoning leads to two basic hypotheses:

> *Hypothesis 1. Working-class egalitarianism.* The more proletarianized is a household, the more housework will tend to be equally divided between husbands and wives. The homogeneous working-class family, therefore, should have the most egalitarian distribution of housework.

> *Hypothesis 2. Petty bourgeois inegalitarianism.* Households within which private ownership of the means of production remains

salient will have a more inegalitarian division of housework. The homogeneous petty bourgeois household should therefore have the least egalitarian distribution of housework.

Sexism and class cultures

One of the persistent images in popular culture is the contrast between the middle-class husband with an apron helping in the kitchen, and the working-class husband tinkering with the car or drinking in a bar with his friends. There are many possible mechanisms which might underwrite this contrast. The premium placed on physical toughness and male solidarity in manual labor may constitute a material basis for an exaggerated masculine identity in the working class. In line with the arguments of Melvin Kohn (1969) about the relationship between work and values, the greater cognitive complexity of middle-class jobs may encourage a more flexible and open set of attitudes towards gender roles. Regardless of the specific mechanism, this image leads to a specific prediction about class and the gender division of labor:

> *Hypothesis 3. Class cultures.* Working-class men will, in general, do proportionately less housework than middle-class men. Homogeneous working-class households should therefore have the most inegalitarian distribution of housework, while homogeneous middle-class households should be the most egalitarian.

Class and power within the family

An important theme in the sociology of gender is the problem of bargaining power between men and women within households. Particularly in an era in which gender roles are being challenged, the division of labor in the household should not be viewed as simply the result of a script being followed by highly socialized men and women. Rather, the amount of housework done by husbands should be viewed as at least in part an outcome of a process of contestation, conflict and bargaining.

The class location of husbands and wives bears on their respective power in the household in two ways. First, as in any bargaining situation, the resources people bring to household bargaining affects their relative power. In these terms, class inequalities between men and women would be expected to be translated into power differentials within the household. The more economically dependent a wife is on her husband, the weaker will be her bargaining position within the household and thus the more inegalitarian the gender division of labor is expected to be. This would imply when wives are in more advantaged class locations than their husbands, housework should be more equally divided. Second, quite apart from sheer material resources, status differentials are likely to play a role in bargaining situation (Coverman 1985). To the extent that wives occupy lower status in the labor force than their husbands, they are thus also likely to be in a weaker bargaining position within the household.

Taking these two issues together, leads to the following hypothesis:

> Hypothesis 4. Class bargaining power. In households in which the wife is in a more privileged class location than her husband she will have greater relative bargaining power and thus her husband is likely to do more housework. Households with middle-class wives and working-class husbands are thus likely to be the most egalitarian.

Autonomy of gender relations

One of the core feminist theses about gender relations in capitalist society is that they have a certain degree of real autonomy with respect to other causal processes. On the one hand, this means that gender is socially constructed rather than a mere expression of biological processes. On the other hand, it means that in the social processes within which this construction takes place, gender is not reducible to any other social phenomena, particularly class or the economy. While there may be important causal interactions between class and gender, gender relations are not mere functions of class or anything else, and in this sense they have some genuine autonomy.

An implication of relatively strong versions of the gender-autonomy thesis is that the amount of housework men do will be primarily determined by the nature of gender relations and gender struggles, not by such things as class. While this does not mean that class would have no effects at all, these effects should be fairly muted. This suggests the following hypothesis:

> Hypothesis 5. Gender autonomy. The degree of equality in the gender division of labor will not vary very much across households with different class compositions.

8.2 Results

As in the previous chapter, we will explore this problem comparatively in Sweden and the United States. Sweden and the United States are almost at opposite poles among developed capitalist countries in terms of economic inequalities in general and the gender dimension of inequality in particular. The Swedish state has poured much greater resources into public childcare, paid parental leaves and other programs which might impact on the gender division of labor within families. A comparison of inequalities in housework in the two countries, therefore, may give some insight into the extent to which this egalitarianism in the public sphere is reflected in greater egalitarianism in the private sphere.

We will present the results in three steps. First, we will examine briefly the overall distributions of housework in the two countries. This is mainly to provide a background context for the rest of our analysis. Second, we will examine the overall patterns of class variation in the husband's performance of housework. Finally, we will examine how these patterns are affected when various other variables are included in the analysis. In particular, we will be concerned to examine the effect of including education in the equation, since it might be thought that what at first looks like class differences in housework performance could in fact be education differences.

Husband's housework contributions: descriptive results

Our basic measure of husband's contribution to housework is a weighted average of five routine housework tasks (routine housecleaning, cooking, meal cleanup, grocery shopping and laundry) and childcare. We also calculated the measure excluding childcare, but none of the results were substantively affected.[2] In the United States, according to our female respondents, husbands in dual earner households performed on average 20.5% of the housework. According to our male respondents, their contribution was 26.2%. In Sweden the corresponding figures are 25.1% and 28.5%. These figures are very much in line with the estimates from other studies, including those which used sophisticated time budgets to calculate male contributions to housework. Most research indicates that in families within which both husbands and wives are in the paid labor force, men do between 20% and 30% of housework in the United States.

---

[2] The details for the construction of this variable can be found in Wright (1997: 304–309).

In both countries, therefore, male respondents report slightly higher contributions to housework than their wives, although the difference is not striking.

Overall, Swedish husbands in two-earner households appear to do a somewhat greater proportion of housework than their American counterparts (25% vs. about 20% according to female respondents). If anything, this is an underestimate of the real difference between the two countries in gender inequality in housework, since a much higher proportion of Swedish married women in the labor force than of American married women are part-time employees. The average number of hours worked per week by the wives in our sample is 30.9 in Sweden and 39.9 in the United States. If we adjust for differences in hours of paid labor force participation, then the difference in husbands' contribution to housework between the two countries is even more striking: in two-earner families in which the wife works 40 hours a week, her husband would be expected to do about 20% of the housework in the United States, whereas in a comparable family in Sweden, the husband would be expected to do over 38% of the housework.[3] While the data do indicate that housework remains unevenly divided in both countries, the degree of gender inequality in the household is clearly greater in the United States than in Sweden.

Variations in husband's housework across class location

Table 8.1 presents the mean amounts of housework performed by husbands within dual-earner families of different class compositions for the United States and Sweden.[4] The most striking feature of these results is how modest are the differences across classes, especially among employee-only households, in both countries. While there are somewhat larger class differences in Sweden than in the United States (although

---

[3] See Wright (1997: 289) for discussion of the technical details of these estimates.

[4] There are reasons to believe that the reports by wives of their husband's contributions to housework are likely to be more accurate than the reports of the husbands themselves, both because women are generally likely to have a more accurate view of the total amount of housework done in a household and because men may be prone to exaggerate their contributions. I have therefore analyzed all of the results in this chapter separately for women as well as for the combined sample. As it turns out, there are no significant differences between the results of these separate analyses, so I will only report the results for the combined sample of men and women respondents in this chapter. Results for women and men separately can be found in Wright (1997: chapter 11).

Table 8.1 *Mean levels of husband's percentage contribution to total housework[a] by family-class composition[b] (dual-earner households only)*

		United States (N = 537)		
		Husband's job class		
		Self-employed	Middle class	Working class
Wife's job class	Self-employed	17.1	22.8	16.1
	Middle class	22.8	23.9	25.5
	Working class	16.1	22.3	27.1

		Sweden (N = 641)		
		Husband's job-class		
		Self-employed	Middle class	Working class
Wife's job class	Self-employed	16.0	25.1	19.6
	Middle class	25.1	32.4	27.8
	Working class	19.6	25.1	28.1

a. "Total Housework" is a weighted average of five household tasks (routine cleaning, cooking, cleaning up after meals, groceries and laundry) and childcare (for families with children under 16 living in the household), and simply of the five housework tasks for families without children in the home. The weights are determined by the average amount of time per week these tasks take according to time-budget studies. For details see Wright (1997: 304–307).

b. Because of sample size limitations for those family-class compositions involving self-employed people, there were not enough cases to generate accurate measures of all of the five cells in which there was one self-employed spouse and one wage-earner spouse. For these cells, therefore, it was necessary to ignore the gender issue. We therefore distinguish such families from families in which there are no self-employed members, but we ignore whether the self-employed spouse is the husband or the wife.

these differences across countries are themselves not statistically significant), in both countries the class variations are very muted. In regression
equations predicting husband's housework, the seven categories distinguishing family-class types only explain about 3% of the variance in
housework in the United States and 6% in Sweden. Very little of the
overall variation in husband's housework, therefore, is accounted for by
variation in household class composition.[5]

If we look a little more closely at the results, there are some moderate
differences between countries that are worth noting. First, among the
four employee-only family-class categories, in Sweden husbands in the
pure middle-class household perform significantly more housework
than husbands in the other three employee-only class categories (32.4%
compared to 25–28% in the other households), whereas in the United
States they do not (23.9% compared to 22–27%). Swedish middle-class
husbands in pure middle-class households do 8.5 percentage points
more housework than their American counterparts (32.4% compared to
23.9%), whereas the differences between the United States and Sweden
in the three other employee family-class locations is only one or two
percentage points.

Turning to the self-employed family-class categories, we find that
there are significant class differences between these households and
some employee households within both countries, although again we
find that in Sweden the class differences are somewhat larger than in the
US. In the United States, husbands in families consisting of two self-
employed persons or one self-employed member and one working-class
member do less housework than in any other family-class location (only
about 16–17% of total housework compared to around 22–27% in other
locations). In Sweden, in both of these family-class locations (households
with both spouses self-employed and households with one self-employed and one worker) husbands also perform less housework than
husbands in any other class location (16–20% in these two types of self-
employed households compared to 25–32% in other households). The
contrast between the pure self-employed household and the pure
middle-class household in Sweden is especially striking. In the former
men perform only half as much housework as in the latter. In both

[5] This low explained variance could be the result of severe measurement problems in the
dependent variable, husband's contribution to housework. However, when we add
other variables besides class to the equation, the explained variation increases to 28% for
the sample of Swedish women and 18% for US women, which suggests that this is not
the case.

countries, therefore, it appears that in what might be thought of as traditional petty bourgeois households a more traditional form of patriarchy exists.

The results for class differences in Table 8.1 do not control for any other attributes of households. It is always possible that, if such controls were added to the equation, class differences might be strengthened. Suppose, for example, that age affects the housework contributions by men (for example, younger men might perform more housework because of historical changes in expectations) and that age also affects class location (younger men are more likely to be working class). This could have the effect of suppressing class differences if, all other things being equal, working-class men do less housework than men in other class locations. If this were the case, then class differences would appear greater in an analysis in which age was controlled.

As it turns out, the inclusion of a fairly wide range of control variables in the analysis – education, hours of paid work, wife's income contribution to the household, total family income, attitudes towards gender, age, the presence of children under 16 in the household – did not significantly affect the magnitude of the class differences observed in the simple analysis in Table 8.1. If anything, the class differences were reduced when some of these controls were included in the analysis (see Wright 1997: 293–300 for details).

8.3 Implications

Overall, the basic implication of these results is that location within the class structure is not a very powerful or systematic determinant of variations in the gender division of labor across households. This is most consistent with Hypothesis 5, the gender autonomy hypothesis. This is decidedly not what I had expected when I began the analysis. Indeed, as part of my general agenda of class analysis, I was initially quite bent on demonstrating that class was a significant part of the explanation of variations in gender practices. When I initially encountered such marginal class effects, I therefore tried many alternative ways of operationalizing the details of the class variable and aggregating the class distinctions. I examined the separate effects of husband's and wife's class rather than simply family-class composition. I changed the boundaries of the sample, restricting it to two-earner families with two full-time workers, or two-earner families with and without children. I even explored the possibility that class was linked to the tails of the distribution of housework – to the contrast between highly egalitarian and inegalitarian households – rather than to the distribution as a whole. None of these manipulations of the data changed the essential contours of the results: class location is simply not a powerful determinant of the amount of housework husbands perform.

This does not mean that class has no relevance whatsoever for the analysis. In Sweden, at least, husbands in property-owning households (especially the purely self-employed households) seem to do significantly less housework than husbands in employee households (even after controlling for the range of variables in the more complex multivariate analysis). These results therefore provide some modest support for part of Engels' classic argument about property ownership and male domination. Still, while this specific class effect does seem robust, it nevertheless is not at the center stage of the process by which variations in gender relations are produced and negotiated within families. And, in any case, there are no consistent, significant class effects on housework in the United States data. On balance, therefore, there is no support in the data at all for the hypotheses 1, 3 and 4 – the working-class egalitarianism hypothesis, the class culture hypothesis and the class bargaining power hypothesis – and at best very limited support in Sweden for Hypothesis 2, the petty bourgeois inegalitarianism hypothesis.

There are possible responses to these results that a staunch defender of class analysis might propose. First of all, we have restricted the analysis to two-earner families. It could certainly be the case that class plays an important role in determining the basic decisions within households concerning wives' labor force participation in the first place, and as all research on the topic indicates, this certainly affects the relative (but not necessarily absolute) amount of housework done by husbands. There is, however, little empirical support for this response in our data. The labor force participation rates of wives do not vary dramatically across husbands' class location either in the United States or in Sweden (Wright 1997: 302). Also, while husbands in all classes do a higher proportion of housework when their wives are in the labor force, the pattern of variation across classes does not itself differ very much between two-earner and single-earner households in either Sweden or the US.

A more promising defense of class analysis shifts the focus from the problem of variations across households to the more institutional issue of the relationship between the political mobilization of classes on the one hand and gender relations on the other. One might argue that the degree of housework egalitarianism in the society as a whole depends, in part, on processes of class politics which reduce or increase overall economic inequality. The greater egalitarianism of the gender division of labor within Swedish households is plausibly linked to the greater societal egalitarianism produced by the combined effects of Swedish social democracy and the labor movement.

While I would not want to minimize the importance of class politics in the formation of the Swedish welfare state, nevertheless it is problematic to attribute Swedish gender politics entirely to the logic of political class formation. Swedish social democracy has not merely produced an amorphous economic egalitarianism driven by working-class progressive politics; it has also supported a specific agenda of gender egalitarianism rooted in political involvement of women. As Moen (1989) indicates, particularly in the 1970s, the Social Democratic government enacted a series of reforms specifically designed to transform the relationship between work, gender and family life: in 1971, separate income-tax assessments were made mandatory for husbands and wives (which established the principle that each partner should be economically independent); in 1974, parental leave was established giving both mothers and fathers the right to share paid leaves after the birth of a child; in 1978 paid leave was extended to 270 days and in 1980 to 360 days; in 1989, parents of infants became legally entitled to six-hour days, thus encouraging the expansion of opportunities for shorter work weeks. Furthermore, as reported by Haas (1981: 958), a specific objective of cultural policy in Swedish education is to encourage gender equality in childcare and, to a lesser extent, domestic chores. It seems likely that the greater egalitarianism within Swedish households has as much to do with these specific family-work policies and educational practices as it does with the more general class-based egalitarianism of Swedish society. To be sure, the class politics of social democracy helped to sustain a set of political and social values favorable to the enactment of such policies; but it seems unlikely that such policies can themselves be primarily explained in class terms.

One final line of response of class theorists to this research could be to shift the problem from the relationship between family-class location and gender to the relationship between class structure as such and gender. Instead of asking how the gender division of labor within families varies across locations within a class structure, the focus of analysis would be on how the gender division of labor varies across different kinds of class structures. Such an investigation could either be posed at the mode of production level of analysis, involving comparisons of capitalist class structures with different kinds of noncapitalist class structures, or at a more concrete level of analysis, involving comparisons across capitalist class structures at different stages of development. It is certainly possible that the central dynamics of capitalism as a specific kind of class system of production provide the most important explanations for the changing forms and degrees of labor force participation of women over the past century in Western capitalist countries, and these changing forms of labor force participation in turn provide the central structural basis for transformations of gender relations within families, reflected in changes in husbands' participation in housework. The trajectory of development of the class structure of capitalism, therefore, might explain much of the trajectory of changes in gender relations even if gender relations do not vary systematically across different locations within a given class structure. For the moment, however, such arguments must remain speculative hypotheses. Much additional research is needed to validate or modify such claims.

Where does this leave us? Feminists have long argued for the autonomy of gender mechanisms in explaining the production and reproduction of male domination. While Marxist class analysis has generally come to acknowledge this autonomy, nevertheless there has remained a tendency for Marxists to see class as imposing systematic limits within which such autonomous gender mechanisms operate. The data analysis in this chapter indicate that, at least in terms of the micro-analysis of variations in gender relations within housework across households, there is basically no support for the view that class plays a pervasive role. The class effects are robustly weak – virtually nonexistent in the United States, and largely confined to the effects of self-employment in Sweden. While *economic* factors do seem quite relevant – the number of hours worked by wives in the labor force is a relatively strong determinant of variations in housework as is the wife's contribution to household income (at least in Sweden) – the relevance of these economic factors is not closely linked to class as such.

9. The gender gap in workplace authority

In this chapter we will explore the intersection of gender inequality and one specific dimension of class relations – the authority structure within workplaces. No one, of course, would be surprised by the general fact that workplace authority is unequally distributed between men and women in all of the countries we examine. What might be surprising to most people, as we shall see, is the specific pattern of cross-national variation in the gender gap in authority. To cite just one example, in the United States the probability of a man in the labor force occupying an "upper" or "top" management position is 1.8 times greater than the probability of a woman occupying such a position, whereas in Sweden, the probability for men is 4.2 times greater than for women. The objective of this chapter is to document and to attempt to explain these kinds of cross-national variations in gender inequality in workplace authority in seven developed, capitalist countries – the United States, Canada, the United Kingdom, Australia, Sweden, Norway and Japan. In doing so we are particularly interested in revealing the extent to which these patterns reflect variations in gender discrimination in various forms.

9.1 Analytical strategy for studying the "gender gap"

The ideal data for analyzing gender discrimination in access to authority would include direct observations of the discriminatory acts that cumulatively shape the outcomes. Since such data are never available in systematic, quantifiable form, research on gender inequalities in labor market outcomes typically relies on indirect methods of assessing discrimination. We will adopt a strategy which can be called the "net gender gap" approach. The basic idea is this. We begin by measuring the "gross gender gap" in authority in a country. This is simply a measure of

159

the relative probabilities of a woman compared to a man having a particular kind of authority. We then examine what happens to these relative probabilities when we control for a variety of attributes of men and women (such as education or job experience). The relative probabilities of women compared to men having authority when these controls are included in the analysis will be called the "net gender gap" in authority. We will treat the magnitude of this net gender gap as an indicator of the degree of direct discrimination in the allocation of authority. In a sense, discrimination is being treated as the "residual explanation" when other nondiscrimination explanations (represented by the control variables in the equation) fail to fully account for gender differences in authority. Of course, even if the net gender gap were zero, this would not prove that discrimination is absent from the social processes generating overall gender differences in authority, since discrimination could systematically affect the control variables themselves. The net gender gap strategy, therefore, is effective only in assessing the extent to which discrimination operates *directly* in the process of allocating authority within organizations.

The net gender gap strategy of analysis is always vulnerable, either because of possible misspecifications of the equation (important nondiscrimination causes of the gender gap might be excluded from the analysis) or because of poor measurement of some of the variables. What looks like a residual "discrimination" gap, therefore, may simply reflect limitations in the data analysis. Nevertheless, if the gender gap in authority remains large after controlling for a variety of plausible factors, then this adds credibility to the claim that direct discrimination exists in the process by which authority is allocated.

The basic statistical device we will use to measure the extent of the gender gap in authority is derived from "odds ratios." We have already encountered these in the analysis of permeability of class boundaries in chapter 5. In that earlier chapter the issue was odds of a person from a particular class location having certain kinds of social ties across particular class boundaries. Here the issue is the odds of women compared to men having particular kinds of authority. The "gender gap coefficient" we will use is, technically, 1 minus the odds ratio of a woman compared to a man having authority. If the odds of having authority for women and men are equal (and thus the ratio of their respective odds is 1), we will say that the gender gap in authority is zero. If no women at all have authority, and thus the odds of a woman having authority is zero, the gender gap will be 1. If it should happen that the odds of women having authority were greater than those of men, the gender gap will be negative.[1]

9.2 Empirical agenda

The data analysis in this chapter revolves around three main tasks: analyzing the net gender gap in authority *within* countries; examining whether the gender gaps in authority within countries take the form of a "glass ceiling"; and, exploring a variety of possible explanations of the cross-national variations in net gender gaps.

Authority variables

The analyses reported in this chapter will mainly revolve around a dichotomous measure of authority referred to as *overall authority dichotomy*. This variable is itself derived from three more specific measures of authority: *sanctioning authority* (the ability to impose positive or negative sanctions on subordinates); *decision-making authority* (direct participation in policy making decisions within the employing organization); and *Formal Position in the authority hierarchy* (occupying a job which is called a managerial or supervisory position in the official hierarchy of an organization). If a person has at least two of these three kinds of authority, then they will have authority on the *overall authority dichotomy*. (For details of the construction of these variables, see Wright 1997:

---

[1] The technical way of generating the coefficient for the *gross* gender gap is to first calculate, for each country, a logistic regressions in which gender is the only independent variable:

$$\text{Log } [\text{Pr}(A{=}1)/\text{Pr}(A{=}0)] = a + B_1\text{Female},$$

where $\text{Pr}(A{=}1)$ is the probability of a person having authority as defined by our various measures, $\text{Pr}(A{=}0)$ is the probability of a person not having authority, and Female is a dummy variable. The significance level of coefficient B_1 in this model is a test of whether men and women differ significantly in their chances of having managerial authority. Taking the antilog of this coefficient yields the odds ratio of women compared to men having authority. The gender gap is then calculated as 1 minus the antilog of B_1. To evaluate the *net* gender gap, we add the compositional control variables to this equation:

$$\text{Log } [\text{Pr}(A{=}1)/\text{Pr}(A{=}0)] = a + B_1\text{Female} + \Sigma_i B_i X_i$$

where the X_i are the firm attribute, job attribute and person attribute compositional variables. This enables us to test whether the bivariate relationship between gender and authority reflects other factors that are correlated with gender and managerial authority. See Wright (1997: 362–363) for definitions of these control variables.

361–367). I also analyzed all of the patterns using a more complex 10–point authority scale. None of the results were substantively different using this variable and thus I will only report the results for the simpler authority dichotomy.

Analyzing the net gender gap in having authority within countries

The core idea of the "net gender gap" approach is to specify plausible explanations of gender differences in authority that do *not* involve direct discrimination in promotions and then to see if the authority gap disappears when these nondiscrimination factors are held constant in an equation predicting authority. We will explore two explanations of this sort of the gender gap in authority: (1) the gender gap is due to gender differences in various personal attributes of men and women and their employment settings; (2) the gender gap is due to the self-selection of women.

1. Compositional factors
We will explore three clusters of compositional factors: *firm attributes* (economic sector, state employment, firm size); *job attributes* (occupation, part-time employment, job tenure); and *personal attributes* (age, education, labor force interruptions). To the extent that women are concentrated in sectors with a lower proportion of managers, or have various job and personal attributes associated with low probabilities of managerial promotions, then once we control for these factors, the authority gap between men and women should be reduced and perhaps even disappear.

It could be objected that some of these compositional factors are in part *consequences* of discrimination in promotions rather than indirect *causes* of the gender gap, and therefore should not be included in the exercise. It could be the case, for example, that one of the reasons women are more likely to work part time is precisely because they are excluded from promotions to managerial positions. Exclusion from positions of authority could thus explain some of these compositional factors rather than vice versa. We have no way in the present data analysis to investigate this possibility. Nevertheless, if the inclusion of these diverse controls does *not* significantly reduce the gender gap in authority, this would add considerable weight to the claim that the gap is to a significant extent the result of direct discrimination in the allocation of authority positions.

2. Self-selection because of family responsibilities

For various reasons, it might be argued, women in similar employment situations and with similar personal attributes to men may simply not want to be promoted into positions of authority as frequently as men, particularly because of family responsibilities. Given the array of feasible alternatives, women may actually prefer the "mommy track" within a career because of the reduced pressures and time commitment this entails even though it also results in lowered career prospects, especially for vertical promotion. Again, this is not to deny that such preferences may themselves reflect the operation of oppressive gender practices in the society. The gender division of labor in the household or the absence of affordable high-quality childcare, for example, may serve to block the options women feel they realistically can choose in the workplace. Nevertheless, self-selection of this sort is a very different mechanism from direct discrimination by managers and employers in promotion practices.

The most often-cited form of gender self-selection centers around the choices women make with respect to family responsibilities and work responsibilities. We can therefore treat the presence of such responsibilities as additional "compositional factors." However, unlike in the simple compositional arguments which are based on *additive* models of compositional effects, the arguments for self-selection require an *interactive* model. For example, the self-selection hypothesis claims that the presence of children in the household leads women to select themselves out of competition for authority promotions whereas it does not for men. This means that in a model predicting authority, the coefficient for a variable measuring the presence of children would be negative for women but zero, or perhaps even positive, for men, if the presence of children increases the incentives for men to seek promotions because of increasing financial needs of the family. To assess the presence of such self-selection, therefore, we have to estimate a model that includes gender-interactions with the self-selection variables (as well as the additive compositional effects), and then assess the gender gap in authority at appropriate values for the interacting independent variables. For this purpose, we include three variables which are plausibly linked to self-selection: marital status, the presence of children in the household and the percentage of housework performed by the husband.

The glass-ceiling hypothesis

One of the most striking metaphors linked to the efforts of women to gain equality with men in the workplace is the "glass ceiling." The image is that, while women may have gained entry through the front door of managerial hierarchies, at some point they hit an invisible barrier which blocks their further ascent up the managerial highrise. In one of the earliest studies of the problem, Morrison et al. (1987: 13) define the glass ceiling as "a transparent barrier that kept women from rising above a certain level in corporations . . . it applies to women as a group who are kept from advancing higher *because they are women."*

The glass-ceiling metaphor therefore suggests not simply that women face disadvantages and discrimination within work settings and managerial hierarchies, but that these disadvantages relative to men *increase* as women move up the hierarchy. Employers and top managers may be willing to let women become supervisors, perhaps even lower- to middle-level managers, but – the story goes – they are very reluctant to let women assume positions of "real" power and thus women are blocked from promotions to the upper levels of management in corporations and other work organizations. This may be due to sexist ideas or more subtle discriminatory practices, but, in any case, the glass-ceiling hypothesis argues that the disadvantages women face relative to men in getting jobs and promotions are greater in the upper levels of managerial hierarchies than at the bottom.

Casual observation seems to confirm this argument. There is, after all, a much higher proportion of bottom supervisors than of chief executive officers who are women. In the class analysis project data, at the bottom of managerial hierarchies perhaps 20–25% of lower level supervisors are women in the United States. In contrast, at most a few percent of top executives and CEOs in large corporations are women. According to Fierman (1990) fewer than 0.5% of the 4,012 highest-paid managers in top companies were women, while fewer than 5% of senior management in the Fortune 500 corporations were women and minorities. Reviewing the data on what they call the "promotion gap," Reskin and Padavic (1994: 84) report that "although women held half of all federal government jobs in 1992 and made up 86 percent of the government's clerical workers, they were only a quarter of supervisors and only a tenth of senior executives." Reskin and Padavic report similar findings for other countries: in Denmark women were 14.5% of all managers and administrators, but only between 1 and 5% of top managers; in Japan women were 7.5% of all administrators and managers but only 0.3% of top management in the private sector. It is hardly surprising with such distributions that it is commonly believed by those working for gender equality that a glass ceiling exists in the American workplace.

However, things may not be what they seem. A simple arithmetic example will demonstrate the point. Suppose, there is a managerial hierarchy with six levels in which 50% of men but only 25% of women get promoted at each level to the next higher level (i.e. men have twice the probability of being promoted than women at every level of the hierarchy). In this situation, if roughly 25% of line supervisors are women, only 1% of top managers will be women. In spite of initial appearances, this example does not fit the story of the "glass ceiling." According to the glass-ceiling hypothesis, the obstacles to women getting managerial positions are supposed to increase as they move up the hierarchy. This could either take the form of a dramatic step function – at some level recruitment and promotion chances for women relative to men plummet to near zero – or it could be a gradual deterioration of the chances of women relative to men. In the example just reviewed, the disadvantages women face relative to men are constant as they move up the hierarchy. And yet, there are almost no women top managers but plenty of women bottom-level supervisors.

What this example illustrates is that the existence of a glass ceiling cannot be inferred simply from the sheer fact that there are many fewer people at the top echelons of organizations who are women than at the bottom levels. The cumulative effect of constant or even declining discrimination can still produce an *increasing* "gender gap in authority" as you move to the top of organizational hierarchies.

The Comparative Class Analysis Project data do not allow us to conduct a fine-grained test of the glass-ceiling hypothesis. Nevertheless, we will make a first cut at the problem by examining the gender gap in authority separately for those people who have made it into the authority hierarchy. If we find that the gender gap in amount of authority for people in the hierarchy is the same or smaller than for the sample as a whole, then this undermines the glass-ceiling hypothesis that gender discrimination is weaker at the port of entry into the hierarchy than in promotions within it. Of course, the glass ceiling could take the form of intensified discrimination only at the very apex of organizations. If this were the case, then we will not be able to observe a glass ceiling in our analysis because of limitations of sample size. If, however, the glass ceiling takes the form of gradually increasing discrimination with higher levels of authority, then the gender gap in how much authority people have conditional upon them having any authority should be greater than the gender gap in simply having authority.

Explaining cross-national variations

We will pursue two different strategies for exploring possible explanations for the cross-national variations in the gender gap in authority. First, we will compare the differences across countries in the *gross* gender gaps in authority (i.e. the country-specific gender gaps not controlling for any compositional effects) with the differences across countries *net* of the various compositional factors. If a significant portion of the gender gap *within* countries is explained by such compositional factors, then these factors may also account for much of the difference across countries in the gender gap.

Second, if significant differences across countries in the gender authority gap remain after controlling for all of the compositional factors, we then examine in a somewhat less formal way a number of possible macro-social explanations by comparing the rank-ordering of the seven countries on the net gender gap in authority with the rank-ordering on the following variables (see Wright: 1997 351–359 for a discussion of the measures used in these analyses):

1. Gender ideology
All things being equal one would expect a smaller gender gap in workplace authority in societies with relatively egalitarian gender ideologies compared to societies with less egalitarian ideologies.

2. Women's reproductive and sexual rights
Developed capitalist societies differ in the array of rights backed by the state in support of gender equality with respect to sexual and reproductive issues, such as rights to abortion, rights to paid pregnancy and maternity leaves from work, and laws concerning sexual violence, abuse and harassment. While such state-backed rights and provisions do not directly prevent discriminatory practices in promotions, they may contribute to the cultural climate in ways that indirectly affect the degree of inequality in promotions and thus in workplace authority. It would therefore be predicted that societies with strong provisions of these rights would have a smaller gender gap in authority than societies with a weaker support for these rights.

3. Gender earnings gap

It might be expected that in societies in which there was a relatively small gender gap in earnings, the gender gap in workplace authority would also be relatively small. The argument is not that greater equality in earnings capacity between men and women is a *cause* of a smaller authority gap (if anything, a smaller gender gap in authority could itself contribute to narrowing the gender earnings gap), but rather that a society that fosters low levels of income inequality between men and women is also likely to foster low levels of authority inequality as well. Low gender differences in earnings would therefore be taken as an indicator of an underlying institutional commitment to gender equality as such.

4. Occupational sex segregation

The logical relationship between occupational sex segregation and gender inequalities in workplace authority is complex. Clearly, the probability of acquiring authority varies from occupation to occupation, and thus occupational sex segregation can reasonably be viewed as one likely cause of inequalities in authority. However, if norms against women supervising men are strong, then, in a limited way, occupational sex segregation might actually open up managerial positions for women in so far as it increases the chances of women being able to supervise only women. Furthermore, promotions into positions of authority often entail changes in occupational titles. This is particularly true for occupations that are formally called "managerial occupations." Barriers to acquiring workplace authority for women, therefore, are also likely to be a cause of occupational sex segregation. In examining variations across countries in occupational sex-segregation, I am thus not suggesting that this variation is itself a direct cause of variation in the net gender gap in authority. Rather, as in the case of the earnings gap, we will treat occupational sex-segregation as an indicator of underlying processes that shape gender inequalities in the society. It would be expected that countries with relatively high levels of occupational sex segregation would also have large gender gaps in authority.

5. The proportion of the labor force with authority

There are two reasons for expecting the gender gap in authority to be greater in countries in which a relatively small proportion of the labor force held positions of authority than in countries in which there are many authority positions. First, it is more difficult for employers and top executives adequately to fill the positions with men in countries in which a high proportion of the employees of organizations have authority. In simple supply and demand terms, therefore, employers have an incentive to fill a higher proportion of authority positions with women in a country with a large proportion of managerial and supervisory positions in the job structure. Second, if as some scholars argue (e.g. Reskin 1988; Acker 1990; Bergman 1986), the gender authority gap is at least partially the result of the interests of men in maintaining male predominance in the authority hierarchy, then the incentive for them to try to do so would be stronger when there were relatively few such positions to go around. A proportionately large managerial structure, therefore increases the incentives for the heads of organizations to recruit women into managerial positions and it reduces the incentives for male managers to engage in restrictive practices to protect their positions.

6. The organized women's movement and political culture
If sex discrimination plays a significant role in the exclusion of women from positions of responsibility and power within work, then it would be expected that one of the determinants of the erosion of such sexist practices would be the extent and forms of women's organized challenge to these practices. Two issues in this respect would seem especially important. First, the *overall strength* of the women's movement is crucial for its ability to challenge the gender gap in workplace authority. Second, and perhaps less obviously, the specific *ideological orientation* of the women's movement may shape the extent to which it directs its energies towards problems of workplace discrimination. In particular, it may matter in the extent to which a women's movement is oriented towards equal *rights* or to the provision of services which benefit women.

9.3 Results

The gross gender grap in authority
Figure 9.1 presents in graphic form the gender authority gap coefficients for the overall authority dichotomy variable, both without any control variables and with the compositional controls used to evaluate the net gender gap. Two results are especially striking about the gross gender gap results.

First, in every country, there is a significant gender gap in authority. In results not reported here (see Wright 1997: 338), this gender gap was also significant for each of the three underlying measures of authority

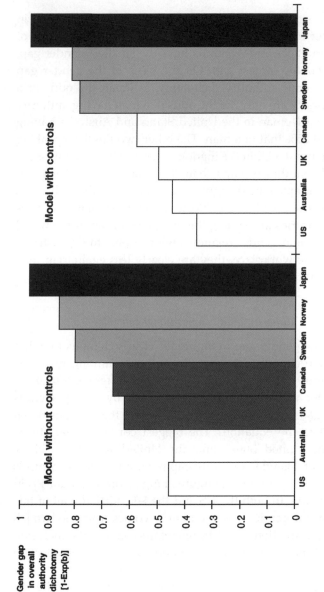

Bars of different shades indicate differences significant at p <.05 or better, with two exceptions: in the model without controls, the UK and Australia differ at the p <.06 level and the UK and the United States differ at the p <.09 level.

Figure 9.1 *The gender gap in authority in seven countries.*

used to construct the overall authority dichotomy. Women are less likely than men to be in the formal authority hierarchy, to have sanctioning power over subordinates and to participate in organizational policy decisions.

Second, there are statistically significant cross-national variations in the degree of gender inequality in authority. On all of the measures of authority, the United States and Australia have the smallest gender gap, and Japan has by far the largest gap. On the basis of the gender gap coefficients in the overall authority dichotomy, in Japan the odds of a woman having authority are only 3% the odds of a man having authority whereas the odds of a woman in the United States and Australia having authority are around 55% that of a man. The other two English-speaking countries – Canada and the United Kingdom – tend to have significantly greater gross gender authority gaps than does the United States and Australia, but – perhaps surprisingly – smaller gaps than the two Scandinavian countries, Sweden and Norway. While in many respects the Scandinavian countries are among the most egalitarian in the world both in terms of class and gender relations, with respect to the distribution of authority in the workplace, they are clearly less egalitarian than the four English-speaking countries in our analysis.

Net gender differences in authority with compositional controls

The results for the net gender gap in Figure 9.1 clearly demonstrate that relatively little of the overall differences in authority among men and women in any country can be attributed to gender differences in these control variables. One way of assessing this is to ask: by what percent is the gross gender gap in authority reduced when the compositional controls are added to the equation? The biggest compositional effects seems to be in the United States and the United Kingdom, where roughly 20% of the total gender authority gap is closed when the controls are added. In the other countries, the figures range from less than 1% in Japan to 12% in Canada. In both the US and the UK, virtually all of this modest reduction in the gender gap in authority comes from the two job attribute variables (occupation and full-time employment); the inclusion of the personal attribute variables in the equation has almost no effect on the authority gap.

The net gender gap results in Figure 9.1 also show that while the significance level of some of the cross national differences declines in the equations controlling for compositional effects, the basic patterns of the results are essentially the same as in the equations for the gross gender gap. In particular, the only change between the model without compositional effects and the model with compositional effects is that in the latter the gender coefficients among the four English-speaking countries no longer differ significantly. For the net gender gap, therefore, we have a very clear grouping of our seven countries: the four English-speaking countries have the smallest net gender gaps in authority, the two Scandinavian countries have significantly larger net gender gaps, and Japan has by far the largest.

While it is always possible that we have omitted some crucial compositional variable from the analysis which might affect the results, nevertheless, these results are strongly supportive of the claim that gender differences in authority, and cross-national patterns of such differences, are not primarily the result of differences in the distributions of relevant attributes of men and women and their employment situations. This adds credibility to the claim that direct discrimination or self-selection in the promotion process itself are likely to be important.

Self-selection models

The self-selection hypothesis states that because of family responsibilities, women voluntarily make themselves less available for promotion into positions of authority in the workplace. The way we will examine this hypothesis is to see how the net gender gap in authority varies for people in different family situations. If selection is a significant factor, then we would expect that the gender gap in authority would be greater among married people than among single people, and greater still among married people with children under sixteen. The gender gap would be especially large among married people with children in which the husbands do very little housework.

The technical strategy for seeing how the gender gap varies across family situation is to examine equations which include interaction terms between gender and the different measures of family situation.[2]

---

[2] The logistic regression used to estimate these interactions is:

$$\text{Log } [\text{Pr}(A=1)/\text{Pr}(A=0)] = a + B_1\text{Female} + B_2\text{Married} + B_3\text{kids} + B_4\text{Husband's Housework} + B_5\text{Female} \times \text{Married} + B_6\text{Female} \times \text{kids} + B_7\text{Female} \times \text{Husband's Housework} + \Sigma_i B_i X_i$$

where the X_i are the compositional control variables used in the analysis of the net gender gap. If self-selection is a powerful force in shaping the gender gap in authority, then at least some of the interactive terms in these equations – B_4, B_5, B_6, B_7 – should be statistically significant.

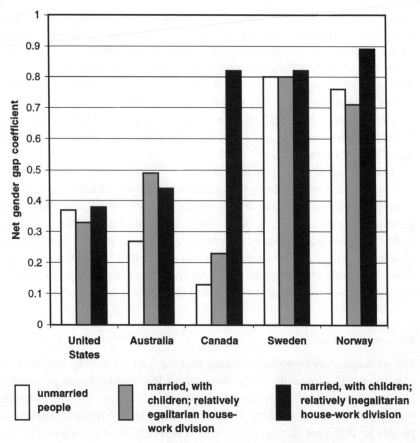

Figure 9.2 *Testing the effects of "self-selection" on the gender gap in authority.*

Figure 9.2 presents the results of our estimates of the gender gap in authority for people in three types of family situations: unmarried people; married people without children and with a relatively egalitarian distribution of housework; married people with children and with an inegalitarian distribution of housework (Japan and the UK are not included because they lacked the housework data). In the United States, Sweden and Australia, none of the interactions are significant. In Norway and Canada, however, some of the interaction terms are significant, indicating that the gender gap in authority does vary with family situation (see Wright 1997: 345–347 for details). In particular, in these two countries, as the proportion of housework done by *husbands* increases, the likelihood of married women having workplace authority also increases. Only in Canada, however, does this interaction term generate a substantively large effect on the gender gap in authority. As Figure 9.2 indicates, the gender gap in authority in Canada for married women without children in the home, living in a relatively egalitarian household (a household in which husbands do 40% of the housework) is 0.23, whereas the gap for married women with children in the home living in an *in*egalitarian household (in which husbands do only 10% of the housework) is 0.82, comparable to the levels in Sweden and Norway. I can offer no explanation for why the patterns in Canada are so different from the other countries. For Canada, therefore, these interactions are consistent with the claims of the self-selection hypothesis that when women have high levels of domestic responsibility they frequently select themselves out of the running for positions of authority. Of course, the negative association between housework inequality and women's workplace authority in Canada could mainly reflect a causal impact of having authority on housework rather than of housework on the likelihood of getting authority and thus not support the self-selection hypothesis. In any case, there is little or no support for the self-selection hypothesis for the other countries in the study.

The glass-ceiling hypothesis

So far we have only discussed the differential likelihood of men and women *having* authority, but not the *amount* of authority that they have if they have any authority. This is a central issue for the "glass-ceiling hypothesis" – the idea that the gender gap in authority increases as one moves up authority hierarchies.

The strategy for evaluating the glass-ceiling hypothesis involves restricting the analysis to respondents in the authority hierarchy and then examining gender gaps in authority within this subsample. To do this, I use the formal position in the authority hierarchy variable as the criterion for restricting the sample: all persons who say that they are at least a supervisor on this question will be treated as in an authority hierarchy. On this restricted sample, we then examine the gender gap in authority for three dependent variables: being a middle-manager or above in the formal hierarchy; having sanctioning authority; and value on the 10-point amount of authority scale. The results for the first of these variables are presented in Figure 9.3. (The results for the other variables are in Wright 1997: 349).

If there is a strong glass-ceiling effect, then the gender gap for people

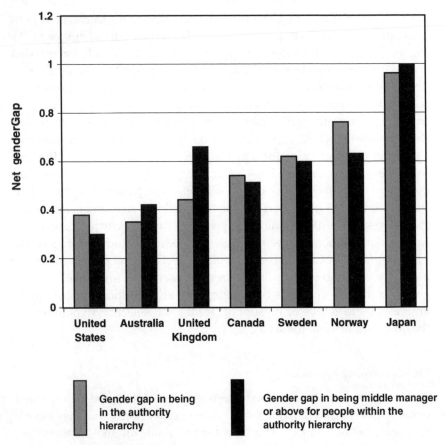

Figure 9.3 *Testing the "glass ceiling"*.

within the authority hierarchy in the odds of a woman compared to a man being a middle-manager or above should be greater than the gender gap in simply being in the authority hierarchy. As the results in Figure 9.3 indicate, this is only nominally the case in three countries – Australia, the United Kingdom and Japan. And in only one of these, the United Kingdom, is the gender gap in authority substantially greater for people inside the hierarchy: in the UK the odds of a woman (net of the various control variables) already inside the hierarchy being a middle manager or above are 66% less than those of a man, whereas the odds of a woman being in the hierarchy altogether are only 44% less than those of a man. In all the other countries, there is either no difference between insiders and everyone in these gender gaps or the gender gaps for people inside the hierarchy are somewhat less than for the labor force as a whole.

The lack of evidence for a glass ceiling is particularly strong in the US data. For all three of the measures of authority – middle manager or above, sanctioning authority, or the 10-point authority scale – the gender gaps in authority actually cease to be statistically significant for people inside of the hierarchy. In all countries except the United States, the gender gap in these measures of authority remain large and statistically significant when we restrict the sample to people in the hierarchy. Overall, therefore, these results do not lend support to the glass-ceiling hypothesis. Especially in the United States, it does not appear that once women are in the hierarchy, the barriers they face to promotion relative to men at least into the middle range of the hierarchy are greater than the barriers they faced in getting into the hierarchy in the first place.

Explaining cross-national variations

We have already examined, and rejected, one possible explanation for the differences across countries in the gender gap in workplace authority. These differences cannot be attributed to differences in the various compositional factors included in our analyses of the net gender gap since the basic pattern of intercountry differences is the same for the gross gender gap and the net gender gap in authority.

We will now explore somewhat less formally a number of general macro-social and cultural factors which might help explain the variations across countries in the gender gap. The results are presented in Table 9.1.

1. Gender ideology

The Comparative project on Class Structure and Class Consciousness contains a limited number of attitude items on gender equality. Respondents were asked how much they agreed, or disagreed with each of the following statements:

1 Ideally, there should be as many women as men in important positions in government and business.
2 If both husband and wife work, they should share equally in the housework and childcare.
3 It is better for the family if the husband is the principal breadwinner outside the home and the wife has primary responsibility for the home and children.

Table 9.1 *Rank ordering of countries from more to less egalitarian by the gender gap in authority and other relevant variables*

Net gender gap in having authority		Gender attitudes[c]		Legal gender egalitarianism[d]	
Rank order of countries[a]	Gender gap[b]	Rank order of countries	Mean score	Rank order of countries	Mean score
US	.36	Sweden	1.77	Norway	1.83
Australia	.45	Norway	1.82	Sweden	1.17
UK	.50	Canada	2.01	US	1.17
Canada	.58	Australia	2.05	Canada	−.48
Sweden	.79	US	2.17	UK	−.48
Norway	.82	Japan	2.43	Australia	−1.02
Japan	.98			Japan	−1.02

Gender earnings gap[e]		Occupational sex segregation (Index of dissimilarity)[f]	
Rank order of countries	Women's hourly earnings as percentage of men's	Rank order of countries	Mean score
Sweden	91.0	Japan	22.2
Norway	81.9	Australia	31.9
Australia	81.7	US	36.6
UK	74.0	Canada	41.0
Canada	66.0	Sweden	41.8
US	65.0	UK	44.4
Japan	51.8	Norway	47.2

Occupational sex segregation ("Ratio index of sex segregation")[g]		Proportion of the labor force in official managerial positions[h]	
Rank order of countries	Mean score	Rank order of countries	Proportion of labor force (%)
US	.65	Australia	15.8
Japan	.72	US	13.7
Canada	.75	Canada	12.2
UK	.92	UK	12.2
Australia	.95	Sweden	10.9
Sweden	.96	Norway	10.4
Norway	.99	Japan	5.9

Table 9.1 (*Continued*)

 a. As indicated in Figure 9.1, the rank ordering of countries is virtually the same for the gross gender gap and the net gender gap.

 b. The gender gap in workplace authority is defined as 1-Exp(b), where b is the coefficient for gender in the logistic regression predicting the overall authority dichotomy.

 c. This is a simple index based on three Likert items concerning sex role attitudes. The lower the score the more egalitarian. The scores range from 1 to 4. The variable was not available for the United Kingdom.

 d. This is a simple factor analytic scale of three legal rights for women: rights to abortion; rights to at least 12 weeks paid pregnancy leave; marital rape is a crime. See Charles (1992: 491–2).

 e. *Sources.* Sweden, Norway, Australia, UK, Canada, US: National Committee on Pay Equity, "Closing the Wage Gap: an international perspective" (Washington, DC: National Committee on Pay Equity, 1988), pp. 10–14. *Japan: The Yearbook of Labor Statistics* (Geneva: International Labor Organization, 51st edn, 1992), pp. 798–804. There are some differences in the definitions for each country: Australia (1985), full time, average weekly earnings; Canada (1986), not specified; Japan (1984), average monthly earnings; Norway (1980), average hourly earnings in manufacturing; Sweden (1985), average monthly earnings, industry; United Kingdom (1985), average hourly earnings; United States (1987), median annual earnings.

 f. Blau and Ferber (1990).

 g. Charles (1992: 489).

 h. This is defined as people in jobs which are described as "managerial positions" (but not supervisory positions) in the formal hierarchy variable.

A gender ideology scale was constructed by adding the responses to each item and averaging over the number of valid items. The scale ranges from 1, indicating a consistently strong egalitarian attitude towards gender roles, to 4, indicating a consistently strong conservative attitude.

As can be seen in Table 9.1, the rank ordering of countries in terms of their degree of ideological gender egalitarianism does not at all parallel the rank ordering for the gender gap in workplace authority. Sweden and Norway are the most ideologically egalitarian but have among the largest gender gaps in authority; the United States is exceeded only by Japan in the level of inegalitarianism ideologically, yet it has the smallest gender gap in authority.

2. Sexual and reproductive rights

Maria Charles (1992) has constructed an index of legally enforced gender egalitarianism based on three dummy variables: (1) abortions available on request, (2) marital rape is a crime, and (3) women are guaranteed at least 12 weeks of paid pregnancy leave from work. The scale values range from 1.83 to −1.02, where positive scores indicate more rights. As can be seen in Table 9.1 the rank order among the seven countries on this variable is both quite different from the rank ordering for gender attitudes and the rank order for the net gender gap in having authority.

3. Gender earnings gap

The gender gap in earnings is one possible indicator of institutional arrangements for gender equality within work which might impact on the gender gap in authority. Contrary to this expectation, however, the data in Table 9.1 indicate that there is no association between the level of the gender gap in hourly earnings and the gender gap in authority. Japan and the United States both have relatively large gender differences in earnings, yet the United States has a small gender gap in authority while Japan has the largest gender gap; Sweden and Norway are both relatively egalitarian in terms of gender differences in earnings, yet they both have relatively large gender gaps in authority.

4. Occupational sex segregation

As in the case of the gender gap in earnings, the expectation that the rank order of countries in sex-segregation of occupations should roughly mirror the gender gap in authority is not supported by the available data. Based on the data of two comparative studies of occupational sex segregation, Blau and Ferber (1990) and Charles (1992), the rank-ordering of our seven countries in terms of overall occupational sex segregation is not at all the same as the rank ordering in terms of the gender gap in authority (see Wright 1997: 354–355 for a more detailed discussion of these results, especially for Japan).

5. The proportion of the labor force with authority

The rank ordering for the size of the managerial category (as measured by the formal hierarchy variable) quite closely mirrors the rank ordering of the gender gap in authority: the four English-speaking countries have the largest proportion of their labor forces in managerial positions, followed by the two Nordic countries and then, with a much smaller figure, Japan. It therefore does appear that the aggregate availability of managerial positions in the society may influence the size of the gender gap in the allocation of authority.

6. The organized women's movement and political culture

I know of no comparative research which systematically assesses women's movements in different countries either in terms of their organizational and political strength or in terms of the details of their ideological stance. Our analysis of these issues, therefore, will have to remain at a relatively impressionistic level.

In terms of the political strength of the women's movement one thing seems particularly clear: the women's movement in Japan is far weaker than in any other country. It is less obvious how to judge the relative strength of women's movements in the other six countries, although it seems clear that the politically organized women's movement in the United States would be among the strongest. On the basis of qualitative research by Katzenstein (1987), the US women's movement has generally been stronger and more powerful than movements in Europe. While this evidence is impressionistic, it seems fairly safe to say that the politically organized women's movement is probably weakest in Japan and strongest in the United States, with the other countries falling somewhere in between.

It is somewhat easier to make some judgments about the ideological orientations of different women's movements, at least if we are willing to assume that these women's movements are likely to reflect to a significant extent the broader political culture of their societies. Esping-Anderson (1990) classified capitalist democracies along a variety of dimensions characterizing the ideological principles within their welfare states. These are presented in Table 9.2. With the exception of the placement of Japan within these rank orderings, these political orderings closely parallel the rank ordering of the gender gap. Specifically, the four English-speaking countries score low on what Esping-Anderson terms "decommodification" (i.e. welfare state policies which reduce the dependency of workers on the market) and high on liberalism of regime characteristics whereas Norway and Sweden score high on decommodification and extremely low on liberalism.

How does this relate to the problem of the gender gap in authority? Liberalism is a doctrine which argues that markets are a legitimate and efficient means of distributing welfare so long as they are "fair." Eliminating ascriptive barriers to individual achievement in labor

Table 9.2 *Rank ordering of countries' political culture and institutions from liberal/commodified to socialist/decommodified*

Degree of "decommodification" in the welfare state [a]		Degree of liberalism in regime attributes[b]		Degree of socialism in regime attributes	
Rank order	Score	Rank order	Score	Rank order	Score
Australia	13.0	United States	12	United States	0
United States	13.8	Canada	12	Japan	2
Canada	22.0	Australia	10	Australia	4
UK	23.4	Japan	10	UK	4
Japan	27.1	UK	6	Canada	4
Norway	38.3	Norway	0	Norway	8
Sweden	39.1	Sweden	0	Sweden	8

a. From Esping-Anderson (1990: 52). This score is a measure of the extent to which the welfare state neutralizes the effects of the market through its welfare policies.

b. From Esping-Anderson (1990: 74). The score indexes the extent to which welfare state interventions follow the principles of classical liberalism. The socialism score indexes the extent to which the regime follows socialist principles. Because in Esping-Anderson's analysis there is a third form of regime, "classical conservatism," the rank ordering for socialism is not necessarily simply the inverse of the rank ordering for liberalism.

markets and employment relations is therefore a central objective of liberal politics. A women's movement animated by a liberal political culture, therefore, would be particularly concerned with equal rights and the elimination of such barriers. In keeping with this expectation, Goldberg and Uremen (1990: 28–30) have emphasized the relatively strong forms of antidiscrimination laws that have been passed in the United States and their relative effectiveness, at least compared to many other countries.

Social democracy, in contrast, questions the legitimacy of market-determined inequalities regardless of the equality of opportunity, and seeks to render human welfare at least partially independent of market mechanisms. A women's movement embedded in a social democratic political culture would be expected to be much less concerned with labor market mechanisms as such, and more concerned with state interventions which directly provide services and resources which enhance the welfare of women. Policy initiatives would therefore concentrate on such things as parental leaves, maternal health care, childcare services and child allowances. Women would certainly benefit in many ways from

such strategies, as many commentators on Scandinavian social democracy have stressed (Goldberg and Uremen 1990: 141–144; Moen, 1989),
but these priorities would not directly impact on barriers to authority
promotions in the workplace. Commenting on the contrast between
American liberal feminism and European social democratic feminism,
Nancy Fraser (1993) argues that the former adopt a "universal breadwinner" model of gender equality which emphasizes employment
rights, whereas the latter adopt a "caregiver parity" model which
stresses the provision of services and resources to equalize the conditions
of life of women engaged primarily in domestic responsibilities. The
relatively large gender gap in workplace authority in the social democratic Nordic countries, therefore, may in part be a by-product of the
relatively lower priority placed on liberal goals of individual competition
and achievement relative to more communal benefits.

Taking these various arguments together, I hypothesize that the variations across countries in the size of the gender gap in workplace
authority is the result of the interaction between the relative scarcity or
abundance of authority positions, on the one hand, and the capacity and
interest of the politically organized women's movement to challenge the
barriers to women being promoted into those positions on the other.
Where there are relatively few managerial positions in the first place and
the women's movement is particularly weak, as in Japan, the gender gap
in authority will be very large. Where there are somewhat more managerial positions, but the women's movement is oriented towards collective
goods and decommodified social provisions, the gender gap will still be
relatively large. When there are relatively abundant managerial positions
in the job structure and where the women's movement is relatively
strong and oriented towards liberal individualist goals, the gender gap
will be most effectively challenged.

Our evidence in support of these interpretations is rather sketchy,
especially because we do not have cases of countries with a high
proportion of the labor force in managerial positions combined with a
weak women's movement, or countries with a strong, liberal women's
movement and relatively few manager positions. Such cases would be
needed to tease out the relative importance of these two factors and the
nature of their interactions. Considerably more research is needed about
the impact of women's struggles and the process by which the gender
gap in authority changes over time within and across countries before
these interpretations could be affirmed with confidence.

9.4 Conclusions

Several conclusions emerge from the research reported in this chapter. First, while a gender gap in authority exists in all of the countries we have studied, there is considerable cross-national variation in the magnitude of this gap: it is smaller in the English-speaking countries, especially in the United States and Australia, relatively large in the Scandinavian countries, and huge in Japan. These results appear quite robust across a variety of measures.

Second, the gender gap in authority within countries and the pattern of cross-national variations do not appear to be significantly the result of compositional factors among men and women in the labor force. Even when we control for a range of attributes of firms, jobs and individuals, the gap within every country and the basic pattern of cross-national differences remain. Furthermore, with the possible exception of Canada, there is little evidence that the gender gap in authority is attributable to self-selection processes by women. Much of the gender gap in workplace authority in the countries we have studied can thus provisionally be attributed to various forms of discrimination, at least some of which occur directly in the promotion process.

Third, the "glass-ceiling" hypothesis (at least in the relatively weak form we were able to investigate) is not supported in most of the countries in the study. While a gender gap in authority generally continues to exist when we restrict the analysis to people already in the authority hierarchy, this gap does not appear to be greater than the gap in acquiring authority in the first place. The commonly held view that the women's movement has been more successful in opening up positions at the bottom of the organizational hierarchy for women and less successful in moving women up the corporate ladder is not supported by these data.

Finally, and more tentatively, we have presented data which suggest that the variations in the gender gap across countries may be the result of the interaction between variations in the relative abundance of authority positions and the effectiveness of different women's movements in challenging barriers women face in moving into those positions. Both political and economic factors thus seem to be important in explaining variability in gender inequality in workplace authority, whereas cultural variations more specifically linked to gender ideology seem less significant.

Part III

Class structure and class consciousness

10. A general framework for studying class consciousness and class formation

In one way or another, most class analysts believe that at the core of class analysis is a relatively simple causal structure that looks something like the diagram in Figure 10.1. There is, of course, much disagreement about precisely how to conceptualize the arrows in this causal stream. Do they mean "determines" or "shapes" or "imposes limits upon"? Is there a clear sense in which the horizontal causal stream in this structure is "more important" or "more fundamental" than the unspecified "other causes"? At one extreme, orthodox historical materialism claimed that one can broadly read off patterns of class struggle directly from the class structure, and these, in turn, determine the fundamental course of history; in the long run, at least, class structures are thought to determine class struggle and class struggles (in conjunction with the development of the forces of production) to determine trajectories of social change. At the other extreme, most non-Marxist class analysts as well as some Marxists view the class structure as at most providing us with the vocabulary for identifying potential actors in class struggles; class structure does not, however, necessarily have a more powerful role in determining actual patterns of class struggle than many other mechanisms (ideology, the state, ethnicity, etc.), and class struggles are only one among a host of change-producing factors.

In this chapter we will explore the elements on the left hand side of Figure 10.1: "Class structure → class struggle." I will propose a general model of the relationship between class structure and class struggle which captures both the core traditional Marxist intuition that class structures are in some sense the fundamental determinant of class struggles, but nevertheless allows other causal factors considerable potential weight in explaining concrete variations across time and place. The core of the model is an attempt to link a micro-conception of the

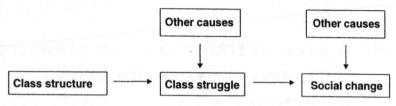

Figure 10.1 *Simple core model of class analysis.*

relationship between class *location* and class *consciousness* with a more macro-level understanding of the relationship between class *structure* and class *formation.*

In section 10.1 of this chapter we will set the stage for this model by briefly elaborating the contrast between micro- and macro-levels of analysis. Section 10.2 will discuss the definitions of a number of the core concepts which we will use, especially class formation and class consciousness. This will be followed in section 10.3 by a discussion of the micro-model, the macro-model and their interconnection.

10.1 Micro- and macro-levels of analysis

The contrast between micro- and macro-levels of analysis is often invoked in sociology, and much is made about the necessity of "moving" back and forth between these levels, but frequently the precise conceptual status of the distinction is muddled. I will use the terms to designate different units of analysis, in which macro-levels of analysis are always to be understood as "aggregations" of relevant micro-units of analysis. The paradigm for this usage is biology: organisms are aggregations of interconnected organs; organs are aggregations of interconnected cells; cells are aggregations of interconnected cellular structures; cellular structures are aggregations of interconnected molecules. The expression "are aggregations of" in these statements, of course, does not simply mean, "haphazard collections of," but rather "structurally interconnected sets of." A given macro-level always consists of *relations* among the relevant constituent micro-units.

What precisely do we mean by "relations" among micro units? This term is often imbued with arcane meanings. I will use it in a fairly straightforward way to designate any systematic pattern of interactions among the micro-units. Relations can thus be strong, well ordered and systematic, involving intensive and repeated interactions among constituent micro-elements, or weak and rather chaotic, involving few and

Table 10.1 *Logic of micro- and macro-levels of social analysis*

Levels of analysis	Constituent sub-units	Nature of relations	Examples of relations
Micro-social level	individuals	inter-individual relations	friendships, point-of-production class relations
Meso-social level	inter-individual relations	bounded organizations and networks (relations among inter-individual relations)	firms, families, unions, schools
Macro-social level	organizations	relations among organizations	nations, economies

erratic interactions among those elements. To analyze any unit of analysis, therefore, is to investigate the nature and consequences of these relations among its sub-units.

In specifying any hierarchy of nested micro- to macro-levels, therefore, we need to define the relevant subunits and the nature of the relations among them. One way of understanding the hierarchy of units of analysis in sociology is represented in Table 10.1 and Figure 10.2

The micro-level of sociological analysis consists of the study of the relations among individuals. Individuals are the constituent elements within these relations, but it is the relations as such that are the object of study of micro-level sociological analysis. The study of interactions among siblings or between bosses and workers are thus both micro-level social phenomena.

The individuals within these relations, of course, can also be considered "units of analysis," and the relations among *their* constituent "parts" can also be studied. The study of such *intra*-individual relations is the proper object of human biology and psychology. The analysis of individuals-qua-individuals is thus at the interface between sociology – in which the individual is the unit within micro-relations – and psychology – in which the individual is the macro-level within which relations of various sorts are studied.

The meso-level of social analysis consists of the investigation of relations among interindividual relations. The units characteristic of such relations-among-relations are normally what we call "organizations," although looser units such as social networks would also consti-

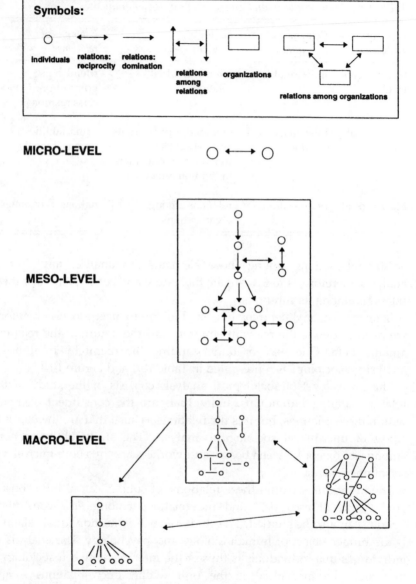

Figure 10.2 *Micro-, meso- and macro-units of analysis.*

tute a meso-level of analysis. The macro-social level of analysis, then, consists of relations among organizations and other forms of meso-level units. At the most macro-level, the "world system" consists of relations among nations and economic regions.

Dividing up the units of sociological analysis in this way is, of course, highly stylized and oversimplified. Depending upon one's theoretical purposes, one can add many intermediate levels of analysis to this simple schema. Organizations, for example, can be analyzed in terms of the relations among a series of suborganizational units – offices, branches, departments – and each of these, in turn, can be analyzed in terms of the relations among sets of inter-individual relations.

The micro–macro distinction understood in this way should not be confused with the abstract-concrete distinction. While it often seems that micro-analysis is more concrete than macro-analysis – since it deals with apparently concrete entities, "individuals" – one can perfectly well develop very abstract concepts for dealing with micro-analyses (as is often done in rational-actor models) or quite concrete concepts for dealing with macro-analyses (as occurs in many historical analyses of institutional development). Individuals are not inherently more concrete than firms or societies, any more than cells are more concrete than organisms.

In terms of class analysis, the concept of "class location" is a preeminently micro-level concept. Individuals, at least in capitalism, are the typical units that occupy the class locations defined by class structures (although in special cases families may be the relevant units). The "capitalist-class location" and the "working-class location" are defined by the social relations of production that link individuals in these locations together. The micro-analysis of class *locations*, therefore, should not be seen as an alternative to the analysis of class *relations*: locations are always specified within relations.

To be "in" a class location is to be subjected to a set of mechanisms that impinge directly on the lives of individuals as they make choices and act in the world. There is some debate, as we will see in section 10.2 below, over what is most salient about these micro-mechanisms attached to the locations within class structures: should they primarily be thought of as determining the material interests of individuals? Or shaping their subjective understandings of the world? Or determining the basic resources they have available to pursue their interests? In any event, to develop a concept of class at the micro-level of analysis is to elaborate the concept in terms of the mechanisms that directly affect individuals within class locations.

The term "class structure," then, is the way of designating the set of class relations and locations within different units of analysis. One can speak, for example, of the class structure of a firm. Some firms are run by a single capitalist entrepreneur who hires a few managers and a homogeneous set of workers. Such a firm has a quite different class structure from a large corporation, with a hierarchically differentiated managerial structure, an external board of directors representing rentier capitalist stockholders and a segmented working class. One can also speak of the class structure of a country, or even, perhaps, of the class structure of the world capitalist system. Some capitalist societies, for example, will have a huge middle class, others a small middle class. The size of the middle class is an attribute of the society itself and depends upon the specific way in which all of the firms of that society are organized and interconnected. All capitalist societies will have state apparatuses and private firms, and among private firms some will be small and some large. The size of the "middle class" in the society as a whole will depend upon the specific mix of these kinds of meso-level employment organizations.

10.2 Basic concepts

The models we will be discussing revolve around a number of interconnected concepts of class analysis: class structure, class location, class interests, class experiences, class consciousness, class formation, class practices and class struggles. Some of these concepts, especially class structure, have been given considerable discussion in previous chapters, so we will not discuss all of them in detail here.

Class structure and class location

I will use the term "class location" as a micro-level concept referring to the location of individuals (and sometimes families) within the structure of class relations, whereas I will use the term "class structure" as concept referring to the overall organization of class relations in some more macro-level of analysis, typically an entire society. To say that someone is "in" a managerial class location is to claim that they are embedded in a set of interindividual interactions (relations) in which they are empowered to give various kinds of commands either directly to their subordinates (i.e. supervisory powers) or indirectly via their control over production decisions. Class structures are aggregations of all of the relations among these micro-level class locations at some more macro-level of analysis.

Class formation

I will use the expression "class formation" either to designate a process (the process of class formation) or an outcome (*a* class formation). In both cases the expression refers to the formation of *collectively organized social forces within class structures in pursuit of class interests*. If class structures are defined by the *antagonistic* social relations *between* class locations, class formations are defined by *cooperative* social relations *within* class structures. Strong, solidaristic relations in which individuals are prepared to make significant sacrifices for collective goals would be one form of class formation, but class formation can also be more narrowly instrumental, without strong solidarities binding people together.

Class formations are important because they constitute a crucial link between class structure and class struggles. Of course, class struggles may also involve various kinds of conflict between people acting strictly as individuals in uncoordinated ways, but, since the capacity of individuals, especially those in exploited classes, to pursue their class interests is so weak when they act alone, people constantly attempt to forge various kinds of collectivities to enhance their capacity for struggle. In these terms, class *formations* are important above all because of the ways in which they shape class *capacities* and thus the balance of power within class struggles.

Understood in this way, the contrast between class structure and class formation is similar to the traditional Marxist distinction between a class *in itself* and a class *for itself*. The class in itself/for itself distinction, however, was linked to a teleological notion of the inevitable trajectory of class struggle within capitalism towards the full, revolutionary formation of the proletariat. The expression "class formation," in contrast, does not imply that the collectively organized social forces within a class structure have any inherent tendency to develop towards revolutionary organization around "fundamental" class interests. "Class formation" is thus a descriptive category which encompasses a wide range of potential variations. For any given class or group of class locations one can speak of "strong" or "weak" class formations; unitary or fragmented class formations; revolutionary, counterrevolutionary or reformist class formations.

Typically, class formations involve creating *formal* organizations (especially political parties and unions) which link together the people within and across different locations in a class structure, but class formation is by no means limited to formal organization. Any form of collectively constituted social relations which facilitate solidaristic action in pursuit of class interests is an instance of class formation. Informal social networks, social clubs, neighborhood associations, even churches, could under appropriate circumstances be elements of class formations. The extensive research on the role of social clubs in coordinating the interests of the ruling class, for example, should be regarded as documenting one aspect of bourgeois class formation.

Class formations should not be thought of as simply in terms of the forming social relations among people within homogeneous class locations in a class structure. The forging of solidaristic relations *across* the boundaries of the locations within a class structure are equally instances of the formation of collectively organized social forces within class structures. Class formation thus includes the formation of class *alliances* as well as the internal organization of classes as such. For example, "populism," to the extent that it provides a context for the pursuit of certain class interests, can be viewed as a form of class formation that forges solidaristic ties between the working class and certain other class locations, typically the petty bourgeoisie (especially small farmers in the American case).

Class practices

Class practices are activities engaged in by members of a class using class capacities in order to realize at least some of their class interests. "Practice" in these terms implies that the activity is *intentional* (i.e. it has a conscious goal); "class" practices implies that the goal is the realization of class-based interests. Class practices include such mundane activities as a worker selling labor on a labor market, a foreman disciplining a worker for poor performance or a stockholder buying stocks or voting in a stockholders' meeting. But class practices also include such things as participating in a strike or busting a union.

Class struggle

The term "class struggle" refers to organized forms of *antagonistic* class practices, i.e. practices that are directed *against* each other. While in the limiting case one might refer to a class struggle involving a single worker and a single capitalist, more generally class struggles involve collectivities of various sorts. Class formations, not atomized individuals, are the characteristic vehicles for class struggles. Class struggles, therefore, generally refer to relatively macro-phenomena. Given the antagonistic nature of the interests determined by class structures, class practices of individuals will have a strong tendency to develop into collective class struggles since the realization of the interests of members of one class generally imply confrontation against the interests of members of other classes.

Class consciousness

I will use the concept of class consciousness to refer to particular aspects of the subjectivity of individuals. Consciousness will thus be used as a strictly micro-concept. When it figures in macro-social explanations it does so by virtue of the ways it helps to explain individual choices and actions. Collectivities, in particular class formations, do not "have" consciousness in the literal sense, since they are not the kind of entities which have minds, which think, weigh alternatives, have preferences, etc. When the term "class consciousness" is applied to collectivities or organizations, therefore, it either refers to the patterned distribution of individual consciousnesses within the relevant aggregate, or it is a way of characterizing central tendencies. This is not to imply, of course, that supra-individual social mechanisms are unimportant, but simply that they should not be conceptualized within the category "consciousness." And it is also not to imply that the actual distribution of individual consciousnesses in a society is not of social significance and causal importance. It may well be; but a distribution of consciousnesses is not "consciousness."[1]

Understood in this way, to study "consciousness" is to study a particular aspect of the mental life of individuals, namely, those elements of a person's subjectivity which are *discursively accessible to the individual's own awareness*. Consciousness is thus counterposed to "unconsciousness" – the discursively inaccessible aspects of mental life. The elements of consciousness – beliefs, ideas, observations, information, theories, preferences – may not continually be in a person's awareness, but they are accessible to that awareness.

This conceptualization of consciousness is closely bound up with the problem of *will* and *intentionality* . To say that something is discursively

---

[1] This is by no means the only way that class consciousness has been understood in the Marxist tradition. In particular, Lukács (1971 [1922]) seems to attribute the category "class consciousness" to the class of workers as a collectivity, not to the empirical individuals who make up that class. For a discussion of Lukács' views on this see Wright (1985: 242).

accessible is to say that by an act of will people can make themselves aware of it. When people make choices over alternative courses of action, the resulting action is, at least in part, to be explained by the particular conscious elements that entered into the intentions of the actor making the choice. While the problem of consciousness is not reducible to the problem of intentionality, from the point of view of social theory one of the most important ways in which consciousness figures in social explanations is via the way it is implicated in the intentions and resulting choices of actions by actors.

This is not to suggest, of course, that the only way *subjectivity* is consequential is via intentional choices. A wide range of psychological mechanisms may directly influence behavior without passing through conscious intentions. Nor does the linkage of consciousness to intentionality and choice imply that in every social situation the most important determinants of outcomes operate through consciousness; it may well be that the crucial determinants are to be found in the processes which determine the range of possible courses of action open to actors rather than the conscious processes implicated in the choice among those alternatives. What is being claimed is that in order to fully understand the real mechanisms that link social structures to social practices, the subjective basis of the intentional choices made by the actors who live within those structures and engage in those practices must be investigated, and this implies studying consciousness.

Given this definition of "consciousness," "class" consciousness can be viewed as those aspects of consciousness *which have a distinctive class character*. To speak of the class "character" of consciousness implies two things. First, it means that the beliefs in question have a substantive class *content* – in one way or another, the beliefs are about class issues. For example, private ownership of means of production is a distinctive structural feature of capitalist class relations; the belief in the desirability of private ownership, therefore, could be viewed as having a class content. Secondly, the class character of consciousness refers to those aspects of consciousness which have effects on how individuals actually operate within a given structure of class relations and effects on those relations themselves. The class dimensions of consciousness are implicated in the intentions, choices and practices which have what might be termed "class-pertinent effects" in the world.

Both of these aspects of the "class character" of consciousness – the content of the beliefs and the effects of beliefs – are necessary if one is to describe something as "class consciousness." Beliefs about gender relations, for example, could have class pertinent effects if, for example, stereotypical beliefs about masculinity undermined solidarity between men and women in class struggles. Yet it would not be useful to describe gender ideologies as *aspects* of class consciousness, although they might certainly be relevant for explaining aspects of class consciousness and class struggle. To count as an aspect of class consciousness, then, the belief in question must *both* have a class content and have class-pertinent effects. If class structure is understood as a terrain of social relations that determine objective material interests of actors, and class struggle is understood as the forms of social practices which attempt to realize those interests, then class consciousness can be understood as the subjective processes with a class content that shape intentional choices with respect to those interests and struggles.

A potential point of terminological confusion needs to be clarified at this point. It is common in Marxist discussions to distinguish between workers who "are class conscious" from those that "are not class conscious." The generic expression "class consciousness" in such usage is being identified with a particular *type* of class consciousness. In the usage of the term I am proposing, this would be a form of class consciousness in which individuals have a relatively "true" and "consistent" understanding of their class interests. I am thus using the term class consciousness in a more general way to designate all forms of consciousness with a class content and class-pertinent effects, regardless of their faithfulness to real or objective interests. In order to specifically indicate the presence of a particular type of class consciousness, therefore, it will be necessary to employ suitable adjectives: proworking-class consciousness, anticapitalist class consciousness, revolutionary working-class consciousness and so forth. When I use the unmodified expression "class consciousness" it will always refer to the general domain of consciousness with a class content relevant to class practices. There will be no implication that such consciousness can always be evaluated as "true" or "false."

This way of understanding class consciousness suggests that the concept can be decomposed into several elements. Whenever people make conscious choices, three dimensions of subjectivity are implicated:[2]

1. Perceptions and observations
In one way or another, conscious choice involves processing information about the world. "Facts," however, are always filtered through categories

---

[2] These three dimensions are derived from Therborn's (1982) analysis of ideology as answers to three questions: what exists? What is possible? What is good?

and beliefs about "what exists." Some workers believe that their employers worry about the welfare of employees, while others believe that employers are only interested in their own profits. Such beliefs about the motivations of employers are an aspect of class consciousness because they are implicated in the way workers are likely to respond to various kinds of class practices of their employers. "Class consciousness," in these terms, involves the ways in which the perceptions of the facts of a situation have a class content and are thus consequential for class actions.

2. Theories of Consequences

Perceptions of the facts by themselves are insufficient to make choices; people also must have some understanding of the expected consequences of given choices of action. This implies that choices involve theories. These may be "practical" theories rather than abstractly formalized theories, they may have the character of "rules of thumb" rather than explanatory principles. One particularly important aspect of such theories is conceptions of what is possible. Workers may decide that there is no point is struggling to establish a union because it is impossible for such a struggle to succeed. "Impossible" does not mean, of course, that one could not try to form a union, but simply that the consequence of such an attempt would not be the desired outcome. Historically, working-class rejections of socialism and communism have as much to do with the belief that such radical alternatives to capitalism would never work or that they are unachievable because of the power of the dominant classes, as with the belief that alternatives to capitalism are undesirable.

3. Preferences

Knowing a person's perceptions and theories is still not enough to explain a particular conscious choice; in addition, of course, it is necessary to know preferences, that is, the evaluation of the desirability of those consequences. "Desirability," in this context, can mean desirable in terms of the material benefits to the person, but there is no necessary restriction of preferences to selfish or egotistical evaluations. Preferences can also involve deep commitment to the welfare of others based on a sense of shared identity and meaning. "Class identity" may therefore figure as a salient aspect of class consciousness insofar as it shapes the extent to which an individual's preferences include a concern for the well-being of other members of a class.

With this understanding of class consciousness, one can begin to develop fairly complex typologies of qualitatively distinct forms of class consciousness in terms of the ways in which perceptions, theories and preferences held by individuals advance or impede the pursuit of class interests. It is possible, for example, to distinguish between "hegemonic," "reformist," "oppositional" and "revolutionary" working-class consciousness in terms of particular combinations of perceptions, theories and preferences. This is essentially what the more sophisticated typologies of class consciousness have tried to do.

In the present study I will not attempt to elaborate a nuanced typology of forms of class consciousness. The data that we will employ could potentially be stretched to operationalize such typologies, but my general feeling is that the limitations of survey research methodology make it preferable to adopt relatively simple and straightforward variables. The measures of class consciousness which we will use, therefore, are designed to tap in a general way the extent to which individuals have attitudes that are consistent with working-class or capitalist-class interests.

Limitation, selection and transformation

In elaborating a micro-model of class consciousness and a macro-model of class formation we will describe the causal relations among the various elements of the models in terms of three different "modes of determination": limitation, selection and transformation. Let me first explain limitation and transformation.

Figure 10.3 illustrates the general abstract relation between limitation and transformation: structures impose limits on practices; practices transform the structures that so limit them. *Limits,* in this context, does not simply mean that given the existence of the social structure in question certain practices are absolutely impossible, i.e. they are "outside" of the limits. In the extreme case, certain forms of practice may become virtually impossible given the existence of a particular structure, but the concept of limits is meant to refer to the effects of the structure on the probabilities of all types of relevant practices occurring. The substantive claim being made when it is said that structures $-limit\rightarrow$ practices is that the structures impose on the actors within those structures various kinds of obstacles and facilitations, sanctions and incentives, risky options and easy opportunities, which make certain kinds of

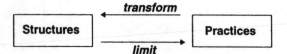

Figure 10.3 *The dialectic of structure and practice.*

practices much more likely and sustainable than others, and some simply impossible.

Transformation refers to the impact of practices on structures. Structures are objects of human intervention. Precisely because they limit action, people either try to change or to maintain them depending upon the effects of those structures on their interests. The structures in question may be embedded in the most macro-settings of social life such the state or the more micro-settings of families and workplaces. The feminist aphorism "the personal is political" is precisely a claim that practices can transform structures in the mundane, micro-arenas of everyday life.

The reciprocal effects "structures $-limit\rightarrow$ practices" and "practices $-transform\rightarrow$ structures" is one way of understanding the basic "dialectic" of structure and agency. To paraphrase Marx, human beings make history (practices transform structures), but not just as they please (structures limit practices). This way of thinking about structure and agency is thus neither a form of structuralism that marginalizes the human agent, nor a form of voluntarism that marginalizes structural constraints. The limits of social structures are real, but they are transformable by the conscious action of human agents.

What about "selection," the third mode of determination? Selection should be understood as "limits within limits." Selection enters the analysis when we are concerned with the interaction of more than one kind of structure with practices. This is illustrated in a general, abstract form in Figure 10.4. We now have two structures, X and Y. Structure X imposes *limits* on practices while structure Y *selects* practices within those limits. In the extreme case, structure Y may narrow the alternatives to the point where only one type of practice is possible. In such a case, we can say that structure Y *determines* the practice within the limits established by structure X. More typically, selection refers to a narrowing of possibilities. With these concepts in hand, we can turn to the problem of the causal models of class consciousness and class formation.

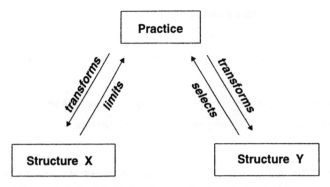

Figure 10.4 *Forms of determination: limits, selects, transforms.*

10.3 The micro-model

If class consciousness is understood in terms of the content of the perceptions, theories and preferences that shape intentional choices relevant to class interests, then the explanatory problem in the analysis of class consciousness is to elaborate the processes which shape the variability in the class content of consciousness. The theory of commodity fetishism in classical Marxism is precisely such a theory: it is an account of how the perceptions and theories of actors are imbued with a particular class content by virtue of the operation of commodity relations. The immediate lived experience of producers in a commodity producing society, the story goes, represents the social relations between people as relations between things (commodities), and this in turn generates the mental structures characterized as "fetishized consciousness." Such consciousness in turn, it is argued, plays an important role in conveying a sense of the permanence and naturalness of capitalism, thus impeding revolutionary projects for the transformation of capitalist society.

The micro-causal model of consciousness formation which we will discuss in this chapter is deliberately simple. Its purpose is to try to capture the most pervasive and systematic determinants at work, rather than to map the full range of complexities that may enter into the class consciousness formation process of any given individual. This bare-bones model is illustrated in Figure 10.5.

The model should be read as follows: class locations impose limits on the consciousness of individuals within those locations and on their class practices. Class consciousness, in turn, selects specific forms of practice within the limits imposed by class locations. Class practices, then, trans-

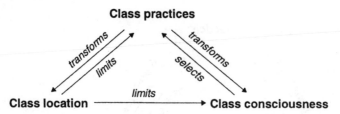

Figure 10.5 *Micro-model of class location, class consciousness and class practice.*

form both class consciousness and class locations. Let me explain each of these causal connections:

1. Class locations − *limits* → class consciousness

Incumbency in a given class location renders certain forms of class consciousness much more likely than others. In the extreme case, certain forms of consciousness may become virtually impossible to sustain for individuals in certain class locations, but the concept of limits need not imply any absolute barrier to any form of consciousness. Capitalists are much more likely to believe in the virtues of unfettered capitalism than are workers, but some capitalists (Frederick Engels, for example) do become revolutionary communists; industrial workers are more likely than capitalists to believe in the desirability of strong unions and work-place participation of workers in management decisions, but some workers believe that nonmanagement employees have no business interfering with the functioning of free markets and the powers of employers. Living within a given class location increases the probability that certain perceptions, certain theories of how society works and certain values will seem more immediately credible than others, but a wide range of other causal factors can intervene to counter these probabilities. Forms of consciousness which seem unlikely by virtue of the class location − *limits* → class consciousness may thus become much more likely because of presence of other, contingent, causal processes.

2. Class locations − *limits* → individual class practices

In a fairly straightforward way, class locations significantly shape the feasible set of what individuals in those locations can do to satisfy their material interests. The crucial mechanism through which being in a class location limits the feasible set of practices is through access to the resources needed to pursue specific courses of action. Being in a working-class location, and thus being deprived of ownership of means of production, means that in order to obtain subsistence both in the present and in the future it is generally necessary to look for paid employment. Certain other options may be relatively easy, at least for some people in working-class locations in some countries. Criminal activities may be an option, or living off welfare. Other options may be more difficult, but still not absolutely impossible. It is generally quite difficult for a worker to get loans to start a business, and most workers are not in a position to save sufficient income to be able to acquire future subsistence in the form of returns on investments, but both of the options are possible under unusual circumstances. More frequently, some workers can invest in various kinds of training which has the potential of enhancing their material interests. And of course, workers may have the option of joining unions and engaging in various kinds of collective practices in pursuit of class interests. The relative ease and difficulty of these alternative courses of action is what is meant by "limits" in the expression: class location *— limits →* class practices.

3. Class consciousness *— selects →* individual class practices
While class locations may shape the feasible set of class practices, the actual choice of specific practices still depends upon the perceptions, theories and values of individuals. In this sense class consciousness selects practices within limits imposed by class locations.

4. Individual class practices *— transforms →* class locations
The most obvious sense in which an individual's class practices can transform that individual's class location is through class mobility. But class practices can also transform various concrete class-pertinent features of jobs – the degree of authority, autonomy, pay – without generating class mobility in the usual sense. When an individual worker engages in various forms of resistance to the domination of a boss, that worker transforms aspects of his or her class location. When employers introduce new technologies and work organization which enhance their capacity to monitor the labor process and extract labor effort from workers, they have engaged in a class practice which transforms a specific property of the class relation to their employees.

5. Individual class practices *— transforms →* class consciousness
One of the classic themes in Marxist theories of consciousness is the idea that in the capitalist labor process workers are constantly producing

themselves while they are producing commodities. This is one of the central themes of Michael Burawoy's numerous studies of workers on the shopfloor (Burawoy 1979, 1985, 1992; Burawoy and Wright 1990). The norms and values of workers, he argues, are not mainly the result of deep socialization outside of the sphere of work, but are generated within production by the practices workers adopt in their efforts to cope with the dilemmas of their situation. Of particular salience in these terms are the ways in which individual participation in class struggles of various sorts contributes to the formation of solidaristic preferences. More generally the claim is that the perceptions of alternatives, theories, and values held by individuals situated in different class locations is not just shaped by where they are but by what they do.

Our empirical objectives in the next chapter are particularly concerned with the relationship between class location and class consciousness. In this micro-model, class location affects class consciousness through two routes: one via the direct impact of being in a class location on consciousness, and the other via the way class locations affect class practices which in turn affect consciousness. One way of thinking about these two causal streams is that in the former concerns things that *happen to people* and the latter concerns things *people do*.

By virtue of being in a class location (understood both as direct and mediated locations in the sense discussed in chapter 7) a person is subjected to certain experiences with greater or lesser probability. Insofar as class location determines access to material resources, being in a class location shapes the mundane material conditions of existence – how comfortable is daily life, how physically and mentally taxing is work, how hungry one is. Class location significantly determines the probability of being the victim of different kinds of crime. Class locations shape the kind of neighborhood one is likely to live in and the nature of the social networks in which one is embedded, and all of these may have an impact on class consciousness. Above all, class locations impose on people a set of trade-offs and dilemmas they face in the pursuit of their material interests. Capitalists have to worry about challenges from competitors, how to extract the maximum labor from their employees, and alternative uses of their investment resources. Workers have to worry about finding a job, about unemployment and job security, about skill obsolescence and job injury, about making ends meet with a paycheck. To say that members of a class share common class interests means that they objectively face similar strategic choices for advancing their material welfare. Such a strategic environment continually generates experiences which shape a person's beliefs about the world.

People do not, however, simply live in a strategic environment; they also adopt specific strategies. And what they actually do also shapes their consciousness. Managers do not simply confront the problems of eliciting work effort from subordinates and impressing their superiors. They also issue orders, discipline subordinates and suck up to higher management and owners. Workers do not simply face the strategic problem of individually competing with fellow workers or solidaristically struggling for higher wages; they also join unions, cross picket lines and quit jobs to find better work. Class consciousness, then, is shaped, on the one hand, by the material conditions and *choices people face* (class location −*limits*→ consciousness) and, on the other, by the *choices people actually make* (class location −*limits*→ practices −*transform*→ consciousness). Consciousness shapes choices; choices change consciousness.

Both of these causal paths have a crucial temporal dimension. Class consciousness is not the instantaneous product of one's present class location and class practices. At any given point in time, consciousness about anything is the result of a life-time history of things that happen to people and things they do, of both choices faced and choices made, of interests and experiences. Most obviously, there is the life-time biographical trajectory of the individual's locations within the class structure (the classical sociological problem of inter- and intra-generational class mobility), but other experiences such as unemployment or strikes are also relevant.

A fully developed theory of consciousness formation would also include an account of the psychological mechanisms through which interests and experiences actually shape perceptions of alternatives, theories and preferences. It is not enough to identify a salient set of experiences and interests through which class locations limit class consciousness; it is also necessary to understand how these limits work through psychological processes within the individual. Jon Elster's (1985: ch. 8) accounts of such cognitive mechanisms as wishful thinking and adaptive preference formation (cognitive dissonance) would be examples.

I will not attempt to elaborate an account of these psychological mechanisms; they will thus remain largely a "black box." Implicitly in my arguments, however, is a fairly naïve form of learning theory which underlies most sociological accounts of the effects of social conditions on consciousness. The basic assumption is that the probability that people will hold beliefs congruent with their class location depends upon the extent to which their life experiences reinforce or undermine such beliefs. All other things being equal, the more a person's life is bound up with a single, coherent set of class experiences, the more likely it is that this person's consciousness will be imbued with a corresponding class content. Perceptions, theories and preferences are the result of learning from experiences, and, to the extent that one's class experiences all push in the same direction, class consciousness will tend to develop a coherent class content.[3]

But, it might be objected, a set of class experiences, no matter how consistent, is not enough to predict a form of consciousness. Experiences are not translated directly into consciousness; they must first be *interpreted*, and interpretations always presuppose some kind of political and cultural context. The same micro-class experiences and interests with the same psychological mechanisms could generate different forms of consciousness depending upon the broader historical context of politics and culture. To understand these issues we must now turn to the macro-model and then to the interaction between the macro- and micro-levels of analysis.

10.4 The macro-model

In the macro-model our object of investigation is no longer individual class consciousness as such, but collective forms of class formation and class struggle. The model is illustrated in Figure 10.6. As in the micro-model, the causal logic revolves around the way structures impose limits on practices and practices in turn transform structures. In the macro-model class structures impose limits on class formations and class struggles. Within those limits, class formations select specific forms of

---

[3] This implicit learning theory of the black-box of consciousness formation is quite similar to Therborn's (1982) view that "ideological interpellation" is the result of the patterns of subjection and qualification which an individual experiences by virtue of the affirmations and sanctions connected to different social positions. It is also close to Bourdieu's (1985) view that daily lived experiences constitute a set of common conditions that generate common conditionings, although Bourdieu is more concerned with the formation of *non*conscious dimensions of subjectivity ("dispositions") than consciousness as such. Bourdieu's concept of *class habitus* is meant to encompass the full range of nonconscious subjective effects on actors that result from such common conditionings/experiences. A class habitus is defined as a common set of dispositions to act in particular ways that are shaped by a common set of conditionings (subject-forming experiences) rooted in a class structure.

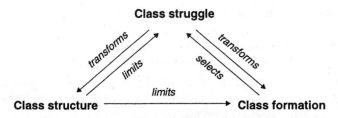

Figure 10.6 *Macro-model of class structure, class formation and class struggle.*

class struggle. Class struggles transform both class formations and class structures. Let us look at each of these connections.

1. Class structure − *limits*→ class formation

To say that class structures impose limits on class formations means that the class structure imposes obstacles and opportunities with which any agent attempting to forge class formations must contend. Within any given class structure, certain class formations will thus be relatively easy to create and are likely to be stable once created, others will be more difficult and unstable, and certain class formations may be virtually impossible. As Przeworski (1985: 47) puts it: "Processes of formation of workers into a class are inextricably fused with the processes of organization of surplus labor. As a result, a number of alternative organizations of classes is possible at any moment of history."

Three kinds of mechanisms are central to this limiting process: (1) the nature of the *material interests* generated by class structures, (2) the patterns of *identities* that emerge from the lived experiences of people in different locations in the class structure and (3) the nature of the resources distributed in the class structure which make certain potential alliances across locations in the class structure more or less attractive. The first two of these are closely tied to the micro-analysis of class locations while the third is more strictly macro- in character.

Material interests. The argument about material interests is the most straightforward. The central thesis of the Marxist theory of class structure is that the underlying mechanisms of exploitation in an economic structure powerfully shape the material interests of people in that structure. Consider the matrix of locations within the class structure which we have adopted in this book. This matrix can be viewed as a map of the degree of inherent antagonism of material interests of people located in different places in the structure: locations relatively "close" to each other will have relatively overlapping material interests whereas more distant locations will have more antagonistic interests. All things being equal, class formations that link locations with relatively similar material interests are thus easier to create than class formations that link locations with quite disparate interests. From the vantage point of working-class locations in the class structure (the lower right-hand corner of the matrix), as you move towards the upper left-hand corner of the matrix (expert managers among employees, and capitalists among property owners) class interests become progressively more antagonistic, and thus class formations joining workers with such locations more and more difficult to forge. This does not mean, it must be emphasized, that material interests alone determine class formations; but they do define a set of obstacles with which parties, unions and other agents of class formation have to contend in their efforts to consolidate and reproduce particular patterns of class formation.

Identities. The second mechanism through which class structures shape the possibilities of class formations centers on the ways class affects the class identities of people, the ways people define who is similar to and who is different from themselves, who are their potential friends and potential enemies within the economic system. As in the case of material interests, it would be expected that class formations that attempt to bind people together with similar identities are likely to be easier to accomplish and more stable than class formations which combine highly disparate and potentially conflicting identities. All things being equal, it would be predicted that class identities would more or less follow the same contours as class interests, and thus common identity would reinforce common interests as a basis for forging class formations.

However, it is rarely the case that all things are equal. Class identities are heavily shaped by idiosyncrasies of personal biographies and by historical patterns of struggles, as well as by the intersection of class with other forms of social collectivity (ethnicity, religion, language, region, etc.). Thus, while it is plausible to argue that there should be some rough association between the objectively given material interests of actors and the kinds of class identities they develop, there is no reason for these two aspects of class to be isomorphic. Class interests and class identities, therefore, may not reinforce each other in linking class structures to class formations.

Resources. The third mechanism that underlies the ways in which class structures limit class formations centers on the effects of the macro-attributes of class structures, in particular the distribution of resources across classes which are relevant for class formations and class struggles. For working-class formations, probably the most important resource is sheer numbers of people, although organizational and financial resources may also be important. As Przeworski (1985, ch. 3) and Przeworski and Sprague (1986) have stressed, in deciding which potential alliances to nourish, the leadership of working-class electoral parties pays particular attention to the potential gains in electoral strength posed by forging different sorts of alliances. The attractiveness of worker-peasant alliances in revolutionary movements in Third World countries or of worker-petty bourgeois alliances in nineteenth-century North American populism is significantly shaped by the power of numbers.

Numbers, however, are not the whole story. Financial resources may also be crucial to the strategies of actors attempting to build class formations. The financial resources available to the middle class give them considerable leverage in forging particular kinds of alliances and coalitions. One of the reasons why working-class parties may put more energy into attracting progressive elements of the middle class than in mobilizing the poorest and most marginalized segments of the population is that the former can potentially make greater contributions.

The combination of these three class-based mechanisms – exploitation→ material interests; lived experiences in a class structure→class identities; distribution of class resources→attractiveness of potential alliances – determines the underlying probabilities that different potential class formations will occur. Figure 10.7 illustrates a range of possible class formations that might be constructed on the same basic class structure. The first two of these follow the contours of the central tendencies generated by the class structure itself: class formations directly mirror the exploitation generated interest configuration. In the first model, a middle-class formation is a buffer between working-class and bourgeois-class formations; in the second model, a pure polarization exists between two "camps." In the third model, the structural division between workers and contradictory locations has been severely muted in the process of class formation: workers have been incorporated into a middle-class ideological block. The fourth and fifth models are perhaps

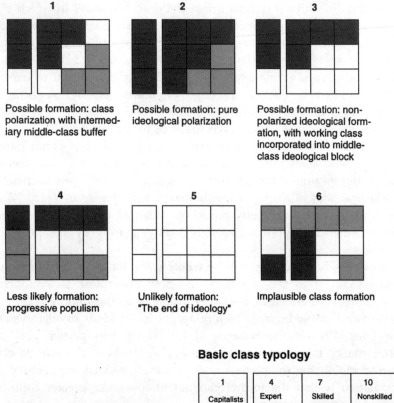

Figure 10.7 *Formable and unformable class formations.*

less likely, but still consistent with the underlying class structure: in model 4 one class formation of capitalists and managers confronts a "populist coalition" of workers, intellectuals (nonmanagerial experts and semi-experts) and petty bourgeois, with a weak intermediary formation; in model 5 a broad cross-class ideological consensus has been forged in which no clear ideological class coalitions appear. Finally, model 6 represents a structurally very improbable class formation: workers, managers and capitalists collectively organized into a working class coalition while experts and petty bourgeois are organized into a bourgeois coalition.

2. Class structure −*limits*→ class struggle

The simplest sense in which class structure limits class struggles is that without the existence of certain kinds of class relations, the relevant actors for certain kinds of class struggles simply do not exist. You cannot have struggles between workers and capitalists without the existence of capitalist class relations. But class structures shape the probabilities of different forms of class struggles in more subtle ways as well. As we discussed in chapter 5, different class structures are characterized by different degrees of permeability of class boundaries, and this will affect the plausibility of people in exploited classes of individualistic strategies pursuing material interests. Where individualistic strategies are closed off (i.e. boundaries are highly impermeable), collective organization and collective struggle become more likely. Class structures also vary in the degree of polarization of material conditions associated with the various dimensions of exploitation. Again, it would be expected that militant forms of struggle are more likely under relatively polarized material conditions than under relatively egalitarian conditions. In these and other ways class structures limit class struggles.

3. Class formation −*selects*→ class struggle

Class structures may set limits on class struggles via the ways in which class structures determine the interests and opportunities of actors, but actual struggles depend heavily upon the collective organizations available for contending actors. It is a telling fact about repressive right-wing political regimes that they are concerned above all with repressing collective organization, especially unions and parties. When such organizations are destroyed, struggles of all sorts are themselves much more easily controlled. It is not, however, merely the sheer existence of organizations of class formation that matter; the specific form of those organizations also has systematic effects on patterns of class struggle. As Joel Rogers (1990) has argued, the degree of centralization or decentralization, unity or fragmentation of the organizational structures of the labor movement has profound consequences for the kinds of working-class struggles in capitalist societies.

4. Class struggles − *transforms* → **class structure**
One of the central objects of class struggle is the class structure itself. In the extreme case, this constitutes and object of revolutionary transformation, when particular forms of class relation are destroyed. More commonly, class struggles transform class structures by transforming particular properties of class relations – the degree of exploitation and polarization of material conditions, the range of powers freely exercised by owners and managers, and the barriers to permeability of boundaries, to name only a few examples. Struggles over the redistributive practices of the state, over the right of capitalists to pollute, or over the representation of workers on the boards of directors of firms are, in this sense, struggles to transform class structures since they bear on the class powers of capitalists and workers.

5. Class struggles − *transforms* → **class formations**
Class struggles are not simply over the material interests rooted in class structures. Class struggles are also directed at the organizational and political conditions which facilitate or impede the struggles themselves. This is the central theme of Przeworski's (1985: 71) analysis of classes when he writes:

> (1) classes are formed as an effect of struggles; (2) the process of class formation is a perpetual one: classes are continually organized, disorganized, and reorganized; (3) class formation is an effect of the totality of struggles in which multiple historical actors attempt to organize the same people as class members, as members of collectivities defined in other terms, sometimes simply as members of "the society."

Working-class struggles to organize unions and state repression of the labor movement are both instances of class struggles transforming class formations.

10.5 Putting the micro- and macro-models together

At several points we have already touched on the interconnection between the micro- and macro-levels of analysis. The claim that class structure limits class formation, for example, depends in part on the arguments about how the material interests and experiences of individuals are shaped at the micro-level by their class locations. Equally, the micro-level claim that class locations limit class practices depends in part on the argument that individuals in different locations face different opportunities and dilemmas in deciding how best to pursue their material interests. Opportunities and dilemmas, however, are not strictly micro-concepts; they depend crucially on properties of the social structure as a whole.

There is a tradition in social theory, sometimes marching under the banner of "methodological individualism," that insists that macro-phenomena are *reducible* to micro-phenomena. Elster (1985: 11) defends this claim explicitly when he defines methodological individualism as "the doctrine that all social phenomena – their structure and their change – are in principle explicable in ways that only involve individuals – their properties, their goals, their beliefs and their actions. To go from social institutions and aggregate patterns of behavior to individuals is the same kind of operation as going from cells to molecules." While it may be necessary for pragmatic reasons to continue to use macro concepts like "class structure," in principle, methodological individualists believe, these could be replaced with purely micro-concepts.

Most sociologists reject this kind of reductionism, preferring instead to talk loosely of the "interaction" of macro- and micro-levels of analysis. Macro-social phenomena are seen as imposing real constraints of various sorts on individuals, constraints which cannot be simply dissolved into the actions of individuals; but individuals are seen as nevertheless making real choices that have real consequences, including consequences for the stability and transformation of the macro-phenomena themselves.

One way of thinking about this micro/macro interaction is illustrated in Figure 10.8: micro-level processes constitute what can be called the *micro-foundations* of the macro-phenomena while macro-level processes *mediate* the micro-processes.

One of the standard ways in which social theorists defend holism against attempts at individualistic reductionism is to state that "the whole is greater than the sum of the parts." The whole, sociologists are fond of saying, has "emergent properties" which cannot be identified with the parts taken one by one and added up. If this were not true, then an adequate description of each part taken separately would be sufficient to generate an adequate description of the whole. Yet it is also true that, without the parts, there would be no whole, and this suggests that in some sense the parts taken together do constitute the whole. These two observations – that the whole is greater than the *sum* of the parts and yet the parts *collectively constitute* the whole – can be reconciled by stating that "the whole equals the sum of the parts *plus* all of the interactions among the parts." The "emergent properties" of

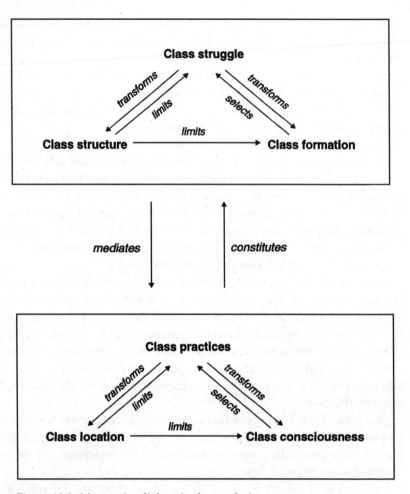

Figure 10.8 *Macro-micro linkage in class analysis.*

the whole can then be identified as properties resulting from the interaction of the parts, not simply their serially aggregated individual properties.

To study the micro-foundations of macro-phenomena is thus to study the ways in which wholes are constituted by the sum and interactions of their parts. Consider class structure. Class structures are constituted by individuals-in-class-locations and all of the interactions among those individuals by virtue of the locations they occupy. To study the micro-foundations of the class structure, therefore, is to explore the ways in which attributes of individuals, their choices and actions, help explain

A general framework   213

the nature of these locations and interconnections. Workers do not own means of production and thus seek employment in order to obtain subsistence; capitalists own means of production and thus seek employees to use those means of production in order to obtain profits. The class relation between worker and capitalist is constituted by the actions of individuals with these attributes (owning only labor power and owning capital) and these preferences (seeking subsistence and seeking profits). The totality of such relations, resulting from these interconnected individual attributes and choices, constitutes the macro-phenomenon we call "class structure."

In a similar way, class formations are constituted by the participation of individuals with varying forms of class consciousness in collective associations organized to realize class interests. Studying the micro foundations of such collective organization involves understanding the process by which solidarities, built around different forms of consciousness, are forged among individuals, and the ways in which this facilitates their cooperation in the collective pursuit of class interests. Different kinds of class formations are grounded in different forms of individual consciousness and solidaristic interdependency.

Finally, to study the micro-foundations of class struggles is to explore the ways in which the attributes, choices and actions of individuals, occupying specific class locations and participating in specific class formations, constitute the collective actions that are the hallmark of class struggle. Take a prototypical example of a class struggle, a strike by a union. The search for micro-foundations insists that it is never satisfactory to restrict the analysis to the "union" as a collective entity making choices and engaging in practices directed at "capitalists" or "management." Since the union as an organized social force (an instance of class formation) is constituted by its members and their interactions, to understand the actions of a union – the decision to call a strike for example – we must understand the attributes, choices and interactions of the individuals constituting that union. This would involve discussions of such things as the free rider problem within unions, the conditions for solidarity to emerge within the membership, the relationship between rank-and-file members and leadership in shaping the decisions of the union, and so on. Class struggles can thus be said to be constituted by the class practices of the individuals within class formations and class structures and all of the interactions among those class practices.

Exploring the micro-foundations of macro-phenomena is only one half of the micro/macro linkage in Figure 10.8. The other half consists of the ways in which macro-phenomena can be said to mediate the effects of micro-processes. To say that the macro- mediates the micro- means that the specific effects of micro-processes depend upon the macro-setting within which they take place. For example, at the core of the micro-model of consciousness formation in Figure 10.5 is the claim that the class consciousness of individuals is shaped by their class location. These micro-level effects, however, are significantly shaped in various ways by macro-level conditions and processes. Occupying a working-class location in a class structure within which the working class is collectively disorganized has different consequences for the likely consciousness of individuals than occupying the same class location under conditions of the cohesive political formation of the class. This is more than the simple claim that macro-conditions of class formation themselves have effects on consciousness; it implies that the causal impact of individual class location on consciousness is enhanced or weakened depending upon the macro-conditions.

In formal terms, this means that the model argues for the interactive effects of micro- and macro-factors rather than simply additive effects. Suppose, for example, we wanted to represent in a simple equation the effects of class location and class formation on class consciousness. The simple additive model would like this:

Consciousness = a + B_1[Class Location] + B_2[Class formation]

where B_1 and B_2 are coefficients which measure the linear effects of these variables on consciousness. The interactive model – the model of macro-mediation of the micro – adds a multiplicative term:

Consciousness = a + B_1[Class Location] + B_2[Class formation] + B_3[Location × formation]

where B_3 indicates the extent to which the effects of class locations vary under different macro-conditions of class formation. It could happen, of course, in a specific empirical setting that B_3 is insignificant, indicating that the effects of class location are invariant under different forms of class formation.

10.6 Using the models in empirical research

The model laid out in Figure 10.8 is incomplete in a variety of ways. First, the model is highly underelaborated in terms of the specification of the relevant range of variation of some of the elements in the model. Thus, while I have proposed a detailed account of the variations in "class locations" in the micro-model that are relevant for explaining class consciousness, the discussions of the relevant range of variation of "individual class practices" in the micro-model or of "class formation" or even "class structure" in the macro-model are quite underdeveloped. Even more significantly, there is no specification of the actual magnitudes of the causal relations included in the model. For example, class location is said to impose "limits" on individual class consciousness, but the model itself leaves open the nature and scope of these limits. The macro-processes of class formation are said to mediate the micro-processes of consciousness formation, yet the model is silent on the precise form and magnitude of these interactive effects. There is thus nothing in the model which would indicate what the relative probabilities of procapitalist or anticapitalist consciousness would be for people in different class locations, nor how these probabilities would themselves vary under different macro-conditions of class formation. Finally, the model is incomplete because it restricts itself to class-related determinants of the elements in the model. A complete theory of class consciousness and class formation would have to include a wide range of other causal processes – from the nature of various nonclass forms of social division (race, ethnicity, gender), to religion, to geopolitics.

Given these limitations, these models should not be seen as defining a general *theory* of class consciousness and class formation, but rather as a *framework for defining an agenda* of problems for empirical research within class analysis. In the multivariate empirical studies of class consciousness and class formation in chapter 11, therefore, we will not directly "test" the models as such. The models constitute a framework within which a range of alternative hypotheses can be formulated and tested, but the framework itself will not be subjected to any direct tests.

11. Class structure, class consciousness and class formation in Sweden, the United States and Japan

This chapter will try to apply some of the elements of the models elaborated in the previous chapter to the empirical study of class formation and class consciousness in three developed capitalist countries – the United States, Sweden and Japan.[1] More specifically, the investigation has three main objectives: first, to examine the extent to which the overall relationship between class locations and class consciousness is broadly consistent with the logic of the class structure analysis we have been using throughout this book; second to compare the patterns of class formation in the three countries; and third to examine the ways in which the micro, multivariate models of consciousness formation vary across the three countries. The first of these tasks centers on exploring the "class location − *limits*→ class consciousness" segment of the model, the second focuses on the "class structure − *limits*→ class formation" segment, and the third centers on the "macro − *mediates*→ micro" aspect of the model.

In the next section we will discuss the strategy we will deploy for measuring class consciousness. This will be followed in section 11.2 with a more detailed discussion of the empirical agenda and the strategies of data analysis. Sections 11.3 to 11.5 will then present the results of the data analysis.

---

[1] In the original edition of *Class Counts*, there are two additional empirical chapters on problems of class consciousness, the first dealing with the interaction between class and state employment in shaping class consciousness, and the second on the relationship between individual class biographies and class consciousness. These had to be dropped from the present edition because of space constraints.

11.1 Measuring class consciousness

Class consciousness is notoriously hard to measure. The concept is meant to denote subjective properties which impinge on conscious choosing activity which has a class content. The question then arises whether or not the subjective states which the concept taps are really only "activated" under conditions of meaningful choice situations, which in the case of class consciousness would imply above all situations of class struggle. There is no necessary reason to assume that these subjective states will be the same when respondents are engaged in the kind of conscious choosing that occurs in an interview. Choosing responses on a survey is a different practice from choosing how to relate to a shopfloor conflict, and the forms of subjectivity which come into play are quite different. The interview setting is itself, after all, a social relation, and this relation may influence the responses of respondents out of deference, or hostility or some other reaction. Furthermore, it is always possible that there is not simply slippage between the way people respond to the artificial choices of a survey and the real choices of social practices, but that there is a systematic inversion of responses. As a result, it has been argued by some (e.g. Marshall 1983) that there is little value in even attempting to measure class consciousness through survey instruments.

These problems are serious ones, and potentially undermine the value of questionnaire studies of class consciousness. My assumption, however, is that there is at least some stability in the cognitive processes of people across the artificial setting of an interview and the real life setting of class struggle and that, in spite of the possible distortions of structured interviews, social surveys can potentially measure these stable elements. While the ability of a survey may be very limited to predict for any given individual the way they would think and behave in a "real life setting," surveys may be able to provide a broad image of how class structure is linked to likely class behaviors.

Deciding to use a questionnaire to tap class consciousness, of course, leaves open precisely what kinds of questionnaire items best measure this concept. Here again there is a crucial choice to be made: should questionnaires be mainly built around open-ended questions or pre-formatted, fixed-option questions. Good arguments can be made that open-ended questions provide a more subtle window on individuals' real cognitive processes. When you ask a person, "What do you think are the main causes of poverty in America?" individuals are more likely to reveal their real understandings of the problem than when you ask the fixed-option question, "Do you strongly agree, somewhat agree, somewhat disagree or strongly disagree with the statement 'One of the main reasons for poverty is that some people are lazy and unmotivated to work hard'?" Fixed-option questions risk putting words into people's mouths, giving them alternatives which have no real salience to them.

On the other hand, open-ended questions often pose severe problems in consistent coding and data analysis. There have been innumerable sociological surveys with ambitious open-ended questions which have never been systematically analyzed because the coding problems proved insurmountable. Open-ended responses often are used primarily anecdotally to add illustrative richness to an analysis, but they frequently are abandoned in the quantitative analysis itself.

The problems with coding open-ended questionnaire responses are greatly compounded in cross-national comparative research. Even if one could somehow devise a common coding protocol for open-ended questions in different languages and cultural contexts, it would be virtually impossible to insure that the coding procedures were applied in a rigorously comparable manner across countries. This has proven exceedingly difficult even in the case of coding occupational descriptions into internationally agreed-upon categories. It would be much more difficult for open-ended responses to attitude questions. In the comparative class analysis project we found it hard enough to get the projects in different countries to stick to a common questionnaire. It would be virtually impossible to enforce acceptable standards of comparability to the coding of open-ended questions.

Thus, while it is probably the case that open-ended questions provide a deeper understanding of an individual's consciousness, for pragmatic reasons our analysis will be restricted to closed questions. In general in research of this kind, systematic superficiality is preferable to chaotic depth.

The survey used in this research contains a wide variety of attitude items, ranging from questions dealing directly with political issues, to normative issues on equal opportunity for women, to explanations for various kinds of social problems. Many of these items can be interpreted as indicators of class consciousness, but for most of them the specific class-content of the items is indirect and presupposes fairly strong theoretical assumptions. For example, Marxists often argue that the distinction between explaining social problems in individualist terms ("the poor are poor because they are lazy") instead of social structural terms ("the poor are poor because of the lack of jobs and education") is an aspect of class consciousness. While this claim may be plausible, it does require a fairly strong set of assumptions to interpret the second of these explanations of poverty as an aspect of anticapitalist consciousness. For the purposes of this investigation, therefore, it seemed advisable to focus on those items with the most direct class implications, and to aggregate these questions into a fairly simple, transparent class consciousness scale.

Five attitude items from the questionnaire will be used to construct the scale. These items are all questions in which respondents were asked whether they strongly agreed, agreed, disagreed or strongly disagreed with each of the following statements:

1 Corporations benefit owners at the expense of workers and consumers.
2 During a strike, management should be prohibited by law from hiring workers to take the place of strikers.
3 Many people in this country receive much less income than they deserve.
4 Large corporations have too much power in American/Swedish society today.
5 The nonmanagement employees in your place of work could run things effectively without bosses.

The responses to each question are given a value of -2 for the strong procapitalist response, -1 for the somewhat procapitalist response, 0 for "Don't know," +1 for the somewhat anticapitalist response and +2 for the strong anticapitalist response. The scores on these individual items were combined to construct a simple additive scale going from -10 (procapitalist extreme value) to +10 (anticapitalist extreme value). (For methodological details on the construction of this variable, see Wright 1997: 450–452.)

11.2 The empirical agenda

Class locations and class consciousness

Before we engage in the detailed discussion of the patterns of class formation and the multivariate models of class consciousness, it will be useful to examine the extent to which the overall relationship between class locations and class consciousness is consistent with the basic logic of the concept of class structure we have been exploring. To recapitulate the basic idea, class structures in capitalist societies can be analyzed in terms of the intersection of three ways people are linked to the process of material exploitation: through the ownership of property, through the positions within authority hierarchies, and through possession of skills and expertise. If class locations defined in this way systematically shape the material interests and lived experiences of individuals, and if these interests and experiences in turn shape class consciousness, then there should be a systematic relationship between class location and class consciousness. Underlying this chain of reasoning is the assumption that, all things being equal, there will be at least a weak tendency for incumbents in class locations to develop forms of class consciousness consistent with the material interests linked to those locations. The perceptions of those interests may be partial and incomplete, but in general, distorted perceptions of interests will take the form of deviations from a full understanding of interests, and thus, on average, there should be a systematic empirical association of class location and consciousness of interests.

In terms of the empirical indicators of class consciousness we are using in this chapter, this argument about the link between class location and consciousness suggests that, as one moves from exploiter to exploited along each of the dimensions of the class structure matrix, the ideological orientation of individuals should become more critical of capitalist institutions. If we also assume that these effects are cumulative (i.e. being exploited on two dimensions will tend to make one more anticapitalist than being exploited on only one), then we can form a rather ambitious empirical hypothesis: Along each of the rows and columns of the class-structure matrix, there should be a monotonic relationship between the values on the anticapitalism scale and class location. In terms of the 12–location class structure matrix with which we have been working, this implies three more specific hypotheses:

> *Hypothesis 1.* The working-class location in the matrix should be the most anticapitalist, the capitalist-class location the most pro-capitalist.

> *Hypothesis 2.* Within the owner portion of the matrix, the attitudes should monotonically become more procapitalist as you move from the petty bourgeoisie to the capitalist class.

> *Hypothesis 3.* Within the employee portion of the matrix attitudes

should become monotonically more procapitalist as you move from the working class corner of the matrix to the expert-manager corner table along both the rows and the columns.

The exploitation-centered class concept does not generate clear hypotheses about the class consciousness of the petty bourgeoisie compared to the contradictory class locations among employees. There is no clear reason to believe that the petty bourgeoisie should be more or less procapitalist than those wage earners who occupy a contradictory relationship to the process of exploitation, managers and experts. On the one hand, petty bourgeois are owners of the means of production and thus have a clear stake in private property; on the other hand, they are often threatened and dominated by capitalist firms in both commodity markets and credit markets, and this can generate quite a lot of hostility. Given that the questions we are using in the class consciousness scale deal with attitudes towards capitalism and capitalists, not private property in general, there may be many petty bourgeois who take a quite anticapitalist stance. In any case, the framework makes no general predictions about whether the petty bourgeoisie will be more or less anticapitalist than the "middle class" (i.e. contradictory class locations among employees).

Class formation

In the previous chapter we defined class formation in terms of solidaristic social relations within class structures. Individuals occupy locations in class structures which impose on them a set of constraints and opportunities on how they can pursue their material interests. In the course of pursuing those interests, collectivities of varying degrees of coherence and durability are forged. The study of class formation involves the investigation of such collectivities – of their compositions, their strategies, their organizational forms, etc.

The research on class formation reported in this chapter is quite limited and focuses entirely on the problem of the class composition of what I will call "ideological class formations." Our approach will be largely inductive and descriptive. The central task will be to map out for the United States, Sweden and Japan the ways in which the various locations in the class structure become grouped into more or less ideologically homogeneous blocks.

The research is thus, at best, an indirect approach to the proper study

of class formation itself. Ideally, to chart out variations in class formations across countries we would want to study the ways in which
various kinds of solidaristic organizations – especially such things as
unions and political parties – link people together within and across
class locations. A map of the ways in which class-linked organizations of
different ideological and political profiles penetrate different parts of the
class structure would provide a basic description of the pattern of class
formation. Data on the class composition of formal membership and
informal affiliation in parties and unions would provide one empirical
way of approaching this.

The data used in this project are not really amenable to a refined
analysis of the organizational foundations of class formation. I will
therefore use a more indirect strategy for analyzing the contours of class
formation in these three countries. Instead of examining organizational
affiliations, we will use the variation across the class structure in
ideological orientation towards class interests as a way of mapping out
the patterns of solidarity and antagonism.

This strategy of analysis may generate misleading results for two
reasons. First, the assumption that the class mapping of attitudes will
roughly correspond to the class mapping of organized collective solidarities is certainly open to question. Even though people in different class
locations may share very similar attitudes, nevertheless they have
different vulnerabilities, control different resources and face different
alternative courses of action – this is, in fact, what it means to say that
they are in different "locations" – and this could generate very different
tendencies to actually participate in the collective actions of class formation.

Second, the method we are using to measure ideological-class coalitions is vulnerable to all of the problems that bedevil comparative survey
research. It is always possible that apparently identical questionnaire
items might actually mean quite different things in different cultural
contexts, regardless of how good the translation might be. A good
example in our questionnaire is the following question: "Do you strongly
agree, somewhat agree, somewhat disagree or strongly disagree with
this statement: workers in a strike are justified in physically preventing
strike-breakers from entering the place of work?" The problem with this
question is that in the Swedish context there is not a well-established
tradition of strikes using picket lines to bar entrance to a place of work.
As a result, the expression "physically prevent" suggests a much higher

level of potential violence to a Swedish respondent than it does to an American. For a Swede to agree with the question, in effect, they must feel it is legitimate for workers to assault a strikebreaker. For this reason, although this item appears in the survey we have not included it in this analysis.

This problem of cultural incommensurability of questionnaire items might mean that cross-national differences in patterns of ideological class formation might simply be artifacts of slippages in the meaning of questions. Our hope is that, with enough discussion among researchers from each of the countries involved and enough pretesting of the questionnaire items, it is possible to develop a set of items that are relatively comparable (or at least that the researchers from each country believe mean the same things). In any event, the precise wording of the items is a matter of record which should facilitate challenges to the comparability of the meanings by skeptics.

Our empirical strategy, then, is to treat the class distribution of class-relevant attitudes held by individuals as an indicator of the patterns of ideological coalitions within class formations. Where individuals in different class locations on average share similar class-relevant attitudes, we will say that these class locations constitute an ideological coalition within the structure of class formations. By using attitudes as an indicator of solidarity and antagonism in this way, I am not implying that class formations can be reduced to the attitudes people hold in their heads about class interests. The claim is simply that the formation of ideological configurations contributes to and reflects solidaristic collectivities and is therefore an appropriate empirical indicator for studying the relationship between class structure and class formation.

The specific methodology we will use to distinguish ideological-class coalitions tests, for each of the twelve locations in the class structure matrix, whether the average person in that location is ideologically closer to the working class, the capitalist class or an ideologically intermediary position between these two poles (for details, see Wright 1997: 453–456). Locations that are closer to the intermediary position will be referred to as part of the middle-class ideological coalition, whereas those closer to the polarized class locations will be referred to as part of the working-class coalition or the bourgeois coalition. The basic objective of this part of the analysis is to examine how these ideological-class coalitions differ in the United States, Sweden and Japan.

Class consciousness

Our analysis of class formation revolves around examining differences and similarities in ideological orientation across locations in the class structure matrix. In the analysis of class consciousness the unit of analysis shifts to the individual. Here the task is to construct a multivariate model of variations in individual consciousness, measured using the same anticapitalism scale, and see how these models vary across countries.

These models contain six clusters of independent variables: *class location* (11 dummy variables); *past class experiences* (dummy variables for working-class origin, capitalist origin, previously self-employed, previously supervisor, and previously unemployed); *current class experiences* (union member, density of ties to the capitalist class, density of ties to the working class); *consumption* (home owner, unearned-income dummy variable, personal income); *demographic variables* (age and gender); and *country* (two dummy variables). (See Wright 1997: 456–457, for precise operationalizations.)

We will first merge the three national samples into a single dataset in which we treat nationality simply like any other variable. This will enable us to answer the following question: which is more important for predicting individuals' class consciousness, the country in which they live or their class location and class experiences? We will then break the data into the three national samples and analyze the micro-level equations predicting class consciousness separately for each country. Here we will be particularly interested in comparing the explanatory power of different groups of variables across countries.

11.3   Results: the overall relationship between locations in the class structure and class consciousness

The results for the overall linkage between class location and class consciousness in Sweden, the United States and Japan are presented in Figure 11.1. With some wrinkles, these results are broadly consistent with each of the three broad hypotheses discussed above.

In all three countries the working-class location in the class structure matrix is either the most anticapitalist or is virtually identical to the location which is the most anticapitalist. Also in all three countries, the capitalist class is either the most procapitalist or has a value which is not significantly different from the most procapitalist location. These results are thus consistent with Hypothesis 1.

SWEDEN

	Owner	Expert	Skilled	Nonskilled	
Capitalist	−3.41	−2.36	0.60	1.05	Manager
Small employer	−0.70	0.56	2.07	3.50	Supervisor
Petty bourgeoisie	0.87	1.98	4.60	4.61	Non-management

UNITED STATES

	Owner	Expert	Skilled	Nonskilled	
Capitalist	−2.17	−2.62	−0.68	−1.09	Manager
Small employer	0.35	−0.73	1.30	2.28	Supervisor
Petty bourgeoisie	1.08	0.16	2.67	2.66	Non-management

JAPAN

	Owner	Expert	Skilled	Nonskilled	
Capitalist	0.17	0.32	2.10	1.83	Manager
Small employer	0.76	0.68	2.68	1.57	Supervisor
Petty bourgeoisie	3.08	1.09	2.61	3.07	Non-management

> The numbers in the cells of the class structure matrix are values on the anti-capitalism attitude scale (range, −10 to +10), in which negative values indicate a procapitalist orientation and positive values a proworking class orientation.

Figure 11.1 *Class structure and class consciousness in Sweden, the United States and Japan.*

The results also support Hypothesis 2 for all three countries. In each case there is a sharp ideological gradient among owners: the capitalist class is 3–4 points more procapitalist than the petty bourgeoisie, with small employers falling somewhere in between.

Hypothesis 3 is strongly supported by the results for Sweden and the

United States, and somewhat more ambiguously supported by the results for Japan. In Sweden, the results nearly exactly follow the predictions of the hypothesis: as you move from the working-class corner of the matrix to the expert-manager corner, the values on the scale decline in a perfectly monotonic manner, whether you move along the rows of the table, the columns of the table, or even the diagonal. Indeed, in the Swedish data the monotonicity extends across the property boundary as well. In the United States the results are only slightly less monotonic: in the employee portion of the matrix, skilled managers are slightly less anticapitalist than unskilled managers. In all other respects, the US data behave in the predicted monotonic manner.

The pattern for Japan is somewhat less consistent. If we look only at the four corners of the employee portion of the matrix, then the predicted monotonicity holds. The deviations from Hypothesis 3 come with some of the intermediary values. In particular, skilled supervisors in Japan appear to be considerably more anticapitalist than unskilled supervisors. The number of cases in these locations is, however, quite small (25 and 19 respectively), and the difference in anticapitalism scores between these categories is not statistically significant at even the 0.20 level. The other deviations from pure monotonicity in the Japanese class structure matrix are even less statistically significant. The results for Japan thus do not strongly contradict the predictions of Hypothesis 3, although they remain less consistent than those of Sweden and the United States.

Overall, then, these results for the three countries suggest that the patterns of variation across the locations of the class structure in class consciousness, as measured by the anticapitalism scale, are quite consistent with the theoretical predictions derived from the multidimensional, exploitation concept of class structure. While empirical consistency by itself cannot definitively prove the validity of a concept, nevertheless it does add credibility to the conceptual foundations that underlie the class analysis of this book.

11.4 Results: the macro-analysis of class formation

The basic patterns of ideological class formation will be presented in two different formats, since each of these helps to reveal different properties of the results. Figure 11.2 presents the results in terms of a one-dimensional ideological spectrum on which the values for the different class locations are indicated and grouped into ideological coalitions. Figure 11.3 represents the patterns as two-dimensional coalition maps as

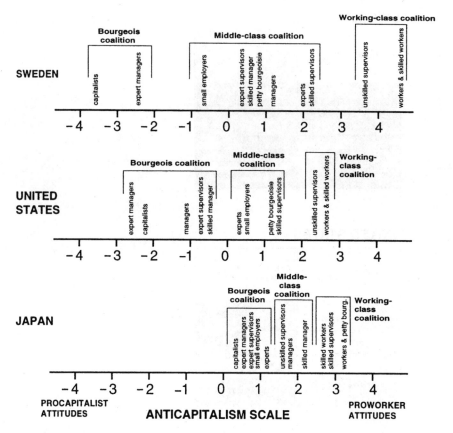

Figure 11.2 *Class and the ideological spectrum in Sweden, the United States and Japan.*

discussed in chapter 10. The numerical data on which these figures are based are presented in Figure 11.1.

Before turning to the rather striking contrasts in patterns of class formation between these three countries, there are two similarities which are worth noting. First, in all three countries skilled workers are in the working-class ideological coalition and have virtually identical scores on the anticapitalism scale as nonskilled workers. This finding supports the common practice of treating skilled and nonskilled workers as constituting "the working class." Second, in all three countries, in spite of the quite different overall configurations of the bourgeois ideological coalition, expert managers are part of this coalition. The most exploitative and dominating contradictory class location among employees (expert

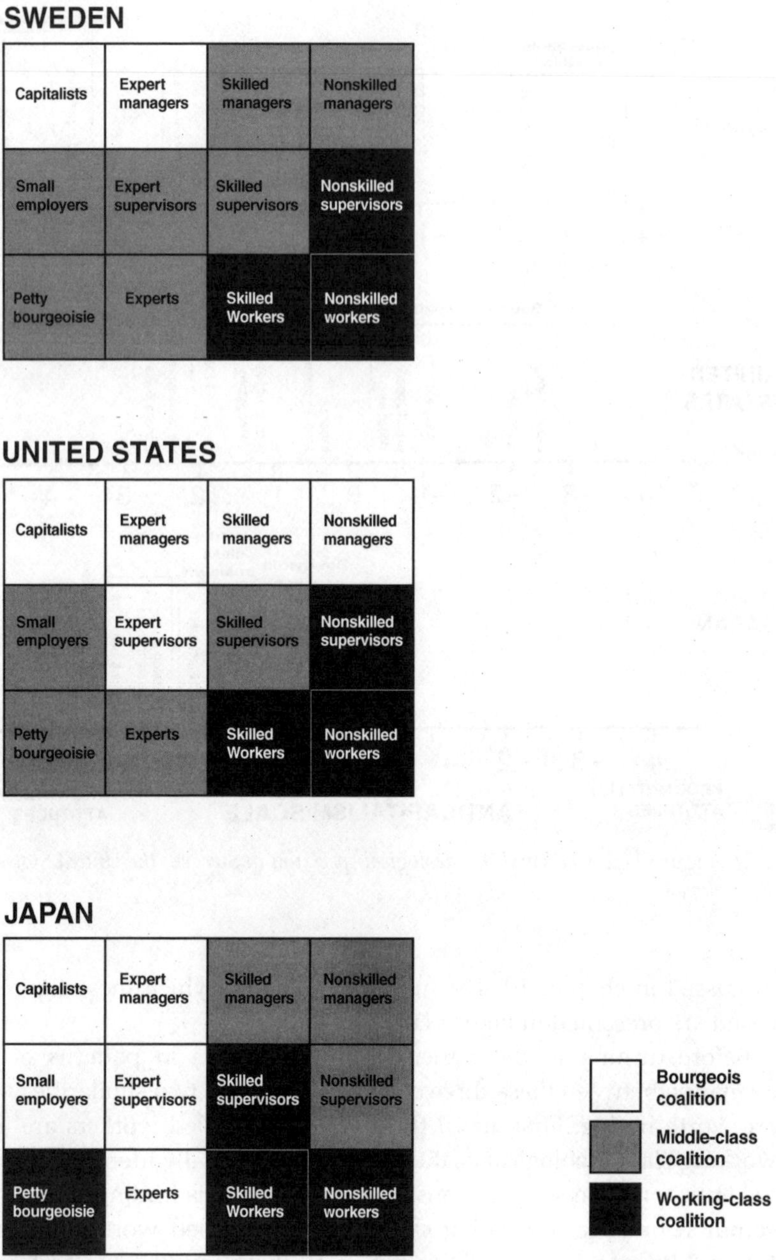

SWEDEN

Capitalists	Expert managers	Skilled managers	Nonskilled managers
Small employers	Expert supervisors	Skilled supervisors	Nonskilled supervisors
Petty bourgeoisie	Experts	Skilled Workers	Nonskilled workers

UNITED STATES

Capitalists	Expert managers	Skilled managers	Nonskilled managers
Small employers	Expert supervisors	Skilled supervisors	Nonskilled supervisors
Petty bourgeoisie	Experts	Skilled Workers	Nonskilled workers

JAPAN

Capitalists	Expert managers	Skilled managers	Nonskilled managers
Small employers	Expert supervisors	Skilled supervisors	Nonskilled supervisors
Petty bourgeoisie	Experts	Skilled Workers	Nonskilled workers

Bourgeois coalition

Middle-class coalition

Working-class coalition

Figure 11.3 *Patterns of ideological class formation.*

managers) is thus consistently part of the capitalist class formation, while the least exploitative and dominating contradictory location (skilled workers) is part of the working-class formation.

In other respects, the three countries we are considering present very different patterns. Let us look at each of them in turn.

Sweden

As indicated in Figure 11.2, the ideological spectrum across the locations of the class structure is larger in Sweden than in the other two countries, spanning a total of over 8 points on the anticapitalism scale. On this ideological terrain, the three ideological-class coalitions are well defined and clearly differentiated from each other. (The mean values on the anticapitalism scale for each of the coalitions differ from each other at less than the 0.001 significance level.)

The working-class coalition contains three class locations: the working class plus the two class locations adjacent to the working class – skilled workers and nonskilled supervisors. This coalition is quite clearly demarcated ideologically from the middle-class coalition. The bourgeois coalition is sharply polarized ideologically with respect to the working-class coalition. It consists of capitalists and only one contradictory class location, expert managers. Like the working-class coalition, the bourgeois coalition is clearly demarcated from the middle-class coalition. Social democracy may have become a stable ideological framework for Swedish politics in general, affecting the policy profiles of even conservative parties, but the Swedish bourgeois coalition remains staunchly procapitalist. Finally, the middle-class coalition in Sweden is quite broad and encompasses most of the employee contradictory locations within class relations as well as the petty bourgeoisie and small employers. This coalition is much more heterogeneous ideologically than either of the other two.

The United States

The ideological class formations constructed on the American class structure are somewhat less ideologically polarized than in Sweden. In particular, the American working-class coalition is clearly less anti-capitalist than the Swedish working-class coalition. The unweighted mean of the American working-class coalition is 2.53 compared to 4.24 in Sweden. In contrast, American capitalists and expert managers (the two locations that are in both the US and Swedish bourgeois coalitions) are only slightly less procapitalist than their Swedish counterpart, -2.40 compared to -2.89. The way to characterize the overall contrast between the ideological spectra in the two countries is thus that the working-class coalition in the US moves significantly towards the center compared to Sweden, while the core of the bourgeois coalitions (capitalists and expert managers) is equally on procapitalist in the two countries. Nevertheless, in spite of this somewhat lower level of polarization, the three ideological-class coalitions all still differ from each other at better than the 0.001 significance level.

The American working-class coalition includes the same three categories as in Sweden. While it is clearly less radical than the Swedish working-class coalition, it is almost as well demarcated from the middle-class coalition. The bourgeois coalition in the United States extends much deeper into the contradictory class locations than in Sweden. All three managerial-class locations as well as expert supervisors are part of the American bourgeois ideological-class formation. Unlike in Sweden, therefore, management is firmly integrated into the bourgeois coalition. The middle-class coalition is somewhat attenuated in the US compared to Sweden reflecting the fact that a much larger part of the contradictory class locations among employees in the US has been integrated ideologically into the bourgeois coalition. The middle-class coalition is also somewhat less sharply demarcated from the bourgeois coalition than it is from the working-class coalition.

Japan

The patterns of ideological class formation in Japan present a sharp contrast to both the United States and Sweden. To begin with, the entire ideological spectrum is much more compressed in Japan than in the other two countries. What is particularly striking is that the capitalist class and expert managers have moved to the center of the anticapitalism scale. These two categories combined are significantly less anticapitalist (at the 0.01 significance level) than the same categories in Sweden and the United States (whereas, as already noted, these categories do not differ between Sweden and the United States). In fact, the values on the anticapitalism scale for the bourgeois coalition in Japan fall entirely within the range for the middle-class coalitions in the other two countries. The Japanese working-class coalition, in contrast, does not differ significantly on the anticapitalism from the American working-class coalition. The conventional image of Japanese society as lacking highly antagonistic class formations is thus broadly supported by these data. While the mean values on the anticapitalism scale for the three ideological coalitions still do differ significantly, the lines of demarcation between these coalitions are much less sharply drawn than in the other two countries.

Not only is the overall degree of ideological polarization of the class structure much less in Japan than in Sweden and the United States, but the pattern of class formation reflected in these ideological cleavages is also quite different. Specifically, in Japan the line of ideological cleavage among employees is much more pronounced between experts and non-experts than it is along the authority dimension. In Sweden and the United States, in contrast, the cleavages along these two dimensions are of roughly comparable magnitude.

The subdued quality of the cleavages along the authority dimension in Japan compared to the other two countries is especially clear among experts and among skilled employees. In Japan, there are no statistically significant differences on the anticapitalism scale across levels of authority for these two categories, whereas in both Sweden and the United States there are sharp and statistically significant differences. For example, consider skilled employees. In Japan, the values on the anti-capitalism scale for managers, supervisors and nonmanagers among skilled employees are 2.1, 2.68 and 2.61 respectively. In the United States the corresponding values are -0.68, 1.30 and 2.67, while in Sweden they are 0.6, 2.07 and 4.60. The differences between managers and workers among skilled employees are thus 0.5 in Japan, 3.3 in the US and 4 in Sweden. With the single exception of the contrast between nonskilled supervisors (anticapitalism score, 1.57) and nonskilled workers (anti-capitalism score, 3.07), there are no statistically significant differences across authority levels in Japan.

In contrast to these patterns for authority, Japan is less deviant from Sweden and the United States in the ideological differences between experts and skilled employees *within* levels of authority. For example, the difference in anticapitalism between expert managers and skilled managers is 3 points in Sweden, 1.9 points in the US and 1.8 points in Japan.

These differences in patterns of ideological cleavage generate very different patterns of class formation in Japan. First, consider the bour-geois coalition. In Japan, experts at all levels of the authority hierarchy are part of the bourgeois ideological coalition, whereas skilled and nonskilled managers are not. This contrasts sharply with the United States in which managers of all skill levels are part of the bourgeois coalition, and Sweden in which only expert managers were part of that coalition.

The working-class coalition in Japan, as measured by our procedures, has a rather odd shape, consisting of skilled and nonskilled workers, and skilled supervisors, but *not* nonskilled supervisors. These results are puzzling, since within the conceptual framework of contradictory class locations one would normally think that in comparison with skilled supervisors, unskilled supervisors would have interests more like those of workers and thus would have a stronger tendency to be part of the working-class ideological coalition. This is certainly the case for Sweden and the United States. I cannot offer a plausible explanation for these specific results. They may reflect some significant measurement problems in operationalizing the distinction between skilled and nonskilled for Japan. But it is also possible that these results reflect some complicated interaction of class location with such things as variations in employment situation, sector of employment, age or some other factor. Unfortunately, because the number of cases in these categories is so small, we cannot empirically explore possible explanations for this apparent anomaly. In any case, as already noted, the difference between skilled and nonskilled supervisors in Japan is not statistically significant even at the 0.10 level.

One final contrast between Japan and the other two countries concerns the petty bourgeoisie. In Japan, the petty bourgeoisie is just as anti-capitalist as is the working-class and is firmly part of the working-class ideological coalition. In both Sweden and the United States, the petty bourgeoisie is part of the middle-class coalition and has an anticapitalist score that is significantly lower than that of the working class. In these terms, the Japanese pattern looks rather like the populism of several generations ago in the United States in which labor–farm coalitions were politically organized against capitalists. Japan continues to have a relatively large petty bourgeoisie and it appears to have an ideological profile that ties it relatively closely to the working class.

Summary of the comparisons of the three countries

Taking all of these results for the macro-analysis of class formation together, three contrasts among the countries we have examined stand out:

1 The degree of ideological polarization across class formations differs significantly in the three cases: Sweden is the most polarized, Japan the least, and the United States is in between. These variations in the degree of polarization do not come from a symmetrical decline in the range of ideological variation across classes. Compared to Sweden, in the United States the working-class coalition is significantly less anticapitalist, but there is little difference between the two countries in the procapitalist attitudes of the core of the capitalist coalition. In Japan, in contrast, both the capitalist-class coalition and the working-class coalition are ideologically less extreme than their Swedish counterparts.

2 While expert managers can be considered the core coalition partner of the capitalist class in all three countries, the overall shape of the bourgeois coalitions varies sharply in the three cases. In Sweden, the bourgeois coalition is confined to this core. In both Japan and the United States the coalition extends fairly deeply into contradictory class locations among employees, but in quite different ways. In Japan contradictory class locations are integrated into the bourgeois-class formation more systematically through credentials than through authority, whereas the reverse is true in the United States. Authority hierarchy thus plays a more central role in processes of bourgeois class formation in the United States than in either other country, and credentials a more central role in Japan.

3 Overall, Sweden and the United States are much more like each other than they are like Japan. The shape of the working-class formation is identical in the US and Sweden and is clearly differentiated ideologically from the middle-class coalition, and even though the bourgeois coalition penetrates more deeply into employee locations in the United States, it does so in a way that is entirely consistent with the underlying patterns in Sweden. Japan, in these terms, is quite different. The working-class formation has a more populist character because of the presence of the petty bourgeoisie and is much less differentiated ideologically from the middle class. The middle-class coalition also looks entirely different from that in the other two countries. Furthermore, whereas in Sweden and the United States, both the skill and authority dimensions among employees are sources of systematic ideological cleavage, in Japan only the contrast between credentialed experts and nonexperts constitutes a consistent source of cleavage among employees.

11.5 Explaining the differences in class formations

It is beyond the capacity of the data in this project to test systematically alternative explanations of the cross-national patterns of class formation we have been mapping out. Ultimately this would require constructing an account of the historical trajectory in each country of class struggles and institution building, especially of unions, parties and states. But we can get some suggestive ideas about explanations by looking at some of the proximate institutional factors that might underpin the ideological configurations that we have been examining. We will first focus on the contrast between the US and Sweden and then turn to the problem of Japan.

The overall differences in patterns of class formation between Sweden and the United States can be summarized in terms of two contrasts: first, the bourgeois-class formation penetrates the middle class to a much greater extent in the United States than in Sweden, and second, the working-class formation is ideologically more polarized with the capitalist class formation in Sweden than in the United States.

In the conceptual framework for the analysis of class formation laid out in chapter 10, class formations were seen as the result of two clusters of causal factors, one linked to the effects of class structure on class formation and the other of class struggle on class formation. Class structure was seen as shaping class formations via the ways in which it influenced the material interests, identities and resources of people; class struggle was seen as shaping class formations by affecting the organizations of collective action. Different patterns of class formation would therefore be expected in cases where the linkage between class location and material interests was quite different or situations in which the linkage between class location and organizational capacities was quite different. We will explore two specific mechanisms reflecting these factors: state employment and unionization.

State employment

State employment might be expected to be particularly important for insulating the middle class from the bourgeois coalition. Within the capitalist corporation, through mechanisms of career ladders, vertical promotions, job security and, in the case of higher-level managers, stock bonuses of various sorts, the material interests of managers and experts tend to be closely tied to the profitability of the corporation itself, and thus the general class interests of the middle-class employed in private corporations tend to be closely tied to those of the bourgeoisie. Within the state, however, this link between middle class interests and bourgeois interests is much less direct. While, in the long run, the salaries of state employees depend upon state revenues, and state revenues depend upon a healthy capitalist economy and thus upon profits, there is in general no direct dependency of the material interests of state employees on the interests of any particular capitalist. State employment, therefore, could potentially constitute a material basis for the middle class to develop a sense of its own class interests relatively differentiated from those of the capitalist class. All things being equal, in a society with a large state sector, therefore, it would be expected that the middle class would be more autonomous ideologically from the bourgeoisie than in a society with a relatively small state sector.

In the United States, the material fate of the middle class is much more directly tied to the fortunes of corporate capitalism than in Sweden. In the United States, only about 18% of the labor force as a whole is employed by the state, and, while the figures are generally higher for those middle-class locations which are not in the working-class coalition (about 23% are employed in the state), it is still the case that most middle-class jobs are in the private sector. In Sweden, in contrast, 38% of the entire labor force, and nearly 50% of the middle-class contradictory locations are directly employed by the state. This makes middle-class interests in Sweden less immediately tied to those of the capitalist class, and thus creates greater possibilities for the formation of a distinctive middle-class ideological coalition.

Some evidence in support of this interpretation is presented in Table 11.1. In the United States, "middle-class" employees (i.e. those that are outside of the working-class ideological coalition) in the state sector have, on average, a significantly less procapitalist ideological orientation than middle-class wage earners in the private sector. This contrast is especially sharp among expert managers, the contradictory class location most closely allied with the capitalist class. Expert managers in the state have a value on the anticapitalism scale of -0.04, whereas those in the private sector have a value of -3.59 (difference significant at the $p < 0.05$ level). Furthermore, US middle-class employees in the state sector do not differ significantly from Swedish middle-class state employees on the anticapitalism scale (1.37 compared to 1.56). The significantly more conservative profile of the middle class in the United States, therefore, is largely concentrated in the private sector of the US economy. In Sweden,

Table 11.1. *Values on the anticapitalism scale for class categories: comparisons of state and private sectors and of union and nonunion members*

	United States		Sweden		Japan	
	State	Private	State	Private	State	Private
Working-class coalition[a]	2.89	2.53	4.16	4.77	4.31	2.74
(N)	(179)	(724)	(300)	(434)	(21)	(283)
Significance level of difference between state and private sectors	p <.15		p <.07		p <.04	
Middle class employees[b]	1.37	−0.23	1.56	0.76	1.92	1.44
(N)	(80)	(271)	(115)	(121)	(9)	(106)
Significance level of difference between state and private sectors	p <.01		p <.20		ns	

	United States		Sweden		Japan	
	Union member	Nonunion member	Union member	Nonunion member	Union member	Nonunion member
Working-class coalition[a]	3.72	2.24	4.97	2.41	2.85	2.84
(N)	(222)	(681)	(606)	(128)	(108)	(196)
Significance level of difference between union and non union members	p <.001		p <.001		ns	
Middle class employees[b]	3.65	−0.27	1.89	−2.72	2.21	1.23
(N)	(36)	(315)	(198)	(38)	(29)	(86)
Significance level of difference between union and nonunion members	p <.001		p <.001		ns	

a. Working-class coalition = nonskilled workers, skilled workers and nonskilled supervisors.
b. Middle-class employees = all employees not in the working-class coalition (i.e. employees in either the bourgeois- or middle-class coalition).

the difference between state and private sector middle-class employees is in the same direction as in the United States, but is not statistically significant. This suggests, perhaps, that under conditions of a large state sector, the middle class as a whole has greater ideological autonomy from the bourgeoisie, not simply those middle class actually employed in the state. The much greater role of state employment in the Swedish class structure, therefore may be one of the reasons why the Swedish bourgeois coalition is restricted to expert managers within the middle class, whereas the American bourgeois coalition penetrates much deeper into managerial class locations (for a much more extended discussion of these issues, see Wright 1997: ch. 15).

Unionization

A second proximate mechanism for consolidating the boundaries of a class formation is collective organization, of which unionization is probably the most important for working-class formation. Where unions are broad-based and organizationally autonomous from the capitalist class, it would be expected that the working-class coalition would be more ideologically polarized with the capitalist-class coalition than in cases where unions were weak and lacked real autonomy.

Sweden and the United States offer clear contrasts in the nature of their respective union movements. While in both countries unions are relatively autonomous organizationally from the capitalist class – company unions are not significant features in either country – the Swedish labor movement has a much broader base than its American counterpart. In the American working-class coalition, 24.4% are union members compared to 82.6% in Sweden. What is even more striking, perhaps, is that in Sweden there is a high rate of unionization among middle-class contradictory class locations as well: 83.9% of the people in middle-class contradictory locations outside of the working-class coalition belong to unions in Sweden compared to only 10.3% in the United States. The low American figures partially reflect the overall weakness of the American labor movement, but more significantly they reflect legal barriers to unionization among people who are formally part of "management." This is reflected in the minuscule unionization rates among people in managerial-class locations (expert managers, skilled managers and nonskilled managers): in the US, out of 92 people in such positions in our sample there were only 2 union members for a rate of 2.2%, whereas, in Sweden, out of 53 people in managerial-class locations, 60.4% belonged to unions.

To what extent, then, does this higher level of unionization in Sweden help to explain the greater ideological polarization between working-class and the bourgeois-class formations in Sweden than in the United States? Table 11.1 indicates that in both the United States and Sweden there are sharp ideological differences between union members and nonmembers within all class locations. What is particularly relevant in these results is that within the working-class coalitions in Sweden and the United States, *non*union members in the two countries do not differ significantly on the anticapitalism scale. The mean value for the non-union segment of the working-class coalition in the United States is 2.24, while in Sweden it is 2.41. The mean values for the unionized segments, on the other hand, do differ significantly ($p < 0.001$): 4.97 in Sweden and 3.72 in the United States.

The overall greater anticapitalism of the Swedish working-class coalition is thus partially due to the fact that Swedish union members are more anticapitalist than American union members, and partially to the fact that the Swedish working-class coalition has a much higher rate of unionization. We can estimate the rough magnitudes of these components by playing a kind of counterfactual game in which we ask two questions:

1 What would the mean value on the anticapitalism scale be for the US working-class coalition if (a) it had the unionization *rate* of the Swedish working-class coalition but (b) union members and nonmembers in the United States working-class coalition still had the same *values* on the scale that they currently have?

2 What would the mean value on the anticapitalism scale be for the US working-class coalition if (a) it had the unionization rate that it actually has, but (b) union members and nonmembers in the United States working-class coalition each had the values on the scale of their Swedish counterparts?

The first question imputes a mean value on the scale to the US working-class coalition under the assumption that all that changes is the union-ization rate in the United States; the second question assumes that all that changes is ideology.

On the basis of these two questions we can decompose the total difference in values on the anticapitalism scale between the working-class coalitions in the two countries into three components: a component reflecting the differences in unionization rates, a component reflecting the differences in ideologies, and a residual interaction component. (For detailed results, see Wright 1997: 438.)

In this counterfactual game, just under 45% of the total difference in the anticapitalism scale between the American and Swedish working-class coalitions is attributable to the higher rate of unionization in Sweden, about 20% is attributable to the fact that Swedish union members are more radical than their American counterparts, and about 35% is attributable to the interaction between these two effects. The sheer fact of higher levels of unionization, therefore, probably contributes substantially to the greater ideological polarization between the Swedish working-class formation and bourgeois formation.

This analysis, of course, is entirely static in character. The counter-factual is completely unrealistic as a dynamic proposition since the degree of ideological polarization enters into the explanation of changes in the rate of unionization. In the dynamic micro–macro model elaborated in the previous chapter, class struggles transform class formations, but those class struggles are themselves constituted by the class practices of individuals with specific forms of consciousness. The greater ideological anticapitalism of union members in the working-class coalition in Sweden compared to the United States is thus both a consequence of the strength of the Swedish labor movement (and of the associated social democratic political party) and part of the historical explanation for the strength of that movement. In the present research, there is no way of sorting out these two sides of the dynamic process.

Japan

Two features of the Japanese case which differentiate it from both the United States and Sweden need to be explained: first, the much lower degree of overall ideological polarization compared to the other two countries, and, second, the absence of significant forms of ideological cleavage along the managerial dimension of the class structure.

The conventional image of Japan is of a society in which firms are organized on a relatively cooperative basis, with high levels of loyalty on the part of most workers, not just managers, and low levels of conflict. Managers in many firms spend significant time on the shop floor doing the work of ordinary workers prior to assuming their managerial responsibilities, which further mutes the sense of vertical antagonism. The pay-off, many observers have argued, is that Japanese firms are able to achieve large productivity gains because relatively little human energy is wasted in destructive conflict.

As numerous commentators have noted, this popular image of Japan is misleading in several important respects. While it is true that general labor-management relations are relatively harmonious by international standards, these high levels of cooperation and loyalty mainly apply to workers in the core of the corporate economy with life-time employment security; the large number of part-time and temporary workers in the core firms, and the workers in the numerous small firms reap few of the benefits of this system (Tsuda 1973; Gordon 1985; Chalmers 1989). Furthermore, as various critical observers of the Japanese factory have stressed, these apparently harmonious relations are combined with intense competition among workers and pervasive surveillance and social control of work performance (Dohse, Jurgens and Malsch 1985; Kamata 1982).

The results for ideological differences between union members and nonmembers in Table 11.1 give us some clue about the underlying processes at work in the Japanese case. The most striking feature of the Japanese data is the virtual absence of ideological differences between union members and nonmembers, especially within the working-class coalition. Whereas in Sweden and the United States union members in the working-class coalition were between 1.5 and 2 points more anti-capitalist than nonmembers, in Japan these groups are virtually identical. The contrast is equally striking for the middle class: in Sweden and the United States union members in the middle-class coalition were roughly 4 points more anticapitalist than nonmembers, whereas in Japan the figure is only about 0.8 points.

These results indicate that in Japan unions are not an organizational basis for formulating and representing distinctive class interests. As critics often note, Japanese unions function basically like company unions, being oriented towards serving corporate interests rather than defending the interests of workers. Without an autonomous organizational basis for the articulation of class interests, class formations become ideologically fuzzy, with diffuse boundaries and weak antagonisms. The result is a pattern of class formation with low levels of polarization that is especially muted along the authority dimension of class relations.

As in the explanation of the differences between Sweden and the United States, this is a purely static explanation: given the existence of company unions and the absence of any autonomous organizational basis for a working-class formation, class formations in Japan will be relatively nonpolarized and poorly demarcated. Dynamically, of course, these ideological configurations themselves contribute to the absence of autonomous working-class organizations and act as obstacles to any strategies for transforming Japanese class formations. In these terms it is worth noting that Japanese class formations were not always so non-antagonistic and unpolarized. The early 1950s were a period of intense labor conflicts and mobilization, with militant unions and periodic wide-spread strikes. It was really only after the defeat and repression of these movements that the current pattern of quasi-company unions was consolidated and integrated with the current forms of "cooperative" labor–management relations.

11.5 The micro-analysis of class consciousness

So far we have focused on macro-patterns of class formation, using ideology as a criterion for mapping the boundaries of class formations. Of course, the process by which individuals acquire their consciousness was implicated in this analysis, both because our measures were all based on responses by individuals to questionnaire items and because it is impossible to talk about the differences between groups without alluding to the differences in the interests and experiences of the individuals that make up those groups. Nevertheless, in the discussion so far we have not been interested in explaining variation across individuals as such. It is to this issue that we now turn.

As discussed in section 11.2, we will engage in two different kinds of analyses of individual class consciousness. In the first, we will merge the data from all three countries into a single dataset and test the relative explanatory power of nationality compared to class. In the second we will investigate the differences in coefficients in more complex multi-variate equations estimated separately for each country.

Additive country effects

Table 11.2 presents the results for the merged sample of all three countries. The numbers reported in this table are the standardized coefficients (beta coefficients) for the different clusters of independent variables considered as groups within a multivariate equation predicting values on the anticapitalism scale (for more detailed results, see Wright 1997: 442–443). In these results, a person's country is a less important determinant of individuals' scores on the anticapitalism scale than is

Table 11.2. *Determinants of class consciousness: micro-level analysis of the United States, Sweden and Japan (standardized regression coefficients)*

Variables	Three countries combined	United States	Sweden	Japan
Class location	.18***	.16***	.27***	.13**
Past class experiences	.13***	.11***	.18***	.12**
Class networks	.07**	.05*	.11***	.03
Consumption	.14***	.15***	.09***	.20***
Union member	.22***	.17***	.23***	.07
Demographics	.05**	.12***	.03	.06
Country	.11***			
Adjusted R^2	.18	.16	.24	.08
N	3,168	1,471	1,089	608

Significance levels (one-tailed tests): ***$P < .001$ **$P < .01$ *$p < .05$.

Definitions of variables:

Class location: dummy variables for the 12-category class location matrix.

Past class experiences: dummy variables for: working-class origin, capitalist-class origin; previously self-employed, previously unemployed.

Class networks: capitalist friendship network; working-class friendship network.

Consumption: personal income; unearned income dummy variable; homeowner dummy.

Union member: dummy variable for member of a union.

Demographics: Gender dummy variable; age.

Country: two dummy variables.

their class location. Indeed, the coefficient for country is smaller than any of the class related variables. If we look at the R^2 in an equation containing only the country variable, it is a fifth of the R^2 for an equation with class location alone (2% compared to 10%). At least within this sample of countries, if you want to predict an individual's class consciousness, therefore, it is more important to know what class they are in than to know what country they are from.

Cross-national comparisons of micro-equations

From what we already know about the cross-national variations in class formation, treating country as an additive variable as we have just done is clearly an unsatisfactory way of modeling the effects of nation on individual consciousness. A more appropriate model involves country interactions in which we estimate the regression equations separately within each national sample and examine cross-national differences in coefficients. The results are also presented in Table 11.2.

There are several striking contrasts in these equations across the three countries. First, the overall predictive power of the equation is strongest in Sweden and, by a considerable margin, weakest in Japan. In Sweden, the regression equation explains 24% of the variance in the anticapitalism scale, which is quite a respectable R^2 for an attitudinal dependent variable. Since a good part of the observed variance in attitude scales is always due to measurement problems and random variation across individuals, the "explainable" variance is much less than the total variance. Accounting for a quarter of the total variance in an attitude variable thus indicates that this dependent variable is quite closely associated with the independent variables in the equation. The 16% R^2 in the American equation is also fairly characteristic of regressions on attitude variables. The 8% explained variance for Japan, however, is rather low, indicating that these variables for Japan do not account for a substantial part of the variance on the anticapitalism scale.

Second, each of the blocks of variables closely linked to class predict consciousness more strongly in Sweden than in the other two countries: the coefficient for the aggregated block of class location dummy variables is 0.27 in Sweden, 0.16 in the US and 0.13 in Japan. Similar differences occur for past class experiences, current class networks and union membership. Class location and class experiences, therefore, seem to shape consciousness most pervasively in Sweden and least pervasively in Japan.

Third, those variables which tap into consumption rather than directly into class – personal income, unearned income and home ownership – are better predictors in the United States and Japan than in Sweden. Taken as a group, the coefficient for the consumption variables is 0.09 in Sweden compared to 0.15 in the US and 0.20 in Japan. This is consistent with the interpretation of the results in chapter 7 concerning the class identities of married women in the labor force in Sweden and the United States: relative to Sweden, class in the US appears to be structured subjectively more around the sphere of consumption than the sphere of production. At least on the basis of the results for the anticapitalism scale, this appears to be even more strongly the case for Japan.

Finally, in no country is gender a significant determinant of class consciousness in the multivariate equation, and only in the United States does age have a significant effect. I do not have a specific interpretation of the age coefficient for the US. Most likely this reflects an effect of historical cohorts in which the younger cohorts of Americans (in 1980), perhaps especially the "60s generation," are more critical of capitalism than older cohorts. If this is the correct interpretation of the age coefficient, then such generational cleavages in ideology appear stronger in the US than in the other two countries, perhaps indicating that the experience of the civil rights and antiwar movements of the 1960s constituted a greater discontinuity in American political life than has occurred in either of the other two countries.

11.6 A brief note on class, race, gender and consciousness

Because of the constraints of sample size, it is impossible with the Comparative Class Analysis Project data to explore systematically the ways class, race and gender interact in the formation of class consciousness. Nevertheless, it is worth briefly looking at the overall pattern of variation in consciousness across race, gender and class categories in the United States since these results are quite suggestive and pose interesting questions for further research.

Figure 11.4 presents the mean values on the anticapitalism scale for black and white males and females in the "extended" working class (nonskilled workers, skilled workers and nonskilled supervisors) and the "middle" class (all types of managers and experts plus skilled supervisors). The most striking feature of these results is that within classes (especially within the working class), racial differences in class consciousness are much greater than gender differences. Within the working class, there are virtually no differences in the values on the anticapitalism scale between white men (2.41) and white women (2.38) or between black men (3.8) and black women (3.5), whereas there are sharp differences between blacks and whites. Indeed, the differences between black and white workers within the US is of the same order of magnitude as the difference between American and Swedish workers.

It is always possible that the explanation of why these racial divisions in consciousness within the working class are greater than gender differences is simply a result of the internal heterogeneity of the class categories. Within the broad category "extended working class" in Figure 11.4, black men and women tend to be concentrated in the most proletarianized and exploited segments. The more anticapitalist value

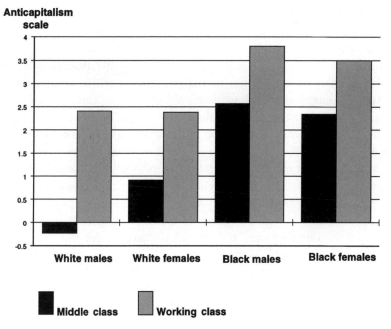

Figure 11.4 *Race and gender differences in class consciousness in the United States.*

for black workers, therefore, could simply be an artifact of the racial differences in composition of this category. These compositional effects would be much more muted between men and women within racial categories because of the effects of household class compositions on class consciousness.

A more interesting explanation centers on the linkage between different forms of oppression in people's lives. A good argument can be made that racial inequality is much more closely linked to class oppression than is gender inequality. In its earliest forms in the United States, racial oppression was virtually equivalent to a specific class relation, slavery. While the race-class linkage has weakened over the past 100 years, it is still the case that the content of the disadvantages racially oppressed groups experience are deeply linked to class. Because of this intimate link to class, racial oppression itself may tend to generate a heightened critical consciousness around issues of class. Gender inequality is less closely linked to class, and thus the experience of gender oppression is less immediately translated into a critical consciousness of class inequality. This may help explain why men and women within the working class have similar levels of class consciousness, whereas black workers are more anticapitalist than white workers.

One other aspect of the results in Figure 11.4 should be noted: class differences between the working class and the middle class are considerably greater among white men than among white women or blacks. Among black men and women, workers score on average about 1.2 points more on the anticapitalism scale than do people in the middle class. Among white women the figure is about 1.5 points higher. Among white men, in contrast, workers score 2.6 points higher than the middle class. As in the results for racial differences within classes, these results could be generated in part by compositional differences in class distributions within groups: among white men a higher proportion of the "middle class" category consists of expert managers than is the case for any of the other groups, and this could account for the sharper ideological difference between the working class and the aggregated "middle class" among white males. But these results could also suggest that, at least in the United States, the class model which we have been using works better among white men than other categories. When class intersects with other forms of oppression in the lives of people, its effects on consciousness may be confounded by the effects of these other relations. In order to pursue these conjectures, research on much larger samples will be needed.

11.7 Conclusion

The relationship between class structure and class formation at the macro-level of analysis and between class location and class consciousness at the micro-level are at the core of class analysis. The Marxist claim that class has pervasive consequences for social conflict and social change crucially hinges on the ways in which class structures shape class formations and class locations shape class consciousness. In these terms, the most important conclusion from the analysis in this chapter is the high degree of variability in these relationships across highly developed capitalist economies. While in very general terms one can say that there is a certain commonality in the patterns of class formation and in the association of class location to class consciousness in the three countries we have examined, what is equally striking is the extent to which these countries vary.

At one end of the spectrum is Sweden. At the macro-level, Sweden is characterized by a pattern of class formation which is both quite polarized and in which there are clear demarcations between the three-class coalitions we examined. At the micro-level, class location and class experiences, past and present, appear to strongly shape the attitudes of individuals towards class issues. Class thus appears to powerfully impinge on the lives and subjectivities of people in Swedish society.

At the other extreme is Japan. At the macro-level class formations are neither very polarized ideologically, nor sharply demarcated. At the micro-level, although class remains significantly associated with consciousness, the effects are much weaker and mainly confined to the indirect effects of class via the sphere of consumption. While the class character of Japanese society may be of great importance for understanding the rhythm of its economic development, the constraints on state policies, the nature of political parties and so on, at the micro-level, variation in class location and class experiences does not appear to pervasively shape variations in class consciousness.

The United States falls somewhere between these two cases, probably somewhat closer to Sweden than to Japan. The patterns of class formation are rather like those in Sweden, only more muted, with a broader bourgeois-class coalition and a working-class coalition that is closer to the middle class. At the micro-level, class location and experiences do systematically shape consciousness, but less strongly than in Sweden and with a greater relative impact of the sphere of consumption.

Part IV

Conclusion

12. Confirmations, surprises and theoretical reconstructions

Class analysis, in the Marxist tradition, stands at the center of a sweeping analysis of the dilemmas of contemporary society and the aspirations for an egalitarian and democratic future for humanity. Class is a normatively charged concept, rooted in ideas of oppression, exploitation and domination. This concept underwrites both an emancipatory vision of a classless society and an explanatory theory of conflicts, institutions and social change rooted in intrinsically antagonistic interests. The ultimate ambition of this kind of class analysis is to link the explanatory theory to the emancipatory vision in such a way as to contribute to the political project of transforming the world in the direction of those ideals. Marxist empirical research of whatever kind – whether ethnographic case studies, historical investigations or statistical analyses of survey data – should further this ambition.

At first glance, it may seem that the empirical studies in this book have little to do with such grand visions. The topics we have explored have revolved around narrowly focused properties of contemporary capitalist societies rather than the epochal contradictions which dynamically shape social change. While I have invoked the themes of transformative struggles, only a pale reflection of "class struggle" has appeared in the actual empirical analyses in the form of attitudes of individuals. And, while the concept of class we have been exploring is conceptualized in terms of exploitation, none of the empirical research directly explores the problem of exploitation as such. In what ways, then, can the coefficients, tables and graphs in this book be said to push forward the central themes and ideas of the Marxist agenda?

Research pushes social theory forward in two basic ways. Where there is a controversy between contending theoretical claims about some problem, research can potentially provide a basis for adjudicating between the alternatives. The more focused and well defined is the problem, and particularly, the more there is agreement among contending views on the precise specification of what needs to be explained, the more likely it is that research can play this role. Our explorations of alternative expectations about the transformations of the class structure or the permeability of class boundaries are in this spirit. Where successful, the results of research can be said to provisionally "confirm" a particular set of expectations linked to a theoretical perspective, at least in the sense of adding significantly to the credibility of those expectations even if it is never possible to absolutely prove theoretical claims. While, at least in social science, such adjudication and confirmation rarely bears directly on the adequacy of broader theoretical perspectives, the cumulative effect of such research can contribute to the erosion of some perspectives and the strengthening of others.

Adjudication and confirmation are at the core of the standard "hypothesis-testing" strategies of contemporary sociology. Although the standard rhetoric is "rejecting the null hypothesis" rather than "adjudicating between rival hypotheses," nevertheless, the underlying logic of inquiry is using evidence to add credibility to a set of expectations derived from one theory versus alternatives. There is, however, a second modality through which research pushes theory forward: the goal of research can be to find interesting surprises, anomalous empirical results that go against the expectations of a theory and thus provoke rethinking. It is all well and good to do research that confirms what one already believes, but the advance of knowledge depends much more on generating observations that challenge one's existing ideas, that are counter-intuitive with respect to received wisdom.

Surprises of this sort may be the by-product of the adjudication between rival hypotheses. After all, what is "surprising" within one theoretical framework may be "commonsense" within another. The accelerating decline of the working class is certainly a surprise within Marxism; it is hardly surprising for post-industrial theorists. Research which seems to confirm the expectations of one's theoretical rivals thus provides crucial raw material for efforts at theory reconstruction.

Empirical anomalies may also occur in research that is not explicitly directed at adjudicating between rival hypotheses. The surprises in our research on housework, for example, grew out of an exploration of the implications of class analysis for gender relations rather than a direct confrontation between alternative theories of housework. In any case, as Burawoy (1990, 1993) has strenuously argued, empirical surprises force the reconstruction of theory, and it is through such reconstruction that social theory moves forward.

"Reconstructions" of theory in the light of empirical surprises, of course, may be purely defensive operations, patching up a sinking ship that is sailing in the wrong direction. There is no guarantee that reconstructions constitute "progressive" developments within a theoretical framework rather than degenerate branches of a research program, to use Imre Lakatos's formulation. Nevertheless, it is through such reconstructions that advances in theoretical knowledge are attempted.

The research in this book involves both of these modalities for linking theory and research. Some of the research was primarily concerned with empirically comparing the expectations of a Marxist class analysis with expectations derived from other theoretical perspectives. Other studies were less focused on adjudicating between well-formulated rival expectations than simply exploring the implications of the Marxist approach itself. Much of this research provides confirmation for what I believed before doing the research, but there were also many surprises, at least some of which may contribute to the ongoing reconstruction of Marxist class analysis.

It is mainly on these surprises that I want to focus in this chapter. In what follows, for each of the major themes in the book I will first present a stylized account of what might be termed the "conventional wisdom" within Marxism. This is not always an easy task, for on some of the topics we have explored Marxists have not had a great deal to say, and in any case there are many Marxisms from which to choose the "traditional view." My characterization of the "traditional understanding," therefore, is bound to be disputed. My intention is not to give an authoritative account of "what Marx really said," but to capture a set of theoretical intuitions shared by many – perhaps most – Marxists. This account of the traditional understanding will serve as the benchmark for assessing the ways in which the results of the various research projects provide confirmations of these conventional expectations or surprises. The inventory of surprises, in turn, will provide the basis for exploring some of the directions in which Marxist class analysis might be reconstructed in light of the research.

These issues will be explored for five broad themes in class analysis which we have examined in this book: 1. the problem of conceptualizing "locations" within the class structure; 2. the variability and transformation of class structure of advanced capitalist societies; 3. the intersection of the lives of individuals and class structures; 4. the effects of class on class consciousness and class formation; and 5. the relationship between class and other forms of oppression, especially gender.

12.1 Conceptualizing "locations" in the class structure

More than any other issue, this research has revolved around the problem of what it means to "locate" a person in the class structure. If we are to link micro- and macro-levels of class analysis by exploring the impact of class on the lives and consciousness of individuals, some sort of solution to this issue is essential. The image is that a structure of class relations generates an array of "empty places" filled by individuals. To pursue micro-level class analysis we must both figure out how to define these empty places and what it means for an individual to be linked to those places.

Traditional understanding

Traditional Marxism developed a systematic conceptualization of class structure only at the highest levels of abstraction. The "empty places" in class relations were defined by the social property relations within specific modes of production. In capitalist societies this led to the rigorous specification of two basic class locations: *capitalists* and *workers* within capitalist relations of production. To these could be added class locations that were rooted in various kinds of precapitalist relations of production, especially the *petty bourgeoisie* within simple commodity production, and in some times and places, various class locations within feudal relations of production. In many concrete analyses, loose references were also made to other class locations, especially to the new middle class of managers and professionals, but these were not given firm conceptual status.

In the traditional account, individuals were linked to these empty places through their direct relationship to the means of production: capitalists owned the means of production and employed workers; workers sold their labor power on a labor market and worked within capitalist firms; the petty bourgeoisie were direct producers using their own means of production. Every class location was therefore in one and only one class. Individuals might, of course, change their class in the course of their lives, but at any given point in time they were located within a specific class.

Initial reconstruction

The framework elaborated in this book attempts to reconstruct the traditional Marxist concept of class structure in two different ways. First, the map of empty places has been transformed through the development of the concept of *contradictory locations within class relations*. Instead of defining class locations simply at the level of abstract modes of production, I have tried to develop a more concrete, multi-dimensional understanding of how jobs are tied to the process of exploitation. Specifically, I have argued that, in addition to the relationship to the ownership of the means of production, the linkage of jobs to the process of exploitation is shaped by their relation to domination within production (authority) and to the control over expertise and skills. This generates the more complex map of locations we have used throughout the book. In this new conceptualization, the "middle class" is not simply a residual category of locations that do not comfortably fit the categories "capitalist" and "worker." Rather, middle-class locations in the class structure are those that are linked to the process of exploitation and domination in contradictory ways. The "empty places" in the class structure, therefore, are no longer necessarily in one and only one class.

The second way in which the traditional view of class locations has been modified is through the concept of mediated class locations. The central point of trying to assign a class location to an individual is to clarify the nature of the lived experiences and material interests the individual is likely to have. Being "in" a class location means that you do certain things and certain things happen to you (lived experience) and you face certain strategic alternatives for pursuing your material well-being (class interests). Jobs embedded within social relations of production are one of the ways individuals are linked to such interests and experiences, but not the only way. Families provide another set of social relations which tie people to the class structure. This is especially salient in families within which different members of the family hold jobs with different class characters. Individuals in such families have both direct and mediated class locations, and these two links to class relations may or may not be the same. This introduces a new level of complexity into the micro-analysis of class which is especially relevant to the interaction of class and gender.

Empirical confirmations

Empirically "testing" concepts is a tricky business. Indeed, there are some traditions of social science which regard concepts as simply linguistic conventions, and thus there is no sense in which a particular conceptualization can be shown to be *wrong*; at most a given concept can be more or less *useful* than others. There is, however, an alternative view which claims that at least some concepts should be treated as attempts at specifying real mechanisms that exist in the world independently of our theories. For such "realist concepts," a definition can be incorrect in the sense that it misspecifies some crucial feature of the relevant causal properties (see Wright 1985: 1–37).

The concept of class being proposed in this book is meant to be a realist concept, not simply an arbitrary convention. The appropriate way of evaluating the concept, therefore, is to examine a variety of effects that the hypothesized class-defining mechanisms are supposed to generate. If a given conceptualization is correct, then these effects should follow certain expected patterns. Anomalies with respect to these expectations, of course, need not invalidate the concept, since failures of prediction of this sort can be due to the presence of all sorts of confounding mechanisms (including the special kind of confounding mechanism we call "measurement problems"). Nevertheless, as in more straightforward hypothesis testing, such surprises pose challenges which potentially provoke reconstructions.

In one way or another, nearly all of the results of this book bear on the problem of evaluating the adequacy of the proposed conceptualization of class structure, even though little of the research is directly geared towards "testing" this conceptualization against its rivals. Still, a few of the results have a particularly clear relation to the theoretical logic which underlies the conceptualization of class in this book.

First, in the analysis of class consciousness, the variation across class locations in individual attitudes towards class issues broadly follows the predictions derived from the three-dimensional class structure matrix. Particularly in Sweden and the United States, the extent to which individuals were likely to hold pro-capitalist or pro-working class attitudes varied monotonically across the three dimensions of the matrix. This does not, of course, decisively prove that this is the appropriate way of specifying the concept of class location within a Marxist framework, but it lends credibility to the approach.

The second specific way the results of this research support the proposed reconceptualization of class is more complex. In the various analyses of the permeability of class boundaries, it was demonstrated that the probabilities of permeability events (mobility, friendships, cross-class marriages) occurring between specific class locations were not simply additive effects of permeability across the three class boundaries we studied – the property boundary, the authority boundary and the skill boundary. For example, the probability of a friendship between a person in a working-class location and one in a capitalist location was not simply the sum of the probabilities of a friendship across the property boundary and across the authority boundary. If the effects of these three boundaries had been strictly additive, then this would have suggested that aggregating the dimensions into a "class structure" was simply a conceptual convenience. Nothing would be lost by disaggregating the class structure into these more "primitive" dimensions and treating them as separate, autonomous attributes of jobs. The consistent interactions among these dimensions in the patterns of class permeability support the claim that these three dimensions should be considered dimensions of a conceptual gestalt – "class structure" – rather than simply separate attributes of jobs.

Third, the credibility of the concept of mediated class locations is demonstrated in the analysis of the class identity of married women in two-earner households. At least in Sweden, the class identity of such women was shaped both by their own job–class and by the class of their husband. While there are complications in this analysis which we will review in the discussion of class consciousness below, these results generally support the idea that individuals' locations in a class structure should be conceptualized in terms of the multiple ways in which their lives are linked to class relations.

Surprises

Most of the empirical results in this book are consistent with the proposed reconceptualization of class structure. There are, however, two specific sets of results that are somewhat anomalous and thus raise questions about the concept of contradictory class locations. Both of these involve the relationship between the authority and expertise dimensions of the class structure matrix, one in the analysis of permeability of class boundaries, the other in the investigation of class consciousness. We will discuss these results in more detail later when we examine the general results for class permeability and for class consciousness. Here I will only focus on how these results bear on the conceptualization of contradictory class locations.

First, in the analyses of permeability of class boundaries, for each of the kinds of permeability we studied the authority boundary was always much more permeable than the expertise boundary (and in some analyses not significantly impermeable in absolute terms), yet, within a Marxist framework, authority is more intimately linked than is skill or expertise to the fundamental class cleavage of capitalism, the capital–labor relation. This relatively high permeability of the authority boundary compared to the expertise boundary is thus in tension with my reconstructed Marxist class concept in which authority constitutes a dimension of the *class* structure among employees rather than simply an aspect of "stratification" or even merely "role differentiation."

Second, in Japan the extremely muted ideological differences across levels of managerial authority compared to a rather sharp ideological cleavage between experts and nonexperts at every level of the authority hierarchy also run against the implications of the contradictory class location concept. Since the items we use as indicators of class consciousness center around capital–labor conflict, if it were the case that managerial authority defines the basis for a contradictory location linked to the capitalist class, then it is surprising that ideological differences along this dimension are so muted in a thoroughly capitalist society like Japan, and it is especially surprising that the expertise cleavage is so much more striking than the authority cleavage.

Further possible reconstructions?

Both of these anomalous results may simply be the result of measurement problems. The Japanese results are obviously vulnerable to all sorts of measurement errors on the attitude questions. But measurement issues may equally undermine the permeability results. Even though we tried to restrict the permeability of the managerial boundary to events that linked proper managers (not merely supervisors) to employees outside of the authority hierarchy, in several of the analyses it was impossible to rigorously distinguish managers and supervisors. Furthermore, even the "manager" category includes people near the bottom of authority structures. The fact that throughout the book we have amalgamated managers in small businesses with managers in multinational corporations may also confound the analyses. It is one thing for the manager of a locally owned retail store or a McDonald's franchise to be good friends with workers and to have come from a working-class family, and another thing for a manager in the headquarters of IBM (let alone an executive) to have such ties. It may well be the case, therefore, that these results would be quite different if we restricted managers to people with decisive power over broad organizational resources and policymaking and distinguished large-scale capitalist production from small business.

However, if these anomalous results turn out to be robust, they may indicate that the concept of "contradictory class locations" does indeed meld a relational concept of class rooted in capitalist property relations with dimensions of gradational stratification. This is most obvious for the skill-expertise dimension, which seems to have a natural gradational logic of having more or less of something. Authority is inherently a relational property of jobs; yet its place within class analysis might better be understood in terms of strata within classes rather than a distinctive kind of class location. This line of reasoning might suggest a fairly radical conceptual shift away from the idea of contradictory locations within class relations: authority and expertise would be treated as the bases for gradational strata within the class of employees defined by capitalist relations of production. Such a class analysis could still claim to be Marxist insofar as the class concept itself remained deeply linked to the problem of exploitation and capitalist property relations, but it would no longer attempt to specify differentiated *class* locations at concrete, micro-levels of analysis among employees. If this conceptual move were embraced, then the distinctively Marxist class concept would primarily inform analyses at the more abstract levels of class analysis, whereas something much more like a gradational concept of social stratification would inform concrete levels of analysis.

I do not believe that these particular results for managers are so compelling as to call for this kind of conceptual transformation. For most of the analyses in this book, the divisions among employees which we have mapped along the authority and expertise dimensions appear to have class-like effects, and the concept of contradictory locations within class relations does a good job of providing an explanatory framework for understanding the results. Taken as a whole, the results of the studies in this book affirm the fruitfulness of the concept of contradictory class locations. Thus, while the conceptual framework does not achieve the level of comprehensive coherence, either theoretically or empirically, which I had hoped for when I first began working on the problem of the middle class, the anomalies are not so pressing as to provoke a new conceptual metamorphosis.

12.2 Class structure and its variations in advanced capitalist societies

Traditional understanding

The traditional Marxist view of the variations across time and place in the class structure of capitalist societies revolves around three broad propositions:

1 *The distribution of the population into different classes within capitalism should depend largely upon the level of development of the "forces of production" (technology and technical knowledge).* This should be particularly true for the distribution of class locations within capitalist production itself. Since our sample is of countries which are all at roughly the same level of economic development, it would be expected that their class distributions should not differ greatly.

2 *The broad tendency of change over time in class distributions within capitalist societies is towards an expansion of the working class.* There are two principle reasons for this expectation: first, the petty bourgeoisie and small employer class locations are eroded by competition from larger capitalist firms, thus expanding the proportion of the labor force employed as wage-earners; and, second, rationalization and technical change within production, designed to maximize capitalist profits, tends to generate a "degradation of labor" – the reduction in the skills, autonomy and power of employees – which results in a relative expansion of proletarianized labor among wage-earners.

3 *As a result of these two propositions, the expectation is that the working class should be the largest class within developed capitalist societies.* The image of developed capitalist societies as becoming largely "middle-class societies" would be rejected by most Marxists, regardless of the specific ways in which they elaborate the concept of class.

Confirmations

Some aspects of these traditional understandings are supported by the data in Part I of this book. In all six of the capitalist societies we examined, the working class remains the single largest location within the class structure, and, when unskilled supervisors and skilled workers are combined with the working-class location, in every country we have examined the "extended working class" is a clear majority (55–60%) of the labor force, and a large majority of employees (generally around 75%). It may well be the case that in terms of the distribution of income and life styles – the characteristic way that the "middle class" is defined in popular culture – a substantial majority of the population is middle class. But in terms of relationship to the process of production and exploitation, the majority of the labor force is either in the working class or in those contradictory class locations most closely linked to the working class. Also as expected, the variation in class distributions, at least among employees, across the six countries we examined is relatively modest: the extended working class constitutes about three-quarters of employees in all of these countries, while the most privileged segment of the middle class (the extended expert-manager location) constitutes about one-ninth of employees.

Surprises

Two principal surprises stand out in the results on class structure. First, there is strong evidence that, at least in the United States, the working class is declining as a proportion of the labor force, and, what is more, this decline is occurring at an accelerating rate. While in the 1960s the decline in the relative size of the working class was entirely attributable to changes in the sectoral composition of the labor force (i.e. the sectors with the smallest proportion of workers were growing the fastest), by the 1980s the working class was declining in all major economic sectors. Experts and expert managers, on the other hand, have generally been expanding as a proportion of the labor force. Second, it also appears in the United States that the long, continuous decline of the petty bourgeois ended in the early 1970s and that since the middle of that decade self-employment has increased almost steadily. A similar growth in self-employment occurred in a variety of other developed capitalist countries. By the early 1990s, the proportion of the labor force self-employed in the US was perhaps as much as 25% greater than 20 years earlier. In the 1980s, this expansion of self-employment was occurring within most economic sectors. Furthermore, between 1980 and 1990 there was an expansion of small employers – not just the petty bourgeoisie – within economic sectors, indicating that the expansion of self-employment is unlikely to be simply a question of disguised forms of wage labor.

Reconstructions

These trends suggest that, while the working class is hardly disappearing, there is clear evidence of an expansion of class locations which are relatively "privileged" in various ways – in terms of autonomy and access to surplus, and even access to capital. The traditional Marxist thesis of deepening proletarianization within developed capitalist economies is therefore called into question.

There are two strategies for rethinking the problem of the transformation of capitalist class structures in light of these results. The first response leaves the basic theory of proletarianization intact, but identifies a misspecification of the empirical context of the analysis. It is possible, for example, that these trends are artifacts of the restriction of the analysis to changes in class structures *within* specific nation states. It has long been recognized that capitalism is a global system of production. This suggests that the proper unit of analysis for understanding the transformation of capitalist class structures should be the world, not specific firms, countries or even regions. It could be the case, for example, that the proportion of the employees of American corporations world-wide who are in the working class has increased, but that there has been a shift of the employment of workers outside the borders of the US. Global capitalism could thus be characterized by increasing proletarianization even if developed capitalism is not.

The second response calls into question more basic elements of the traditional Marxist understanding. As various theorists of "post-industrial" society have argued, the dramatic new forces of production of advanced capitalist societies may have fundamentally altered the developmental tendencies of capitalist class relations. Of particular importance in this regard are the implications of information technologies for the class location of various kinds of experts and managers. One scenario is that a decreasing proportion of the population is needed for capitalist production altogether, and, among those who remain employed in the capitalist economy, a much higher proportion will occupy positions of responsibility, expertise and autonomy. This implies a broad decline of the working class and purely supervisory employees, an increase of the "relative surplus population," and an expansion of experts and proper managers. Of course, this may simply be a short-lived phase, not a permanent reconfiguration of capitalist class structures. It is possible that once these new technologies have been in place for a while, a process of systematic deskilling and proletarianization might once again dominate changes in class distributions. But it may also be the case that these new forces of production stably generate a class structure different from earlier industrial technologies.

12.3 Individual lives and the class structure

Traditional understanding

Marxism has never developed a systematic theory of the way the lives of individuals intersect class structures, and thus there is not a strong set of expectations about the class patterns of intergenerational mobility, friendship formation, and family composition. There is nothing in the Marxist concept of class to logically preclude the possibility of two class structures with very similar distributions of *locations* having quite different trajectories of individual lives across locations.

Nevertheless, the underlying spirit of Marxist class analysis suggests that in a stable capitalist class structure most people's lives should be fairly well contained within specific class locations. Specifically, Marxism suggests three general propositions about the permeability of class boundaries:

1 *The relative impermeability of the property boundary.* The antagonistic material interests and distinctive forms of lived experience linked to class locations should make friendships, marriages, and mobility across the basic class division of capitalist societies – the division between capitalists and workers – relatively rare. Such events should certainly be less common than parallel events that spanned the authority and skill dimensions of the class structure. In the language developed in chapter 5, the property boundary in the class structure should be less permeable to mobility, friendships and families than either the expertise or authority boundary.

2 *The authority boundary.* A weaker expectation within a Marxist class analysis is that the authority boundary should be less permeable than the skill/expertise boundary. Insofar as the class antagonisms generated by managerial authority are more closely linked to the basic class cleavage of capitalism than is skill or expertise, there should be greater barriers to intimate social interaction across the authority boundary than across the skill boundary.

3 *Variations in permeability across capitalist societies.* On the assumption that the degree of impermeability of a class boundary is based on the

antagonism of material interests generated around that boundary, then the more purely capitalistic is a class structure, the less permeable its property boundary should be, both absolutely and relatively to other class boundaries.

Confirmations

The core results of our investigations of the permeability of class boundaries are quite consistent with the first and third of these expectations. In particular, the property boundary is generally less permeable than either the authority or skill boundaries to intergenerational mobility, friendship formation and cross-class marriages. Also, as expected, the property boundary is generally less permeable in North America than in Scandinavia, especially for intergenerational mobility. The contrast is especially striking in the comparison of the United States and Sweden: the chances of intergenerational mobility or friendships across the property boundary are over twice as great in Sweden as in the United States. Where capitalism is the most unconstrained and thus capitalist property relations make the biggest difference in the material interests of actors, the barriers to intergenerational mobility and friendship ties across the property boundary appear to be greatest.

Surprises

Not all of the results in our analyses of class-boundary permeability fit comfortably with Marxist intuitions. First, even though the property boundary is the least permeable of the three class boundaries we explored, nevertheless it can hardly be described as highly impermeable. Roughly speaking, mobility, friendships and cross-class marriages across the property boundary occur at about 25–30% of the rate that would be expected if the boundary were completely permeable. Furthermore, in the broader analysis of the petty bourgeoisie in the United States in chapter 4, we observed that well over 50% of all workers say that they would like to be self-employed some day, and over 60% have some kind of personal connection with the petty bourgeoisie – through previous jobs, class origins, second jobs, spouses or close personal friendships. The extent to which the lives of people in capitalist societies cross the property boundary is thus greater than suggested by the traditional Marxist image of capitalist class relations.

Second, as already noted in the discussion of anomalies in the concept of contradictory class location, the authority boundary turns out to be highly permeable to all three social processes we have explored in all four countries. Recall that for the purposes of these analyses we have tried to define the permeability of the authority boundary relatively restrictively – except for the mobility analysis, it involves a connection between proper managers (not mere supervisors) and nonmanagerial employees. With that definition, for many of the results the authority boundary creates almost no barriers. Again, while Marxist theory does not contain strong predictions about how individual lives intersect authority relations within work, given the importance of domination within production to Marxist class analysis, this degree of permeability is at least in tension with certain traditional Marxist themes.

Third, cross-class families are more common in all of the countries we studied than many Marxists would have expected. In roughly a third of all dual-earner families in these countries, husbands and wives were in different class locations. This is particularly important theoretically, since families are units of consumption with shared material interests. The existence of cross-class families, therefore, means that for many people their direct and mediated class locations will be different.

Reconstructions

It is an old theme in sociology, especially in the Weberian tradition, that social mobility is a stabilizing process in contemporary societies. It is generally assumed that a class structure that rigidly constrains the lives of individuals will ultimately be more fragile than one with relatively high levels of fluidity. These issues have been largely neglected within the Marxist tradition of class analysis. Much more attention has been paid to the levels of inequality across class locations and the exploitative practices thought to generate that inequality than to the way individual lives are organized within those class structures.

The patterns of class-boundary permeability which we have explored indicate that this issue needs to be taken seriously within Marxist class analysis. The results suggest that the durability of capitalism in the developed capitalist societies is probably not simply due to its capacity to generate growth and affluence for a substantial proportion of their populations, but also because of the extent to which individual lives and interactions cross the salient divisions within the class structure. This is particularly the case for the permeability of the secondary class divisions in capitalist societies – class boundaries constituted by authority and expertise – but it is also true for the primary class division. Of course, none of our analyses examine the probability of life events linking the working class and large capitalists, let alone the "ruling class." Nevertheless, the personal linkages between workers and small employers are not rare events in developed capitalist societies.

This permeability of class boundaries has potentially important consequences for both the class identities and interests of actors. Insofar as identities are shaped by biographical trajectories of lived experiences, the relative frequency of cross-class experiences would be expected to dilute class identity. Even more significantly, to the extent that class boundaries are permeable to *intra*generational mobility (a problem we have not explored) and family ties, then class interests would no longer be narrowly tied to individual class locations. Class interests define the strategic alternatives individuals face in pursuing their material welfare. Those alternatives are quite different where individual families contain members in different class locations or where individuals have a reasonable expectation that their future class location might be different from their present one. Class analysis needs to incorporate these facts about the interweaving of lives and structures.

12.4 Effects of class structure: class consciousness and class formation

Traditional understanding

Forms of consciousness – at least those aspects of consciousness bound up with class – are deeply affected by the ways class structure shapes lived experiences and material interests. While political and cultural processes may affect the extent to which such consciousness develops a coherent ideological expression and becomes linked to collectively organized social forces, nevertheless, a strong and systematic association between class location and the subjectivities of actors should be generated by the class structure itself. While Marxism does not predict politically conscious, collectively organized class struggles to be a universal feature of capitalism, it does predict that, at the level of individual subjectivity, there should be a systematic association between location in the class structure and forms of class consciousness.

This general Marxist perspective on class location and class consciousness, suggests five broad theses about the empirical problems we have been exploring:

1 *The point of production thesis.* Within the Marxist tradition, class has its effects on people's subjectivity not mainly through the standard of living generated by class positions (the "sphere of consumption"), but by the experiences and interests generated within production itself. Therefore, in cases in which there is a disjuncture between a person's direct class location and their mediated class location, their class consciousness should be more powerfully shaped by their direct class.

2 *The polarization thesis.* Class structures should be ideologically polarized between workers and capitalists on aspects of consciousness concerning class interests.

3 *The multidimensional exploitation thesis.* Among employees, the extent of working-class consciousness should vary monotonically with a person's location within the two-dimensional matrix class locations among nonproperty-owners. Even if one does not buy into all of the details of the concept of contradictory class locations, still most Marxists would predict that the more fully proletarianized is a class location along either the expertise or authority dimensions, the more likely it is that persons in that class location will have proworking-class consciousness.

4 *The macro-mediation thesis.* While class location should be systematically linked to class consciousness everywhere, the strength of this linkage at the micro-level will vary across countries depending upon the strength of working-class formations.

5 *Class formation thesis.* Within the common patterns postulated in the polarization thesis and the multidimensional exploitation thesis, the specific line of demarcation between class formations will vary cross-nationally depending upon a range of historically contingent processes, especially the political legacies of class struggles.

Confirmations

With the partial exception of some results concerning the point of production thesis (see below), the basic patterns of the relationship between class location and class consciousness in our various analyses are broadly consistent with these hypotheses. Even though we only have data on relatively small capitalist employers, in all three of the countries we studied, capitalists and workers are ideologically polarized in their attitudes towards class issues. Among employees, workers and expert managers are also polarized, with nonexpert managers and nonmanagerial experts having ideological positions somewhere between these extremes. Furthermore, as suggested by the macro-mediation thesis, the strength of the micro-level association between class location and various aspects of class consciousness does vary across countries. Specifically, this association is consistently very strong in Sweden where working-class formations are politically and ideologically strong, while the association is moderate in the United States and quite weak in Japan. Finally, as suggested by the class formation thesis, the specific ideological coalitions that are formed on the basis of these common underlying patterns are quite different in the three countries we examined. At least for Sweden and the United States, these differences can plausibly be interpreted in terms of the divergences in the two countries in the historical trajectories and institutional legacies of political class struggles.

Surprises: direct and mediated class locations

The results of the study of the effects of family-class composition on class identity partially contradict the point of production thesis. For men, the thesis holds in both the United States and Sweden: class identity is much more decisively shaped by the class character of the individual's own job than by the class composition of the household within which men live. For women, in contrast, mediated class locations (i.e. their links to the class structure through their spouses' job) matter much more than they do for men. In Sweden, for wives in two-earner households, direct and mediated class locations have roughly the same impact on the probability of their having a working-class identity; in the United States, for wives in two-earner households, direct class location has almost no effect on class identity net of the effect of mediated class location. At least for the study of the class identity of married women in two-earner households, therefore, this aspect of class subjectivity is affected at least as much by mediated class locations as by their direct position within the system of production, contradicting the point of production thesis.

Surprises: class consciousness and class formation

While the patterns of class structure and consciousness we observed are broadly consistent with Theses 2–5, the extent of cross-national variation in the strength of association of class location and consciousness is greater than suggested by traditional Marxist intuitions. In particular, the Japanese case falls outside of the range of variability that would be expected within Marxist class analysis. While class location is a statistically significant predictor of class consciousness in Japan, nevertheless it accounts for a very modest amount of the variance in our attitude scales in Japan (about 5%) – about half of the variance accounted for by class in the United States and less than a third of the figure for Sweden. Even when an array of other class-related experiences and conditions are added to the equation, the explained variance in the Japanese data remains quite small compared to the other two countries.

The patterns of ideological class formation in Japan also do not conform with standard Marxist expectations. While it is the case that the basic monotonic relationship between class location and consciousness postulated in the multidimensional exploitation hypothesis roughly holds for Japan, the variation in consciousness along the authority dimension is highly attenuated compared to either the United States or Sweden. Divisions along the dimension of skill (especially between experts and skilled employees) clearly have much deeper effects on consciousness in Japan than divisions along the dimension of managerial authority. As already noted, given that domination (and thus managerial authority) is more closely linked to capitalist exploitation than is expertise, Marxism would generally expect that proworking-class consciousness should not vary more sharply across categories of skill and expertise than across levels of managerial hierarchies. Sweden and the United States conform to this expectation; Japan does not.

Reconstructions: direct and mediated class locations

The results for Swedish and American married women in the study of class identity suggest that the relative weight of the sphere of production compared to the sphere of consumption in shaping class consciousness depends upon the nature of the class formations within which class experiences are generated and translated into subjectivity. In Sweden, as a result of the cohesiveness of the labor movement and its strength within production, "class" is formed collectively at the point of production itself. In the United States, class is highly disorganized and atomized at the point of production, and is formed as a collective category primarily within the sphere of consumption, especially in terms of standards of living and the character of residential neighborhoods. When politicians talk about a "middle-class tax cut" they mean "a middle-income tax cut." This difference between Sweden and the United States in the sites within which class is constructed, then, is translated into different salience accorded production and consumption in the formation of class identities. The point of production thesis, therefore, is not wrong; it is simply underspecified. To the extent that class becomes collectively organized within production, class experiences and interests generated within production itself will more strongly shape class identity than will experiences and interests in the sphere of consumption; where class formations remain highly disorganized within production, the sphere of consumption will have greater weight in shaping class subjectivities.

Reconstructions: class consciousness and class formation

The main results for class consciousness and class formation which are somewhat anomalous for the traditional Marxist understanding of these issues come from Japan. As in other cases, it is always possible that the surprising results for Japan are simply artifacts of measurement problems. The survey instrument used in this project was designed and tested within a broadly Western European cultural context. While there are still potential problems in the comparability of the meaning of identically worded questions between countries such as the United States and Sweden due to the differences in their political cultures, we tried to minimize such problems in the selection and wording of questions. The Japanese research team was not part of that process, and in any event it is possible that the differences in cultural meanings between Japan and the other countries might have undermined any attempt at generating genuinely comparable questions. With a more suitable survey instrument, therefore, it might turn out that Japan was not so different from the United States and Sweden after all.

On the assumption that these results do not merely reflect measurement issues, they are consistent with the conventional image of Japanese society in which significant segments of the working class have high levels of loyalty to their firms and in which the social distance between managers and workers is relatively small. In terms of the Marxist understanding of class consciousness, this suggests that the concrete organizational context of class relations may have a bigger impact on the micro-relationship between individual's class locations and class consciousness than is usually suggested within Marxist class analysis. Capitalism may universally be characterized by processes of exploitation and domination, but firms can be organized in ways which significantly mute the subjective effects of these relations. These organizational contexts may thus affect not merely the extent to which the class experiences and class interests of workers can be mobilized into collective action, but also the way these experiences and interests are transformed into identities and beliefs.

12.5 Class and other forms of oppression: class and gender

Traditional understanding

While there has always been some discussion within the Marxist tradition of the relationship between class and other forms of oppression, until recent decades this has not been given concentrated theoretical attention. Traditionally, Marxist discussions have emphasized two somewhat contradictory themes. On the one hand, there is the classical formulation by Marx that the development of capitalism will destroy all traditional, ascriptive forms of oppression which act as impediments to the expansion of the market. Racism and sexism erect barriers to the free movement of labor and thus block the functioning of fully commodified, competitive labor markets. Marx – along with many contemporary neoclassical economists – believed that the long-term tendency in capitalism is for these barriers to be destroyed.

On the other hand, many contemporary Marxists have downplayed the corrosive effects of the market on ascriptive oppressions, and instead have stressed the ways in which both racial and gender oppression are functional for reproducing capitalism, and therefore are likely to persist and perhaps even be strengthened with capitalist development. A variety of possible functional effects are then posed: racism divides the working class and thus stabilizes capitalist rule; racial oppression facilitates super-exploitation of specific categories of workers; gender oppression lowers the costs of labor power by providing for unpaid labor services in the home; gender oppression underwrites a sharp split between the public and private spheres of social life, which reinforces consumerist culture and other ideological forms supportive of capitalism.

Such functionalist accounts do not necessarily imply the absence of any autonomous causal mechanisms for gender and racial oppression, and they certainly do not logically imply that the best way to combat racism and sexism is simply to struggle against class oppression. The *existence* of specific forms of racism or sexism could be functionally explained by their beneficial effects for capitalism, yet the ultimate *destruction* of these forms of oppression could require concentrated struggle directly against them and could be achieved in spite of their functionality for capitalism. Nevertheless, these kinds of arguments do imply an explanatory primacy to class and suggest that whatever autonomy racial and gender mechanisms might have is circumscribed by the functional imperatives of the class system.

More recent discussions have tended to reject such functionalist arguments and have stressed greater autonomy for nonclass forms of oppression. Nevertheless, there is still a general expectation by Marxists that class and nonclass forms of oppression will tend to reinforce each other. This generates two broad theses about the interconnection of class and other forms of oppression:

1 *Nonclass oppression translates into class oppression.* Marxists would generally expect that social groups that are significantly oppressed through nonclass mechanisms will tend to be especially exploited within class relations. This can either be because the nonclass oppression affects the access of groups to the resources which matter for class, or because of direct discriminatory mechanisms within class relations themselves. In either case, it would be predicted that nonclass oppressions will be translated into class oppressions so that women and racially oppressed groups should be overrepresented in the working class and underrepresented in the most privileged class locations.

2 *Class oppression translates into nonclass oppression.* "Oppression" is a variable, not a constant. While all capitalist societies may be exploitative, the degree of inequality generated by capitalist relations varies considerably across capitalisms. Similarly, both racial and gender oppressions vary considerably. One of the factors which shape such variation in the intensity of nonclass oppression, Marxists would argue, is the power and interests of exploiting classes. Nonclass oppression will be more intense to the extent that exploiting classes, on the one hand, are able to take advantage of nonclass oppressions to further their own interests, and, on the other, are able to block popular mobilizations which might effectively challenge these forms of nonclass oppression. This does not imply that nonclass oppressions are *created* by exploiting classes, but it does imply that exploiting classes have interests in perpetuating such oppressions and have the capacity to act on those interests. A class analysis of nonclass oppression, therefore, would generally predict that, at any given level of capitalist

development, *the more oppressive and exploitative are class relations within capitalism, the more oppressive these other forms of oppression will tend to be as well.*

Confirmations

The results in our various explorations of class and gender distributions are broadly consistent with the expectations of the first thesis. In particular, in every country we examined, women in the labor force are universally much more proletarianized than are men. In general, roughly 50–60% of women in the labor force are in the working class, compared to only 35–45% of men. Similarly, in our analysis of gender and authority, significant gender inequality in authority was present in all of the countries we examined. This gender gap in authority was quite robust, being present for a variety of different measures of authority as well as in equations in which a wide range of individual, job and firm attributes were included as controls. Our brief exploration of race and class also indicates that blacks are significantly more proletarianized than whites, and black women – subjected to both racial and gender forms of oppression – are the most proletarianized of all race and gender categories. These results correspond to the general expectation that inequalities generated by nonclass forms of oppression will be reflected in class inequalities as well.

Surprises

Two results run counter to broad Marxist expectations about the intersection of class and gender. Most striking, perhaps, are the results for the rank ordering of countries in the gender gap in authority. The thesis that class exploitation intensifies nonclass oppressions would lead to the prediction that the Scandinavian countries should have the smallest gender gap in authority. On every measure, the United States has considerably greater class inequality than Sweden and Norway, yet the gender gap in workplace authority is much smaller in the US than in these social democratic countries. These results run directly counter to the expectation in the second nonclass oppressions thesis above that gender inequalities will be greatest where class inequalities are greatest.

The results for the study of housework also run counter to Marxian expectations. While Marxist theory does not explicitly generate explanations of the *variations* in the sexual division of labor across households, nevertheless, most Marxists would expect the class composition of households to have at least some effects on the amount of housework men do. Specifically, in classical Marxism the most homogeneously proletarianized households would be predicted to be the most egalitarian, whereas in contemporary neo-Marxism households in which the wife was in a relatively more privileged class location than her husband would be predicted to be the most egalitarian. Neither of these predictions are supported in either Sweden or the United States – husbands did little housework regardless of the class composition of the household.

Reconstructions

The results for authority and housework reinforce the standard feminist thesis that gender relations are quite autonomous from class relations. While many Marxists acknowledge this thesis, nevertheless there remains an expectation that empirically class and gender inequalities will be closely tied to each other. While the specific issues we have been exploring here are fairly limited in scope, they indicate that these two forms of oppression can vary relatively independently of each other.

This does not imply that struggles for women's liberation do not confront obstacles generated by existing class relations. Demands for quality, inexpensive childcare, for example, may be constrained by the difficulty of democratic states raising taxes in the context of global capitalism; equal pay for equivalent work may be impeded by the labor market for credentialed labor, an important aspect of the skill/expert dimension of class relations; and fully degendered authority hierarchies may be undermined by the competitive pressures of corporate organizations. Nevertheless, the degree of independent variation of class and gender relations supports the general claim that the struggles over gender inequality may have more scope for success inside of capitalism than Marxists have usually been willing to acknowledge.

This book was written for two rather different audiences: non-Marxists who are skeptical about the fruitfulness of Marxism as a theoretical framework for pursuing systematic empirical research, and radicals who are skeptical about the fruitfulness of quantitative research as a strategy for pursuing class analysis.

To the first audience I wanted to show that Marxist class analysis could be carried out with the same level of empirical rigor as non-Marxist stratification research, and that it could generate sociologically interesting empirical results. To accomplish this I faced three principal tasks. First, I had to clarify the core concepts of Marxist class analysis so that they could be deployed in quantitative empirical research. Second, I had to show that Marxist theory generated interesting questions which could be productively addressed using quantitative methods. And third, I had to operationalize the concepts in such a way as to generate answers to these questions. Much of this book has attempted to carry out these tasks.

To the left-wing audience, my central objective was not to affirm the importance of class analysis, but to show that knowledge within class analysis could be pursued using conventional quantitative research methods. Left-wing scholars, especially Marxists, are generally skeptical of quantitative analysis and have traditionally relied primarily on historical and qualitative methods in their empirical research. In part this skepticism is rooted in the substantive concerns of Marxism – social change and epochal transitions, transformative struggles, dynamic processes in the historically specific lived experiences of actors. Since these themes in the Marxist tradition are not easily amenable to precise measurement and quantitative treatment, Marxist scholars have understandably primarily engaged in qualitative research.

The traditional Marxist skepticism towards quantitative methods, however, goes beyond simply a judgment about the appropriate kinds of data needed to answer specific theoretical and empirical questions. It has also reflected a general hostility by many (although not all) Marxists to anything that smacked of "bourgeois social science." The terms of this hostility are familiar to anyone who has engaged the Marxist tradition of scholarship: Marxism, it has been claimed, is dialectical, historical, materialist, antipositivist and holist, while bourgeois social science is undialectical, ahistorical, idealist, positivist and individualist. This litany of antinomies has frequently underwritten a blanket rejection of "bourgeois" research methods on the grounds that they were unredeemably tainted with these epistemological flaws.

One of the main objectives in this book has been to counter this current within Marxist thought by demonstrating that quantitative methods could illuminate certain important problems in class analysis. This objective is part of a larger project for reconstructing Marxist thought in which the distinctiveness of Marxism is seen as lying not in its "Method" or epistemology, but in the concepts it deploys, the questions it asks, and the answers it proposes. Here I have attempted to show that there are important problems of class analysis in which knowledge can usefully be generated with systematic quantitative research.

In pursuing this dual agenda of demonstrating the usefulness of class analysis to non-Marxists and the usefulness of quantitative analysis to Marxists and other radical scholars, we have examined a diverse set of substantive problems. Some of these, like the study of patterns of class formation, the transformation of the class structure, or the problem of the class location of married women in dual-earner households, are central to class analysis. Others, like the permeability of class boundaries to friendships or the relationship between class and housework, are somewhat more peripheral. For all of these topics, however, I believe that our knowledge of class analysis has been pushed forward in ways that would not have been possible without systematic quantitative investigation.

In some cases, this advance in knowledge has taken the form of confirming various expectations that were grounded in less systematic observations. In other cases, the new knowledge has emerged from surprises, from unexpected results. And, out of these unexpected results, new questions and unresolved problems have been posed for future empirical research and theoretical reconstruction.

References

Acker, J. 1973. "Women and Social Stratification: A Case of Intellectual Sexism," *American Journal of Sociology* 78, 4: 936–945.

1990. "Hierarchies, Jobs, Bodies: A Theory of Gendered Organization," *Gender and Society* 4: 139–158.

Akerloff, G. A. and J. L. Yellen (eds.). 1986. *Efficiency Wage Models of the Labor Market*. Cambridge: Cambridge University Press.

Atwood, Margaret. 1987. *The Handmaid's Tale*. New York: Ballantine Books.

Barrett, Michele. 1984. "Rethinking Women's Oppression: A Reply to Brenner and Ramas," *New Left Review* 146: 123–128.

Bechhofer, Frank and B. Elliott. 1985. "The Petite Bourgeoisie in Late Capitalism," *Annual Review of Sociology* 11: 181–207.

Bell, Daniel. 1973. *The Coming of Post-Industrial Society*. New York: Harper and Row.

Bergman, Barbara. 1986. *The Economic Emergence of Women*. New York: Basic Books.

Blau, Francine D. and Marianne A. Ferber. 1990. "Women's Work, Women's Lives: A Comparative Perspective," National Bureau of Economic Research, Working Chapter No. 3447. Cambridge.

Bourdieu, Pierre. 1984. *Distinction: A Social Critique of the Judgement of Taste*. Translated by Richard Nice. London and New York: Routledge and Kegan Paul.

1985. "The Social Space and the Genesis of Groups," *Theory and Society* 14: 723–744.

1987. "What Makes a Social Class? On the Theoretical and Practical Existence of Groups," *Berkeley Journal of Sociology* 32: 1–17.

Bourdieu, Pierre and Jean-Claude Passeron. 1990. *Reproduction in Education, Society and Culture*. 2nd ed. London: Sage.

Bowles, Samuel and Herb Gintis. 1990. "Contested Exchange: New Microfoundations for the Political Economy of Capitalism," *Politics & Society* 18, 2: 165–222.

Braverman, Harry. 1974. *Labor and Monopoly Capital: The Degradation of Work in the Twentieth Century*. New York: Monthly Review Press.

Brenner, Johanna and Maria Ramas. 1984. "Rethinking Women's Oppression," *New Left Review* 144: 33–71.

Burawoy, Michael. 1979. *Manufacturing Consent*. Chicago: University of Chicago Press.

1985. *The Politics of Production*. London: Verso.

1990. "Marxism as Science: Historical Challenges and Theoretical Growth," *American Sociological Review* 55, 6: 775–793.

1992. *The Radiant Past*. Chicago: University of Chicago Press.

1993. *Ethnography Unbound*. Berkeley: University of California Press.

Burawoy, Michael and Erik Olin Wright. 1990. "Coercion and Consent in Contested Exchange," *Politics & Society*, June, reprinted in Wright (1994), chapter 4.

Burris, Val. 1987. "The Neo-Marxist Synthesis of Marx and Weber on Class," in N. Wiley (ed.) *The Marx–Weber Debate*. Newbury Park, CA: Sage Publications.

Capp, Al. 1992. *Li'L Abner*, vol. 14: 1948. Princeton, WI: Kitchen Sink Press.

Chalmers, Norma. 1989. *Industrial Relations in Japan: The Peripheral Workforce*. London and New York: Routledge.

Charles, Maria. 1992. "Cross-National Variations in Occupational Sex Segregation," *American Sociological Review* 57 (August): 483–502.

Cohen, G. A. 1978. *Karl Marx's Theory of History: A Defense*. Princeton: Princeton University Press.

1988. *History, Labour, and Freedom*. Oxford: Oxford University Press.

Coverman, Shelley. 1985. "Explaining Husbands' Participation in Domestic Labor," *The Sociological Quarterly* 26, 1: 81–97.

Currie, Elliott and Jerome H. Skolnick. 1983. *America's Problems: Social Issues and Public Policy*. 2nd edn, Glenview, IL: Scott, Foresman.

Dahrendorf, Ralf. 1959. *Class and Class Conflict in Industrial Society*. London: Routledge and Kegan Paul.

Dale, Angela. 1986. "Social Class and the Self-Employed," *Sociology* 20, 3: 430–434.

Delphy, Christine. 1984. *Close to Home: A Materialist Analysis of Women's Oppression*. London: Hutchinson.

Dohse, Knuth, Ulrich Jurgens and Thomas Malsch. 1985. "From 'Fordism' to 'Toyotism'? The Social Organization of the Labor Process in the Japanese Automobile Industry," *Politics & Society* 14, 2: 115–146.

Domhoff, G. William. 1971. *The Higher Circles*. New York: Vintage Books.

Elster, Jon. 1985. *Making Sense of Marx*. Cambridge: Cambridge University Press.

Engels, Frederick. 1968 [1884]. *The Origin of the Family, Private Property and the State*. Reprinted in *Karl Marx and Frederick Engels, Selected Works in One Volume*. London: Lawrence and Wishart. 455–593.

Erickson, Robert and John H. Goldthorpe. 1993. *The Constant Flux: a Study of Class Mobility in Industrial Societies*. Oxford: Oxford University Press.

Esping-Anderson, Gosta. 1990. *The Three Worlds of Welfare Capitalism*. Princeton: Princeton University Press.

Feld, Scott L. 1981. "The Focussed Organization of Social Ties," *American Journal of Sociology* 86: 1015–1035.

Fierman, Jaclyn, 1990. "Why Women Still Don't Hit the Top," *Fortune* 122, 3: 40.

Fraad, Harriet, Stephen Resnick and Richard Wolff. 1994. *Bringing it All Back Home: Class, Gender and Power in the Modern Household*. London: Pluto Press.

Fraser, Nancy. 1993. "After the Family Wage: What Do Women Want in Social Welfare?" Unpublished manuscript. Department of Philosophy, Northwestern University.

Fuchs, Victor R., 1968 *The Service Economy*. New York: Columbia University Press.

Gardiner, Jean. 1975. "Women's Domestic Labour." *New Left Review* 89 (January–February): 47–58. Reprinted in Z. Eisenstein (ed.) *Capitalist Patriarchy and the Case for Socialist Feminism*. New York: Monthly Review Press, 1979.

Gerth, Hans and C. W. Mills. 1958. *From Max Weber*. New York: Oxford University Press.

Giddens, Anthony. 1973. *The Class Structure of the Advanced Societies*. New York: Harper and Row.

Ginsberg, Norman. 1992. *Divisions of Welfare: A Critical Introduction to Comparative Social Policy*. London: Sage.

Glenn, Evelyn Nakano. 1992. "From Servitude to Service Work: Historical Continuities in the Racial Division of Paid Reproductive Work," *Signs* 18, 11: 1–43.

Goldberg, Gertrude Schaffner and Eleanor Ureman (eds.). 1990. *The Feminization of Poverty: Only in America?* New York: Praeger.

Goldthorpe, John. 1982. "On the Service Class," in Anthony Giddens and Gavin Mackenzie (eds.), *Social Class and the Division of Labor*. Cambridge University Press, 162–185.

    1983. "Women and Class Analysis: In Defence of the Conventional View," *Sociology* 17: 465–488.

    1984. "Women and Class Analysis: A Reply to the Replies," *Sociology* 18: 491–499.

    1987. *Social Mobility and Class Structure in Modern Britain*. 2nd edn, Oxford: Clarendon Press. (With Catriona Llewellyn and Clive Payne.)

Gordon, Andrew. 1985. *The Evolution of Labor Relations in Japan: Heavy Industry, 1853–1955*. Cambridge, MA: Council on East Asian Studies, Harvard University.

Haas, Linda. 1981. "Domestic Role Sharing in Sweden," *Journal of Marriage and the Family* (November): 955–967.

Halaby, Charles and David Weakliem. 1993. "Ownership and Authority in the Earnings Function," *American Sociological Review* 58, 1 (February): 16–30.

Hartmann, Heidi. 1979. "Capitalism, Patriarchy and Job Segregation by Sex." Pp. 206–247 in Zillah Eisenstein (ed.) *Capitalist Patriarchy and the Case for Socialist Feminism*. New York: MR Press.

Heath, A. and N. Brittain. 1984. "Women's Jobs Do Make a Difference: A Reply to Goldthorpe," *Sociology* 18, 4: 475–490.

Humphries, Jane. 1977. "Class Struggle and the Persistence of the Working Class Family," *Cambridge Journal of Economics* 1, 3: 241–258.

Jefferson, Thomas. 1786. [1984] *Writings*. New York: Literary Classics of the United States, Viking Press.

Kamata, Satoshi. 1982. *Japan in the Passing Lane*. New York: Pantheon.

Katzenstein, Mary Fainsod. 1987. "Comparing the Feminist Movements of the

United States and Western Europe: An Overview." In Mary Fainsod Katzenstein and Carol McClurg Mueller (eds.) *The Women's Movements of the United States and Western Europe.* Philadelphia: Temple University Press.

Kohn, M. 1969. *Class and Conformity.* Holmwood: The Dorsey Press.

Lerner, Gerda. 1986. *The Creation of Patriarchy.* New York: Basic Books.

Lewis, Jane. 1985. "The Debate on Sex and Class," *New Left Review* 149: 108–120.

Lincoln, Abraham. 1907 [1865]. *Life and Works of Abraham Lincoln: Centenary Edition,* Marion Mills Miller (ed.). New York: Current Literature.

Lukács, Georg. 1971 [1922]. *History and Class Consciousness.* Cambridge: MIT Press.

Marsh, A., P. Heady and J. Matheson. 1981. *Labour Mobility in the Construction Industry.* London: HMSO.

Marshall, Gordon. 1983. "Some Remarks on the Study of Working Class Consciousness," *Politics & Society* 12, 3: .263–302.

Mishel, Lawrence and David Frankel. 1991. *The State of Working America.* New York.

Moen, Phyllis. 1989. *Working Parents: Transformations in Gender Roles and Public Policies in Sweden.* Madison: University of Wisconsin Press.

Molyneux, Maxine. 1979. "Beyond the Domestic Labour Debate," *New Left Review* 116: 3–27.

Morrison, Ann M., R. P. White, E. Van Velsor, and the Center for Creative Leadership. 1987. *Breaking the Glass Ceiling.* New York: Addison Wesley.

Pakulski, Jan and Malcolm Waters. 1996. *The Death of Class.* London: Sage.

Parkin, Frank. 1974. "Strategies of Social Closure in Class Formation." In Frank Parkin (ed.) *The Social Analysis of the Class Structure.* London: Tavistock.

1979. *Marxism and Class Theory: A Bourgeois Critique.* New York: Columbia University Press.

Piore, Michael and Charles Sabel. 1984. *The Second Industrial Divide.* New York: Basic Books.

Przeworski, Adam. 1985. *Capitalism and Social Democracy.* Cambridge: Cambridge University Press.

Przeworski, Adam and John Sprague. 1986. *Paper Stones: A History of Electoral Socialism.* Chicago: University of Chicago Press.

Public Reports of the Presidents of the United States. Ronald Reagan. 1983. Book 1. Washington DC: United States Government Printing Office, 1984.

Reskin, Barbara. 1988. "Bringing Men Back In: Sex Differentiation and the Devaluation of Women's Work," *Gender and Society* 2, 1: 58–81.

Reskin, Barbara and Lrene Padavic. 1994. *Women and Men at Work.* Thousand Oaks, CA: Pine Forge Press.

Rogers, Joel. 1990. "Divide and Conquer: Further Reflections on the Distinctive Character of American Labor Laws," *Wisconsin Law Review* 1, 1: 1–147.

Secombe, Walley. 1974. "The Housewife and her Labour under Capitalism," *New Left Review* 83 (January–February): 3–24.

Shelton, Beth and Ben Agger. 1993. "Shotgun Wedding, Unhappy Marriage, No-Fault Divorce? Rethinking the Feminism–Marxism Relationship." Pp. 25–42 in Paul England (ed.) *Theory on Gender / Feminism on Theory.* New York: Aldine de Gruyter.

Singelmann, Joachim. 1978. *From Agriculture to Services*. Beverly Hills: Sage Publications.

Sorensen, Annemette and Sara McLanahan. 1987. "Married Women's Economic Dependency, 1940–1980," *American Journal of Sociology* 93, 3: 659–687.

Stanworth, Michelle. 1984. "Women and Class Analysis: A Reply to John Goldthorpe," *Sociology* 18: 159–170.

Therborn, Göran. 1982. *The Power of Ideology and the Ideology of Power*. London: Verso.

Touraine, Alain. 1971. *The Post Industrial Society*. New York: Random House.

Tsuda, Masumi. 1973. "Personnel Administration at the Industrial Plant Level." In K. Okochi, B. Karsh and S. B. Levine (eds.) *Workers and Employers in Japan: The Japanese Employment Relations System*. University of Tokyo Press.

Wilson, William Julius. 1982. *The Declining Significance of Race*. Chicago: University of Chicago Press.

1987. *The Truly Disadvantaged*. Chicago: University of Chicago Press.

Wright, Erik Olin. 1978. *Class, Crisis and the State*. London: New Left Books.

1985. *Classes*. London: New Left Books.

1989. "Rethinking, Once Again, The Concept of Class Structure." Pp. 269–348 in Wright, et al. (1989).

1993. "Typologies, Scales and Class Analysis: A Comment on Halaby and Weakliem," *American Sociological Review* 58, 1 (February): 31–34.

1994. *Interrogating Inequality*. London: Verso.

1997. *Class Counts: Comparative Studies in Class Analysis*. Cambridge University Press.

Wright, Erik Olin, Carolyn Howe and Donmoon Cho. 1989. "Class Structure and Class Formation." In Melvin Kohn (ed.), *Comparative Sociology*. Beverly Hills: Sage ASA Presidential Volume.

Wright, Erik Olin, Andrew Levine and Elliott Sober. 1992. *Reconstructing Marxism: Essays on Explanation and the Theory of History*. London: Verso.

Wright, Erik Olin, Uwe Becker, Johanna Brenner, Michael Burawoy, Val Burris, Guglielmo Carchedi, Gordon Marshall, Peter Meiksins, David Rose, Arthur Stinchcombe, Phillipe Van Parijs. 1989. *The Debate on Classes*. London: Verso.

Zaretsky, Eli. 1976. *Capitalism, the Family and Personal Life*. New York: Harper & Row.

Index of names

Index of subjects

abstract/concrete, 158, 189
achievement vs. ascription, 179–80
African-Americans, 24
agriculture, 133
  and mobility, 71–2
anomalies and theory construction, 252–3
anticapitalist attitudes, 219, 224–32, 235–41, 243–61
Australia, gender and authority in, 170, 172, 174, 178, 182
authority, 16–21, 255
  anomalous findings, 257–9, 265
  and class formation, 231–2, 233
  cross-class families, 104–6, 108
  Dahrendorf's views on, 96–7
  distribution in US and Sweden, friendship permeability, 95–103
  and gender, 49, 51, 272–4
  Goldthorpe's treatment of, 19–20
  loyalty rent and, 17, 30–1
  measures and measurement problems, 82, 258–9
  mobility permeability, 87–8, 89, 90
autonomy (in work), 58, 260, 262

base/superstructure, 116–17; *see also* historical materialism
biography in class analysis, 80–1; *see also* class trajectory
boundary (social), 81
"bourgeois social science," 275

Canada, 45, 50
  authority and gender in, 170–2, 173–4
  permeability, 93–5, 101
  petty bourgeoisie in, 68
capitalism, 2, 9, 13–15, 56–7, 65–6, 69, 88–9, 109, 260
  class model within, 13–14, 20–1
  dynamics of, 56, 57–8, 260, 271

and exploitation, 13–14
globalization of, 65, 262
mobility involving, 86–7
and patriarchy, 117, 146–7
polarized classes within, 15–19
underclass in, 24–5
capitalists
  antagonistic interests with workers, 7–9, 14, 32, 213, 267
  class consciousness of, 224–5
  class formations of, 227–30, 233
  definition of, 13–14, 213, 254–5
  and domination (power), 14, 16, 32
  gender distribution of, 49, 51–2
  race distribution of, 52–4
  size of, 44–6
  wealth of, 44 n.2
childcare, 119
children, 21–2, 85–7, 119–20, 122, 132–3, 148, 173
class alliances, 192, 207
class analysis, 1–3, 185–6, 251
  basic concepts within, 190–8
  definition of, 1
  as an independent variable discipline, 1, 115
  macro-model, 204–15
  micro-model, 199–204, 210–15
  Weberian tradition, xiv, 2, 27–9
  Weberian and Marxist traditions compared, 30–3
Class Analysis Project, xiii–xvi
class capacity, 32, 207
class consciousness, 2, 193–7, 201–4
  anomalous results, 268–9
  and class location, 199–200, 219–21, 224–6, 256
  confirmations of traditional Marxist views, 256–7, 267–8
  definition of, 2, 193–5

284